White's Grammar School Texts

THE FIFTH BOOK

OF

VIRGIL'S ÆNEID

WITH A VOCABULARY

BY

JOHN T. WHITE, D.D. OXON.

1876

PREFACE.

FOR some long time past it has been widely felt that a reduction in the cost of *Classical Works* used in schools generally, and more especially in those intended for boys of the middle classes, is at once desirable and not difficult of accomplishment. For the most part only portions of authors are read in the earlier stages of education, and a pupil is taken from one work to another in each successive half-year or term; so that a book needlessly large and proportionably expensive is laid aside after a short and but partial use.

In order, therefore, to meet what is certainly a want, Portions of the *Classical Writers* usually read in Schools are now being issued under the title of GRAMMAR SCHOOL TEXTS; while, at the request of various Masters, it has been determined to add to the series some of the *Gospels in Greek*.

Each TEXT is provided with a VOCABULARY of the words occurring in it. In every case the origin of a word, when known, is stated at the commencement of the article treating of it, if connected with another Latin, or Greek, word; at the end of it, if derived from any other source. Further still, the primary or etymological meaning is always given, within inverted commas, in Roman type, and so much also of each word's history as is needful to bring down its chain of meanings to the especial force, or forces, attaching to it in the particular "Text."

Moreover, as an acquaintance with the principles of GRAMMAR, as well as with ETYMOLOGY, is necessary to the understanding of a language, such points of construction as seem to require elucidation are concisely explained under the proper articles, or a reference is simply made to that rule in the *Public Schools Latin Primer*, or in *Parry's Elementary Greek Grammar*, which meets the particular difficulty. It occasionally happens, however, that more information is needed than can be gathered from the above-named works. When such is the case, whatever is requisite is supplied, in substance, from Jelf's Greek Grammar, Winer's Grammar of New Testament Greek, or the Latin Grammars of Zumpt and Madvig.

LONDON: *January*, 1876.

ARGUMENT.

THE flames of Dido's funeral-pile seen by Æneas and the Trojans while sailing towards Italy. Trojan fleet driven by a storm to the coast of Sicily. Acestes. Æneas resolves to celebrate funeral-games on the anniversary of his father's death. Pours out libations and sacrifices at his father's tomb. The funeral-games: viz. the rowing-match; the foot-race; the fight with the cæstus; shooting at a pigeon fastened to the mast of a ship. Acestes discharges his arrow with such force that it becomes ignited. Representation of an equestrian fight by three bands of boys. Said by Virgil to be the origin of the Roman game, *Troja*. At the instigation of Iris, who is sent by Juno, the Trojan women set fire to the ships. Four ships destroyed; the rest being saved by a heavy rain sent by Jupiter. Nautes counsels Æneas to leave in Sicily such of his followers as are wearied of their wanderings, together with the old men and the women. Anchises appears to Æneas in a vision, and bids him adopt the advice given. Informs him that he must descend with the Sibyl to the lower world, and that there he will see the long line of his descendants. *Æneas founds a city for those whom he is about to leave in Sicily. Places them under the rule of Acestes. Sets sail for Italy. Venus* entreats Neptune to grant him a favourable voyage. Neptune recounts how he had beforetime succoured him, and promises to befriend him still. Foretells the death of one of his followers. Calms the sea, and disperses the storm-clouds. The fleet proceeds on its course. Somnus, the sleep-god, assuming the shape of Phorbas, tries to induce Palinurus to quit the helm and take repose. Failing in his purpose, sprinkles Palinurus with water from Lēthē, and throws him headlong into the sea. The fleet approaches the rocks of the Sirens. Æneas discovers the loss of Palinurus, and takes his place at the helm. Laments the loss of his friend.

P. VIRGILII MARONIS ÆNEIDOS

LIBER V.

Interea medium Æneas jam classe tenebat
Certus iter, fluctūsque atros Aquilone secabat,
Mœnia respiciens, quæ jam infelicis Elissæ
Collucent flammis: quæ tantum accenderit ignem,
Causa latet; duri magno sed amore dolores   5
Polluto, notumque, furens quid femina possit,
Triste per augurium Teucrorum pectora ducunt.
   Ut pelagus tenuere rates, nec jam ampliùs ulla
Occurrit tellus, cœlum undique et undique pontus:
Olli cæruleus supra caput astitit imber,   10
Noctem hiememque ferens; et inhorruit unda tenebris.
Ipse gubernator puppi Palinurus ab altā:
" Heu! quianam tanti cinxerunt æthera nimbi?
Quidve, pater Neptune, paras?" Sic deinde loquutus,
Colligere arma jubet, validisque incumbere remis,
Obliquatque sinūs in ventum, ac talia fatur: 15
" Magnanime Ænea, non, si mihi Jupiter auctor

Spondeat, hoc sperem Italiam contingere cœlo.
Mutati transversa fremunt et vespere ab atro
Consurgunt venti; atque in nubem cogitur aër. 20
Nec nos obniti contrà, nec tendere tantum
Sufficimus : superat quoniam Fortuna, sequamur ;
Quòque vocat, vertamus iter. Nec litora longè
Fida reor fraterna Erycis portūsque Sicanos ;
Si modò rite memor servata remetior astra." 25
Tum pius Æneas : " Equidem sic poscere ventos
Jamdudum et frustra cerno te tendere contrà.
Flecte viam velis. An sit mihi gratior ulla,
Quòve magis fessas optem dimittere naves,
Quàm quæ Dardanium tellus mihi servat Acesten,
Et patris Anchisæ gremio complectitur ossa?" 31
Hæc ubi dicta, petunt portūs, et vela secundi
Intendunt Zephyri : fertur cita gurgite classis :
Et tandem læti notæ advertuntur arenæ.

At procul excelso miratus vertice montis 35
Adventum sociasque rates occurrit Acestes,
Horridus in jaculis et pelle Libystidis ursæ :
Troïa Crimiso conceptum flumine mater
Quem genuit. Veterum non immemor ille parentum
Gratatur reduces, et gazā lætus agresti 40
Excipit, ac fessos opibus solatur amicis.

Postera quum primo stellas oriente fugârat
Clara dies, socios in cœtum litore ab omni
Advocat Æneas, tumulique ex aggere fatur :

"Dardanidæ magni, genus alto a sanguine divûm,
Annuus exactis completur mensibus orbis, 46
Ex quo relliquias divinique ossa parentis
Condidimus terrā, mœstasque sacravimus aras.

Jamque dies, ni fallor, adest, quem semper acerbum,
Semper honoratum, sic di voluistis, habebo.　　50
Hunc ego Gætulis agerem si Syrtibus exsul,
Argolicove mari deprensus et urbe Mycenæ,
Annua vota tamen sollennesque ordine pompas
Exsequerer, strueremque suis altaria donis.
Nunc ultro ad cineres ipsius et ossa parentis　　55
(Haud equidem sine mente, reor, sine numine divûm)
Adsumus; et portūs delati intramus amicos.
Ergo agite, et lætum cuncti celebremus honorem;
Poscamus ventos, atque hæc mea sacra quotannis
Urbe velit positā templis sibi ferre dicatis.　　60
Bina boum vobis Trojā generatus Acestes
Dat numero capita in naves: adhibete Penates
Et patrios epulis, et quos colit hospes Acestes.
Præterea, si nona diem mortalibus almum
Aurora extulerit radiisque retexerit orbem,　　65
Prima citæ Teucris ponam certamina classis;
Quique pedum cursu valet, et qui viribus audax,
Aut jaculo incedit melior levibusve sagittis,
Seu crudo fidit pugnam committere cæstu;
Cuncti adsint, meritæque exspectent præmia palmæ.
Ore favete omnes et cingite tempora ramis."　　71
　　Sic fatus velat maternā tempora myrto:
Hoc Helymus facit, hoc ævi maturus Acestes,
Hoc puer Ascanius: sequitur quos cetera pubes.
Ille e concilio multis cum millibus ibat　　75
Ad tumulum, magnā medius comitante catervā.
Hìc duo rite mero libans carchesia Baccho
Fundit humi, duo lacte novo, duo sanguine sacro;
Purpureosque jacit flores, ac talia fatur:

'Salve, sancte parens : iterum salvete, recepti   80
Nequiquam cineres, animaeque umbraeque paternae.
Non licuit fines Italos fataliaque arva
Nec tecum Ausonium, quicumque est, quaerere
   Tybrim."
Dixerat haec, adytis quum lubricus anguis ab imis
Septem ingens gyros, septena volumina traxit,   85
Amplexus placidè tumulum, lapsusque per aras ;
Caeru'eae cui terga notae, maculosus et auro
Squamam incendebat fulgor : ceu nubibus arcus
Mille jacit varios adverso sole colores.
Obstupuit visu Æneas : ille agmine longo   90
Tandem inter pateras et levia pocula serpens
Libavitque dapes, rursusque innoxius imo
Successit tumulo, et depasta altaria liquit.
Hoc magìs inceptos genitori instaurat honores,
Incertus geniumne loci famulumne parentis   95
Esse putet ; caedit binas de more bidentes,
Totque sues, totidem nigrantes terga juvencos ;
Vinaque fundebat pateris, animamque vocabat
Anchisae magni Manesque Acheronte remissos.
Necnon et socii, quae cuique est copia, laeti   100
Dona ferunt, onerantque aras mactantque juvencos :
Ordine aëna locant alii ; fusique per herbam
Subjiciunt verubus prunas, et viscera torrent.
   Exspectata dies aderat, nonamque serenā
Auroram Phaëthontis equi jam luce vehebant,   105
Famaque finitimos et clari nomen Acestae
   Excierat : laeto complêrant litora coetu
   Visuri Æneadas ; pars et certare parati.
Munera principio ante oculos circoque locantur

In medio, sacri tripodes viridesque coronæ   110
Et palmæ, pretium victoribus ; armaque, et ostro
Perfusæ vestes, argenti auri que talenta :
Et tuba commissos medio canit aggere ludos.
  Prima pares ineunt gravibus certamina remis
Quatuor, ex omni delectæ classe, carinæ.   115
Velocem Mnestheus agit acri remige Pristin,
Mox Italus Mnestheus, genus a quo nomine Memmî
Ingentemque Gyas ingenti mole Chimæram,
Urbis opus, triplici pubes quam Dardana versu
Impellunt ; terno consurgunt ordine remi ;   120
Sergestusque, domus tenet a quo Sergia nomen,
Centauro invehitur magnā ; Scyllāque Cloanthus
Cæruleā, genus unde tibi, Romane Cluenti
  Est procul in pelago saxum spumantia contra
Litora, quod tumidis submersum tunditur olim 125
Fluctibus, hiberni condunt ubi sidera Cori :
Tranquillo silet immotāque attollitur undā
Campus, et apricis statio gratissima mergis.
Hìc viridem Æneas frondenti ex ilice metam
Constituit, signum nautis, pater ; unde reverti   130
Scirent, et longos ubi circumflectere cursūs.
Tum loca sorte legunt ; ipsique in puppibus auro
Ductores longè effulgent ostroque decori:
Cetera populeā velatur fronde juventus,
Nudatosque humeros oleo perfusa nitescit.   135
Considunt transtris, intentaque brachia remis ;
Intenti exspectant signum ; exsultantiaque haurit
Corda pavor pulsans laudumque arrecta cupido.
  Inde ubi clara dedit sonitum tuba, finibus omn-
  es—   139

Haud mora—prosiluere suis; ferit æthera clamor
Nauticus; adductis spumant freta versa lacertis.
Infindunt pariter sulcos, totumque dehiscit
Convulsum remis rostrisque tridentibus æquor.
Non tam præcipites bijugo certamine campum
Corripuere ruuntque effusi carcere currūs;   145
Nec sic immissis aurigæ undantia lora
Concussere jugis, pronique in verbera pendent.
Tum plausu fremituque virûm studiisque faventûm
Consonat omne nemus, vocemque inclusa volutant
Litora; pulsati colles clamore resultant.   150
Effugit ante alios primisque elabitur undis
Turbam inter fremitumque Gyas; quem deinde
   Cloanthus
Consequitur melior remis; sed pondere pinus
Tarda tenet. Post hos æquo discrimine Pristis
Centaurusque locum tendunt superare priorem; 155
Et nunc Pristis habet; nunc victam præterit ingens
Centaurus; nunc unà ambæ junctisque feruntur
Frontibus et longā sulcant vada salsa carinā.
  Jamque propinquabant scopulo, metamque ten-
   ebant;
Quum princeps medioque Gyas in gurgite victor 160
Rectorem navis compellat voce Mencæten:
"Quò tantum mihi dexter abis? huc dirige gressum;
Litus ama; et lævas stringat sine palmula cautes;
Altum alii teneant." Dixit: sed cæca Menœtes
Saxa timens, pròram pelagi detorquet ad undas: 165
"Quò diversus abis? iterum, pete saxa, Menœte,"
Cum clamore Gyas revocabat: et ecce! Cloanthum
Respicit instantem tergo, et propiora tenentem.

Ille inter navemque Gyæ scopulosque sonantes
Radit iter lævum interior, subitusque priorem   170
Præterit, et metis tenet æquora tuta relictis.
Tum verò exarsit juveni dolor ossibus ingens,
Nec lacrimis caruere genæ ; segnemque Menœten,
Oblitus decorisque sui sociûmque salutis,
In mare præcipitem puppi deturbat ab altā.   175
Ipse gubernaclo rector subit, ipse magister,
Hortaturque viros, clavumque ad litora torquet.
At gravis ut fundo vix tandem redditus imo est
Jam senior, madidāque fluens in veste, Menœtes
Summa petit scopuli, siccāque in rupe resedit.   180
Illum et labentem Teucri et risere natantem,
Et salsos rident revomentem pectore fluctūs.

Hìc læta extremis spes est accensa duobus,
Sergesto Mnestheique, Gyan superare morantem.
Sergestus capit antè locum, scopuloque propinquat:
Nec totā tamen ille prior præeunte carinā,   186
Parte prior ; partem rostro premit æmula Pristis.
At mediā socios incedens nave per ipsos
Hortatur Mnestheus : "Nunc, nunc insurgite remis,
Hectorei socii, Trojæ quos sorte supremā   190
Delegi comites ; nunc illas promite vires,
Nunc animos, quibus in Gætulis Syrtibus usi,
Ionioque mari, Maleæque sequacibus undis.
Non jam prima peto Mnestheus, neque vincere
    certo ;
Quamquam o !—sed superent, quibus hoc, Neptune,
    dedisti.   195
Extremos pudeat rediisse : hoc vincite, cives,
Et prohibete nefas." Olli certamine summo

Procumbunt : vastis tremit ictibus ærea puppis,
Subtrahiturque solum ; tum creber anhelitus artūs
Aridaque ora quatit : sudor fluit undique rivis. 200
   Attulit ipse viris optatum casus honorem.
Namque furens animi dum proram ad saxa suburge
Interior spatioque subit Sergestus iniquo ;
Infelix saxis in procurrentibus hæsit.
Concussæ cautes, et acuto in murice remi   205
Obnixi crepuere, illisaque prora pependit.
Consurgunt nautæ, et magno clamore morantur :
Ferratasque sude et acutā cspide contos
Expediunt, fractosque legunt in gurgite remos.
At lætus Mnestheus, successuque acrior ipso,   210
Agmine remorum celeri, ventisque vocatis,
Prona petit maria et pelago decurrit aperto.
Qualis speluncā subitò commota columba,
Cui domus et dulces latebroso in pumice nidi,
Fertur in arva volans, plausumque exterrita pennis
Dat tecto ingentem ; mox aëre lapsa quieto,   216
Radit iter liquidum celeres neque commovet alas:
Sic Mnestheus, sic ipsa fugā secat ultima Pristis
Æquora : sic illam fert impetus ipse volantem.
Et primùm in scopulo luctantem deserit alto   220
Sergestum brevibusque vadis, frustraque vocantem
Auxilia, et fractis discentem currere remis.
Inde Gyan ipsamque ingenti mole Chimæram
Consequitur ; cedit, quoniam spoliata magistro est.
Solus jamque ipso superest in fine Cloanthus ;   225
Quem petit et summis adnixus viribus urget.
Tum verò ingeminat clamor, cunctique sequentem
ıstigant studiis, resŏnatque fragoribus æther.

Hi proprium decus et partum indignantur honorem,
Ni teneant, vitamque volunt pro laude pacisci. 230
Hos successus alit ; possunt, quia posse videntur.
Et fòrs æquatis cepissent præmia rostris ;
Ni palmas ponto tendens utrasque Cloanthus
Fudissetque preces, divosque in vota vocâsset :
" Dî, quibus imperium est pelagi, quorum æquora
 curro, 235
Vobis lætus ego hoc candentem in litore taurum
Constituam ante aras voti reus, extaque salsos
Porriciam in fluctūs, et vina liquentia fundam."
Dixit, eumque imis sub fluctibus audiit omnis
Nereïdum Phorcique chorus, Panopeaque virgo ;
Et pater ipse manu magnā Portunus euntem 241
Impulit : illa Noto citiùs volucrique sagittā
Ad terram fugit, et portu se condidit alto.
 Tum satus Anchisā, cunctis ex more vocatis,
Victorem magnā præconis voce Cloanthum 245
Declarat, viridique advelat tempora lauro,
Muneraque in naves ternos optare juvencos,
Vinaque, et argenti magnum dat ferre talentum.
Ipsis præcipuos ductoribus addit honores :
Victori chlamydem auratam, quam plurima circum
Purpura Mæandro duplici Melibœa cucurrit, 251
Intextusque puer frondosā regius Idā
Veloces jaculo cervos cursuque fatigat,
Acer, anhelanti similis ; quem præpes ab Idā
Sublimem pedibus rapuit Jovis armiger uncis. 255
Longævi palmas nequiquam ad sidera tendunt
Custodes, sævitque canum latratus in auras.
At, qui deinde locum tenuit virtute secundum,

Levibus huic hamis consertam auroque trilicem
Loricam, quam Demoleo detraxerat ipse   260
Victor apud rapidum Simoënta sub Ilio alto,
Donat habere viro, decus et tutamen in armis.
Vix illam famuli Phegeus Sagarisque ferebant
Multiplicem, connixi humeris ; indutus at olim
Demoleus cursu palantes Troas agebat.   265
Tertia dona facit geminos ex ære lebetas,
Cymbiaque argento perfecta atque aspera signis.
 Jamque adeo donati omnes, opibusque superbi,
Puniceis ibant evincti tempora tænîs ;
Quum sævo e scopulo multā vix arte revulsus,   270
Amissis remis, atque ordine debilis uno,
Irrisam sine honore ratem Sergestus agebat.
Qualis sæpe viæ deprensus in aggere serpens,
Ærea quem obliquum rota transiit, aut gravis ictu
Seminecem liquit saxo lacerumque viator,   275
Nequiquam longos fugiens dat corpore tortūs,
Parte ferox ardensque oculis et sibila colla
Arduus attollens ; pars vulnere clauda retentat
Nexantem nodis seque in sua membra plicantem.
Tali remigio navis se tarda movebat ;   280
Vela facit tamen, et plenis subit ostia velis.
Sergestum Æneas promisso munere donat,
Servatam ob navem lætus sociosque reductos.
Olli serva datur, operum haud ignara Minervæ,
Cressa genus, Pholoë, geminique sub ubere nati.
 Hoc pius Æneas misso certamine tendit   286
Gramineum in campum, quem collibus undique
 curvis
Cingebant silvæ ; mediāque in valle theatri

Circus erat, quò se multis cum millibus heros
Consessu medium tulit, exstructoque resedit. 290
Hìc, qui fortè velint rapido contendere cursu,
Invitat pretiis animos, et præmia ponit.
Undique conveniunt Teucri, mistique Sicani:
Nisus et Euryalus primi ;
Euryalus formā insignis viridique juventā ; 295
Nisus, amore pio pueri : quos deinde sequutus
Regius egregiā Priami de stirpe Diores :
Hunc Salius, simul et Patron ; quorum alter Acarn-
an ;
Alter ab Arcadiā, Tegeææ sanguine gentis.
Tum duo Trinacrii juvenes, Helymus Panopesque,
Assueti silvis, comites senioris Acestæ. 301
Multi præterea, quos fama obscura recondit.
Æneas quibus in mediis sic deinde loquutus :
 " Accipite hæc animis lætasque advertite mentes :
Nemo ex hoc numero mihi non donatus abibit. 305
Gnosia bina dabo levato lucida ferro
Spicula, cælatamque argento ferre bipennem ;
Omnibus hic erit unus honos. Tres præmia primi
Accipient, flavāque caput nectentur olivā.
Primus equum phaleris insignem victor habeto. 310
Alter Amazoniam pharetram, plenamque sagittis
Threïciis ; lato quam circùm amplectitur auro
Balteus, et tereti subnectit fibula gemmā.
Tertius Argolicā hac galeā contentus abito." 314
 Hæc ubi dicta, locum capiunt, signoque repente
Corripiunt spatia audito, limenque relinquunt
Effusi, nimbo similes ; simul ultima signant.
Primus abit longèque ante omnia corpora Nisus

Emicat, et ventis et fulminis ocior alis.
Proximus huic, longo sed proximus intervallo, 320
Insequitur Salius. Spatio pòst deinde relicto
Tertius Euryalus,
Euryalumque Helymus sequitur. Quo deinde sub ipso
Ecce volat, calcemque terit jam calce Diores,
Incumbens humero : spatia et si plura supersint,
Transeat elapsus prior, ambiguumve relinquat. 326
  Jamque ferè spatio extremo fessique sub ipsam
Finem adventabant, levi quum sanguine Nisus
Labitur infelix ; cæsis ut fortè juvencis
Fusus humum viridesque super madefecerat herbas.
Hìc juvenis, jam victor ovans, vestigia presso 331
Haud tenuit titubata solo; sed pronus in ipso
Concidit immundoque fimo sacroque cruore.
Non tamen Euryali, non ille oblitus amorum,
Nam sese opposuit Salio per lubrica surgens : 335
Ille autem spissā jacuit revolutus arenā.
Emicat Euryalus, et munere victor amici
Prima tenet, plausuque volat fremituque secundo.
Pòst Helymus subit, et nunc tertia palma Diores.
Hìc totum caveæ consessum ingentis et ora 340
Prima patrum magnis Salius clamoribus implet,
Ereptumque dolo reddi sibi poscit honorem.
Tutatur favor Euryalum lacrimæque decoræ,
Gratior et pulchro veniens in corpore virtus.
Adjuvat et magnā proclamat voce Diores, 345
  Qui subiit palmæ, frustraque ad præmia venit
Ultima, si primi Salio redduntur honores.
  Tum pater Æneas, "Vestra," inquit, " munera vobis

ÆNEIDOS LIB. V. 13

Certa manent, pueri, et palmam movet ordine nemo.
Me liccat casūs misereri insontis amici." 350
Sic fatus tergum Gætuli immane leonis
Dat Salio, villis onerosum atque unguibus aureis.
Hìc Nisus, " Si tanta," inquit, " sunt præmia victis,
Et te lapsorum miseret ; quæ munera Niso
Digna dabis, primam merui qui laude coronam ;
Ni me, quæ Salium, fortuna inimica tulisset?" 356
Et simul his dictis faciem ostentabat, et udo
Turpia membra fimo. Risit pater optimus olli,
Et clypeum efferri jussit, Didymaonis artes,
Neptuni sacro Danais de poste refixum. 360
Hoc juvenem egregium præstanti munere donat.
Pòst, ubi confecti cursūs, et dona peregit :
" Nunc, si cui virtus animusque in pectore præsens,
Adsit et evinctis attollat brachia palmis."
Sic ait, et geminum pugnæ proponit honorem : 365
Victori velatum auro vittisque juvencum ;
Ensem atque insignem galeam solatia victo.
Nec mora : continuò vastis cum viribus effert
Ora Dares, magnoque virûm se murmure tollit :
Solus qui Paridem solitus contendere contra ; 370
Idemque ad tumulum, quo maximus occubat Hector,
Victorem Buten immani corpore, qui se
Bebryciā veniens Amyci de gente ferebat,
Perculit, et fulvā moribundum extendit arenā.
Talis prima Dares caput altum in prœlia tollit, 375
Ostenditque humeros latos, alternaque jactat
Brachia protendens, et verberat ictibus auras.
Quæritur huic alius : nec quisquam ex agmine
  tanto

Audet adire virum, manibusque inducere caestūs.
Ergò alacris cunctosque putans excedere palmā
Æneæ stetit ante pedes ; nec plura moratus 381
Tum laevā taurum cornu tenet, atque ita fatur :
"Nate deā, si nemo audet se credere pugnae,
Quæ finis standi ? quò me decet usque teneri ?
Ducere dona jube." Cuncti simul ore fremebant
Dardanidæ reddique viro promissa jubebant. 386
Hìc gravis Entellum dictis castigat Acestes,
Proximus ut viridante toro consederat herbæ :
"Entelle, heroum quondam fortissime frustra,
Tantane tam patiens nullo certamine tolli 390
Dona sines ? ubi nunc nobis deus ille, magister
Nequiquam memoratus, Eryx? ubi fama per omnem
Trinacriam, et spolia illa tuis pendentia tectis ?"
Ille sub hæc : "Non laudis amor nec gloria cessit
Pulsa metu ; sed enim gelidus tardante senectā 395
Sanguis hebet, frigentque effetæ in corpore vires.
Si mihi, quæ quondam fuerat, quāque improbus iste
Exsultat fidens, si nunc foret illa juventa,
Haud equidem pretio inductus pulchroque juvenco
Venissem ; nec dona moror." Sic deinde loquutus,
In medium geminos immani pondere caestūs 401
Projecit ; quibus acer Eryx in proelia suetus
Ferre manum, duroque intendere brachia tergo.
Obstupuere animi : tantorum ingentia septem
Terga boum plumbo insuto ferroque rigebant. 405
Ante omnes stupet ipse Dares, longèque recusat :
Magnanimusque Anchisiades, et pondus, et ipsa
uc illuc vinclorum immensa volumina versat.

Tum senior tales referebat pectore voces :
" Quid, siquis cæstūs ipsius et Herculis arma   410
Vidisset tristemque hoc ipso in litore pugnam?
Hæc germanus Eryx quondam tuus arma gerebat.
Sanguine cernis adhuc sparsoque infecta cerebro.
His magnum Alciden contra stetit : his ego suetus,
Dum melior vires sanguis dabat, æmula necdum
Temporibus geminis canebat sparsa senectus.   416
Sed si nostra Dares hæc Troïus arma recusat,
Idque pio sedet Æneæ, probat auctor Acestes ;
Æquemus pugnas. Erycis tibi terga remitto,
Solve metūs ; et tu Trojanos exue cæstūs."   420
Hæc fatus duplicem ex humeris rejecit amictum,
Et magnos membrorum artūs, magna ossa, lacertos-
    que
Exuit, atque ingens mediā consistit arenā.
    Tum satus Anchisā cæstūs pater extulit æquos
Et paribus palmas amborum innexuit armis.   425
Constitit in digitos extemplo arrectus uterque,
Brachiaque ad superas interritus extulit auras.
Abduxere retro longè capita ardua ab ictu,
Immiscentque manūs manibus, pugnamque lacess-
    unt.
Ille, pedum melior motu, fretusque juventā ;   430
Hic, membris et mole valens ; sed tarda trementi
Genua labant, vastos quatit æger anhelitus artūs.
Multa viri nequiquam inter se vulnera jactant,
Multa cavo lateri ingeminant, et pectore vastos
Dant sonitūs ; erratque aures et tempora circum
Crebra manus ; duro crepitant sub vulnere malæ. 436
Stat gravis Entellus nisuque immotus eodem ;

Corpore tela modò atque oculis vigilantibus exit.
Ille—velut celsam oppugnat qui molibus urbem,
Aut montana sedet circum castella sub armis— 440
Nunc hos nunc illos aditūs omnemque pererrat
Arte locum, et variis assultibus irritus urget.
Ostendit. dextram insurgens Entellus et altè
Extulit : ille ictum venientem a vertice velox
Prævidit, celerique elapsus corpore cessit. 445
Entellus vires in ventum effudit, et ultro
Ipse gravis graviterque ad terram pondere vasto
Concidit : ut quondam cava concidit aut Erymantho,
Aut Idā in magnā radicibus eruta pinus.
Consurgunt studiis Teucri et Trinacria pubes ; 450
It clamor cœlo : primusque accurrit Acestes,
Æquævumque ab humo miserans attollit amicum.
At non tardatus casu neque territus heros
Acrior ad pugnam redit, ac vim suscitat irā :
Tum pudor incendit vires et conscia virtus, 455
Præcipitemque Daren ardens agit æquore toto,
Nunc dextrā ingeminans ictūs nunc ille sinistrā.
Nec mora, nec requies : quàm multā grandine nimbi
Culminibus crepitant, sic densis ictibus heros
Creber utrāque manu pulsat versatque Dareta. 460
Tum pater Æneas procedere longiùs iras,
Et sævire animis Entellum haud passus acerbis,
Sed finem imposuit pugnæ ; fessumque Dareta
Eripuit, mulcens dictis, ac talia fatur :
"Infelix! quæ tanta animum dementia cepit ? 465
Non vires alias conversaque numina sentis ?
Cede deo." Dixitque et prœlia voce diremit.

ÆNEIDOS LIB. V.

Ast illum fidi æquales, genua ægra trahentem,
Jactantemque utroque caput, crassumque cruorem
Ore rejectantem mistosque in sanguine dentes, 470
Ducunt ad naves; galeamque ensemque vocati
Accipiunt; palmam Entello taurumque relinquunt.
Hìc victor, superans animis tauroque superbus:
" Nate deā, vosque hæc, inquit, cognoscite Teucri,
Et mihi quæ fuerint juvenili in corpore vires, 475
Et quā servetis revocatum a morte Dareta."
Dixit, et adversi contra stetit ora juvenci,
Qui donum astabat pugnæ; durosque reductā
Libravit dextrā media inter cornua cæstūs
Arduus, effractoque illisit in ossa cerebro. 480
Sternitur exanimisque tremens procumbit humi bos.
Ille super tales effudit pectore voces :
" Hanc tibi, Eryx, meliorem animam pro morte
  Daretis
Persolvo : hìc victor cæstūs artemque repono."
  Protinus Æneas celeri certare sagittā 485
Invitat, qui fortè velint, et præmia ponit :
Ingentique manu malum de nave Seresti
Erigit, et volucrem trajecto in fune columbam,
Quò tendant ferrum, malo suspendit ab alto.
Convenere viri, dejectamque ærea sortem 490
Accepit galea; et primus clamore secundo
Hyrtacidæ ante omnes exit locus Hippocoontis:
Quem modò navali Mnestheus certamine victor
Consequitur, viridi Mnestheus evinctus olivā.
Tertius Eurytion, tuus, o clarissime, frater, 495
Pandare; qui quondam, jussus confundere fœdus,
In medios telum torsisti primus Achivos.

C

Extremus galeāque imā subsedit Acestes,
Ausus et ipse manu juvenum tentare laborem.
  Tum validis flexos incurvant viribus arcūs, 500
Pro se quisque, viri et depromunt tela pharetris :
Primaque per cœlum nervo stridente sagitta
Hyrtacidæ juvenis volucres diverberat auras ;
Et venit adversique infigitur arbore mali.
Intremuit malus, timuitque exterrita pennis 505
Ales, et ingenti sonuerunt omnia plausu.
Pòst acer Mnestheus adducto constitit arcu
Alta petens, pariterque oculos telumque tetendit :
Ast ipsam miserandus avem contingere ferro
Non valuit ; nodos et vincula linea rupit, 510
Queis innexa pedem malo pendebat ab alto.
Illa Notos atque atra volans in nubila fugit.
Tum rapidus jamdudum arcu contenta parato
Tela tenens fratrem Eurytion in vota vocavit ;
Jam vacuo lætam cœlo speculatus et alis 515
Plaudentem nigrā figit sub nube columbam.
Decidit exanimis, vitamque reliquit in astris
Aëriis, fixamque refert delapsa sagittam.
Amissā solus palmā superabat Acestes :
Qui tamen ætherias telum contendit in auras, 520
Ostentans artemque pater arcumque sonantem.
Hìc oculis subitò objicitur magnoque futurum
Augurio monstrum : docuit pòst exitus ingens,
Seraque terrifici cecinerunt omina vates. 524
Namque volans liquidis in nubibus arsit arundo,
Signavitque viam flammis, tenuesque recessit
Consumpta in ventos : cœlo ceu sæpe refixa
Transcurrunt crinemque volantia sidera ducunt.

Attonitis hæsere animis superosque precati
Trinacrii Teucrique viri : nec maximus omen   530
Abnuit Æneas; sed lætum amplexus Acesten
Muneribus cumulat magnis, ac talia fatur :
"Sume, pater ; nam te voluit rex magnus Olympi
Talibus auspiciis exsortem ducere honores.
Ipsius Anchisæ longævi hoc munus habebis,   535
Cratera impressum signis, quem Thracius olim
Anchisæ genitori in magno munere Cisseus
Ferre sui dederat monumentum et pignus amoris."
Sic fatus cingit viridanti tempora lauro,
Et primum ante omnes victorem appellat Acesten.
Nec bonus Eurytion prælato invidit honori,   541
Quamvis solus avem cœlo dejecit ab alto.
Proximus ingreditur donis, qui vincula rupit ;
Extremus, volucri qui fixit arundine malum.
   At pater Æneas, nondum certamine misso,   545
Custodem ad sese comitemque impubis Iüli
Epytiden vocat, et fidam sic fatur ad aurem :
"Vade age ; et, Ascanio, si jam puerile paratum
Agmen habet secum cursūsque instruxit equorum,
Ducat avo turmas, et sese ostendat in armis,   550
Dic," ait. Ipse omnem longo decedere circo
Infusum populum et campos jubet esse patentes.
Incedunt pueri, pariterque ante ora parentum
Frenatis lucent in equis ; quos omnis euntes
Trinacriæ mirata fremit Trojæque juventus.   555
Omnibus in morem tonsā coma pressa coronā :
Cornea bina ferunt præfixa hastilia ferro,
Pars leves humero pharetras ; it pectore summo
Flexilis obtorti per collum circulus auri.

Tres equitum numero turmæ ternique vagantur
Ductores ; pueri bis seni quemque sequuti 561
Agmine partito fulgent paribusque magistris.
Una acies juvenum, ducit quam parvus ovantem
Nomen avi referens Priamus, tua clara, Polite,
Progenies, auctura Italos : quem Thracius albis
Portat equus bicolor maculis, vestigia primi 566
Alba pedis frontemque ostentans arduus albam.
Alter Atys, genus unde Atti duxere Latini ;
Parvus Atys, pueroque puer dilectus Iülo.
Extremus, formāque ante omnes pulcher, Iülus 570
Sidonio est invectus equo, quem candida Dido
Esse sui dederat monumentum et pignus amoris.
Cetera Trinacriis pubes senioris Acestæ
Fertur equis. 574
  Excipiunt plausu pavidos gaudentque tuentes
Dardanidæ, veterumque agnoscunt ora parentum.
Postquam omnem læti consessum oculosque suorum
Lustravere in equis ; signum clamore paratis
Epytides longè dedit, insonuitque flagello.
Olli discurrêre pares, atque agmina terni 580
Diductis solvêre choris ; rursusque vocati
Convertêre vias, infestaque tela tulere.
Inde alios ineunt cursūs, aliosque recursūs,
Adversi spatiis ; alternosque orbibus orbes 584
Impediunt, pugnæque cient simulacra sub armis.
Et nunc terga fugā nudant, nunc spicula vertunt
Infensi, factā pariter nunc pace feruntur.
Ut quondam Cretā fertur labyrinthus in altā
Parietibus textum cæcis iter ancipitemque
Mille viis habuisse dolum, quà signa sequendi 590

ÆNEIDOS LIB. V.

Falleret indeprensus et irremeabilis error;
Haud aliter Teucrûm nati vestigia cursu
Impediunt, texuntque fugas et prœlia ludo,
Delphinum similes, qui per maria humida nando
Carpathium Libycumque secant, luduntque per
    undas. 595
Hunc morem cursūs, atque hæc certamina primus
Ascanius, Longam muris quum cingeret Albam,
Rettulit, et priscos docuit celebrare Latinos,
Quo puer ipse modo, secum quo Troïa pubes.
Albani docuere suos; hinc maxima porrò 600
Accepit Roma et patrium servavit honorem;
Trojaque nunc, pueri, Trojanum dicitur agmen.
  Hac celebrata tenus sancto certamina patri.
Hìc primùm Fortuna fidem mutata novavit.
Dum variis tumulo referunt sollennia ludis, 605
Irim de cœlo misit Saturnia Juno
Iliacam ad classem, ventosque aspirat eunti,
Multa movens, necdum antiquum saturata dolorem.
Illa viam celerans per mille coloribus arcum,
Nulli visa, cito decurrit tramite virgo. 610
Conspicit ingentem concursum; et litora lustrans
Desertosque videt portūs classemque relictam.
At procul in solā secretæ Troades actā
Amissum Anchisen flebant, cunctæque profundum
Pontum aspectabant flentes: heu! tot vada fessis
Et tantum superesse maris, vox omnibus una. 616
Urbem orant; tædet pelagi perferre laborem.
Ergò inter medias sese haud ignara nocendi
Conjicit, et faciemque deæ vestemque reponit.
Fit Beroë, Ismarii conjux longæva Doryclî, 620

Cui genus et quondam nomen natique fuissent.
Ac sic Dardanidûm mediam se matribus infert :
"O miseræ, quas non manus," inquit, "Achaïca belli
Traxerit ad letum, patriæ sub mœnibus ! o gens
Infelix ! cui te exitio fortuna reservat ? 625
Septima post Trojæ excidium jam vertitur æstas ;
Quum freta, quum terras omnes, tot inhospita saxa
Sideraque emensæ ferimur ; dum per mare magnum
Italiam sequimur fugientem, et volvimur undis. 629
Hìc Erycis fines fraterni, atque hospes Acestes :
Quis prohibet muros jacere, et dare civibus urbem ?
O patria, et rapti nequiquam ex hoste Penates !
Nullane jam Trojæ dicentur mœnia ? nusquam
Hectoreos amnes, Xanthum et Simoënta videbo ?
Quin agite, et mecum infaustas exurite puppes. 635
Nam mihi Cassandræ per somnum vatis imago
Ardentes dare visa faces : hìc quærite Trojam ;
Hìc domus est, inquit, vobis : jam tempus agit res.
Nec tantis mora prodigiis ; en quatuor aræ 639
Neptuno ! deus ipse faces animumque ministrat."
 Hæc memorans, prima infensum vi corripit ignem :
Sublatāque procul dextrā connixa coruscat
Et jacit. Arrectæ mentes stupefactaque corda
Iliadum. Hìc una e multis, quæ maxima natu,
Pyrgo, tot Priami natorum regia nutrix : 645
"Non Beroë vobis ; non hæc Rhœteïa, matres,
Est Dorycli conjux : divini signa decoris,
*Ardentes*que notate oculos : qui spiritus illi,
Qui vultus, vocisve sonus, vel gressus eunti.
Ipsa egomet dudum Beroën digressa reliqui 650

Ægram, indignantem tali quòd sola careret
Munere, nec meritos Anchisæ inferret honores."
Hæc effata.
  At matres primò ancipites oculisque malignis
Ambiguæ spectare rates miserum inter amorem
Præsentis terræ fatisque vocantia regna :   656
Quum dea se paribus per cœlum sustulit alis,
Ingentemque fugā secuit sub nubibus arcum.
Tum verò attonitæ monstris, actæque furore,   659
Conclamant, rapiuntque focis penetralibus ignem :
Pars spoliant aras, frondem ac virgulta facesque
Conjiciunt : furit immissis Vulcanus habenis
Transtra per, et remos, et pictas abiete puppes.
  Nuntius Anchisæ ad tumulum cuneosque theatri
Incensas perfert naves Eumelus : et ipsi   665
Respiciunt atram in nimbo volitare favillam.
Primus et Ascanius, cursūs ut lætus equestres
Ducebat, sic acer equo turbata petivit
Castra ; nec exanimes possunt retinere magistri.
" Quis furor iste novus? quò nunc, quò tenditis,"
    inquit,   670
" Heu miseræ cives! non hostem inimicaque castra
Argivûm ; vestras spes uritis. En ego vester
Ascanius !" Galeam ante pedes projecit inanem,
Quā ludo indutus belli simulacra ciebat.
Accelerat simul Æneas, simul agmina Teucrûm ;
Ast illæ diversa metu per litora passim   676
Diffugiunt, silvasque et sicubi concava furtim
Saxa petunt : piget incepti lucisque ; suosque
Mutatæ agnoscunt ; excussaque pectore Juno est.
Sed non idcirco flammæ atque incendia vires   680

Indomitas posuere : udo sub robore vivit
Stuppa, vomens tardum fumum ; lentusque carinas
Est vapor, et toto descendit corpore pestis ;
Nec vires heroum infusaque flumina prosunt.
    Tum pius Æneas humeris abscindere vestem,
Auxilioque vocare deos, et tendere palmas :   686
"Jupiter omnipotens, si nondum exosus ad unum
Trojanos, si quid pietas antiqua labores
Respicit humanos ; da flammam evadere classi
Nunc, pater, et tenues Teucrûm res eripe leto :   690
Vel tu, quod superest, infesto fulmine morti,
Si mereor, demitte ; tuāque hîc obrue dextrā."
Vix hæc ediderat ; quum effusis imbribus atra
Tempestas sine more furit, tonitruque tremiscunt
Ardua terrarum et campi, ruit æthere toto   695
Turbidus imber aquā densisque nigerrimus Austris,
Implenturque super puppes, semusta madescunt
Robora, restinctus donec vapor omnis, et omnes,
Quatuor amissis, servatæ a peste carinæ.
    At pater Æneas casu concussus acerbo,   700
Nunc huc ingentes, nunc illuc pectore curas
Mutabat ; versans, Siculisne resideret arvis
Oblitus fatorum, Italasne capesseret oras.
Tum senior Nautes, unum Tritonia Pallas
Quem docuit multāque insignem reddidit arte,   705
Hæc responsa dabat, vel quæ portenderet ira
Magna deûm, vel quæ fatorum posceret ordo.
Isque his Æneam solatus vocibus infit :
"Nate deā, quò fata trahunt retrahuntque, sequ-
    amur.
Quicquid erit, superanda omnis fortuna ferendo est.

ÆNEIDOS LIB. V.

Est tibi Dardanius divinæ stirpis Acestes; 711
Hunc cape consiliis socium et conjunge volentem.
Huic trade, amissis superant qui navibus, et quos
Pertæsum magni incepti rerumque tuarum est;
Longævosque senes, ac fessas æquore matres, 715
Et quicquid tecum invalidum, metuensque pericli
  est,
Delige; et his habeant terris sine mœnia fessi.
Urbem appellabunt permisso nomine Acestam."
  Talibus incensus dictis senioris amici:
Tum verò in curas animus deducitur omnes. 720
Et Nox atra polum bigis subvecta tenebat.
Visa dehinc cœlo facies delapsa parentis
Anchisæ subitò tales effundere voces:
" Nate, mihi vitā quondam, dum vita manebat,
Care magìs: nate, Iliacis exercite fatis; 725
Imperio Jovis huc venio, qui classibus ignem
Depulit, et cœlo tandem miseratus ab alto est.
Consiliis pare, quæ nunc pulcherrima Nautes
Dat senior: lectos juvenes, fortissima corda,
Defer in Italiam: gens dura atque aspera cultu
Debellanda tibi Latio est. Ditis tamen antè 731
Infernas accede domos; et Averna per alta
Congressūs pete, nate, meos. Non me impia nam-
  que
Tartara habent tristesque umbræ; sed amœna
  piorum
Concilia, Elysiumque colo. Huc casta Sibylla 735
Nigrarum multo pecudum te sanguine ducet.
Tum genus omne tuum, et, quæ dentur mœnia,
  disces.

Jamque vale : torquet medios Nox humida cursūs,
Et me sævus equis oriens afflavit anhelis."
Dixerat, et tenues fugit, ceu fumus, in auras. 740
Æneas, " Quò deinde ruis ? quò proripis ? " inquit,
" Quem fugis ? aut quis te nostris complexibus
  arcet ? "
Hæc memorans cinerem et sopitos suscitat ignes ;
Pergameumque Larem, et canæ penetralia Vestæ
Farre pio et plenā supplex veneratur acerrā. 745
  Extemplo socios primumque arcessit Acesten,
Et Jovis imperium et cari præcepta parentis
Edocet ; et quæ nunc animo sententia constet.
Haud mora consiliis, nec jussa recusat Acestes.
Transcribunt urbi matres, populumque volentem
Deponunt, animos nil magnæ laudis egentes. 751
Ipsi transtra novant, flammisque ambesa reponunt
Robora navigiis, aptant remosque rudentesque,
Exigui numero ; sed bello vivida virtus.
  Interea Æneas urbem designat aratro, 755
Sortiturque domos : hoc Ilium, et hæc loca Trojam,
Esse jubet ; gaudet regno Trojanus Acestes,
Indicitque forum, et patribus dat jura vocatis.
Tum vicina astris Erycino in vertice sedes
Fundatur Veneri Idaliæ ; tumuloque sacerdos 760
Et lucus latè sacer additur Anchiseo.
Jamque dies epulata novem gens omnis, et aris
Factus honos ; placidi straverunt æquora venti ;
Creber et aspirans rursus vocat Auster in altum.
Exoritur procurva ingens per litora fletus ; 765
Complexi inter se noctemque diemque morantur.
Ipsæ jam matres ; ipsi, quibus aspera quondam

Visa maris facies et non tolerabile nomen,
Ire volunt, omnemque fugæ perferre laborem.
Quos bonus Æneas dictis solatur amicis, 770
Et consanguineo lacrimans commendat Acestæ.
Tres Eryci vitulos, et Tempestatibus agnam
Cædere deinde jubet, solvique ex ordine funem.
Ipse caput tonsæ foliis evinctus olivæ,
Stans procul in prorā, pateram tenet, extaque salsos
Porricit in fluctūs, ac vina liquentia fundit. 776
Prosequitur surgens a puppi ventus euntes :
Certatim socii feriunt mare, et æquora verrunt.
  At Venus interea Neptunum exercita curis
Alloquitur, talesque effundit pectore questūs : 780
" Junonis gravis ira neque exsaturabile pectus
Cogunt me, Neptune, preces descendere in omnes :
Quam nec longa dies pietas nec mitigat ulla,
Nec Jovis imperio fatisve infracta quiescit.
Non mediā de gente Phrygum exedisse nefandis
Urbem odiis satis est, nec pœnam traxse per omnem 786
Relliquias ; Trojæ cineres atque ossa peremptæ
Insequitur. Causas tanti sciat illa furoris.
Ipse mihi nuper Libycis tu testis in undis
Quam molem subitò excierit : maria omnia cœlo
Miscuit, Æoliis nequiquam freta procellis ; 791
In regnis hoc ausa tuis.
Per scelus, ecce, etiam Trojanis matribus actis,
Exussit fœdè puppes et classe subegit
Amissā socios ignotæ linquere terræ. 795
Quod superest, oro, liceat dare tuta per undas
Vela tibi, liceat Laurentem attingere Tybrim ;

Si concessa peto, si dant ea mœnia Parcæ."
 Tum Saturnius hæc domitor maris edidit alti :
" Fas omne est, Cytherea, meis te fidere regnis, 800
Unde genus ducis, merui quoque : sæpe furores
Compressi et rabiem tantam cœlique marisque.
Nec minor in terris, Xanthum Simoëntaque testor,
Æneæ mihi cura tui. Quum Troïa Achilles
Exanimata sequens impingeret agmina muris, 805
Millia multa daret leto, gemerentque repleti
Amnes, nec reperire viam atque evolvere posset
In mare se Xanthus; Pelidæ tunc ego forti
Congressum Æneam, nec dîs nec viribus æquis,
Nube cavā rapui; cuperem quum vertere ab imo
Structa meis manibus perjuræ mœnia Trojæ. 811
Nunc quoque mens eadem perstat mihi: pelle timorem;
Tutus, quos optas, portūs accedet Averni.
Unus erit tantùm, amissum quem gurgite quæret;
Unum pro multis dabitur caput." 815
 His ubi læta deæ permulsit pectora dictis,
Jungit equos auro genitor spumantiaque addit
Frena feris, manibusque omnes effundit habenas.
Cæruleo per summa levis volat æquora curru :
Subsidunt undæ, tumidumque sub axe tonanti 820
Sternitur æquor aquis; fugiunt vasto æthere nimbi.
Tum variæ comitum facies; immania cete,
Et senior Glauci chorus, Inoüsque Palæmon,
Tritonesque citi, Phorcique exercitus omnis.
Læva tenent Thetis et Melite, Panopeaque virgo,
Nesæe, Spioque, Thaliaque, Cymodoceque. 826
Hic patris Æneæ suspensam blanda vicissim

Gaudia pertentant mentem ; jubet ociùs omnes
Attolli malos, intendi brachia velis. 829
Unà omnes fecere pedem ; pariterque sinistros,
Nunc dextros solvêre sinūs ; unà ardua torquent
Cornua detorquentque : ferunt sua flamina classem.
Princeps ante omnes densum Palinurus agebat
Agmen : ad hunc alii cursum contendere jussi. 834
  Jamque ferè mediam cœli Nox humida metam
Contigerat ; placidā laxârant membra quiete
Sub remis fusi per dura sedilia nautæ ;
Quum levis ætheriis delapsus Somnus ab astris
Aëra dimovit tenebrosum, et dispulit umbras,
Te, Palinure, petens, tibi tristia somnia portans
Insonti ; puppique deus consedit in altā, 841
Phorbanti similis, fuditque has ore loquelas :
"Iaside Palinure, ferunt ipsa æquora classem,
Æquatæ spirant auræ, datur hora quieti.
Pone caput, fessosque oculos furare labori. 845
Ipse ego paulisper pro te tua munera inibo."
Cui vix attollens Palinurus lumina fatur :
"Mene salis placidi vultum fluctūsque quietos
Ignorare jubes ? mene huic confidere monstro ?
Æneam credam quid enim fallacibus Austris 850
Et cœli toties deceptus fraude sereni ?"
Talia dicta dabat : clavumque affixus et hærens
Nusquam amittebat, oculosque sub astra tenebat.
Ecce deus ramum Lethæo rore madentem, 854
Vique soporatum Stygiā, super utraque quassat
Tempora, cunctantique natantia lumina solvit.
Vix primos inopina quies laxaverat artūs,
Et super incumbens cum puppis parte revulsā

Cumque gubernaclo liquidas projecit in undas
Præcipitem, ac socios nequiquam sæpe vocantem.
Ipse volans tenues se sustulit ales in auras.   861
Currit iter tutum non seciùs æquore classis,
Promissisque patris Neptuni interrita fertur.
Jamque adeò scopulos Sirenum advecta subibat,
Difficiles quondam, multorumque ossibus albos 865
(Tum rauca assiduo longè sale saxa sonabant),
Quum pater amisso fluitantem errare magistro
Sensit, et ipse ratem nocturnis rexit in undis,
Multa gemens, casuque animum concussus amici :
"O nimiùm cœlo et pelago confise sereno,   870
Nudus in ignotā, Palinure, jacebis arenā."

VOCABULARY.

ABBREVIATIONS.

a. *or* act.	active.	interrog.	interrogative
abl.	ablative.	irr. *or* irreg.	irregular.
acc.	accusative.	m.	masculine.
acc. to	according to.	n. *or* neut.	neuter.
adj.	adjective.	nom.	nominative.
adv.	adverb.	num.	numeral.
c = cum	with.	obsol.	obsolete.
cf. = confer	compare.	ord.	ordinal.
comm. gen.	common gender.	P. *or* part.	participle.
comp.	{ compar..tive degree. }	pa.	participial adj.
		pass.	passive.
conj.	conjunction.	perf.	perfect.
contr.	contracted.	pers.	person, personal.
dat.	dative.	pluperf.	pluperfect.
def. *or* defect.	defective.	plur.	plural.
dem. *or* demonstr.	} demonstrative.	pos.	positive degree.
		poss.	possessive.
dep.	deponent.	prep.	preposition.
desid.	desiderative.	pres.	present.
dissyll.	dissyllable.	prob.	probably.
esp.	especially.	pron.	pronoun.
etym.	etymology.	[§]	{ paragraph in Public Schools Latin Primer. }
f.	feminine.		
folld.	followed.		
follg.	following.	rel.	relative.
fr.	from.	Sans.	Sanscrit.
freq.	frequentative.	semi-dep.	semi-deponent.
fut.	future.	sing.	singular.
gen.	genitive.	subj.	subjunctive.
gov.	governing.	sup.	{ superlative; supine. }
Gr.	Greek.		
imperf.	imperfect.	trisyll.	trisyllable.
inch.	inchoative.	t. t.	technical term.
ind. *or* indic.	indicative.	uncontr.	uncontracted.
indecl.	indeclinable.	v. a.	verb active.
indef.	indefinite.	v. dep.	verb deponent.
inf. *or* infin.	infinitive.	v. n.	verb neuter.
intens.	intensive.	voc.	vocative.
interj.	interjection.	=	equal to.

N.B.—The figures before v. a., v. dep., and v. n., denote the conjugation of the verb.

Where the etymology is not given, the word is of very uncertain or unknown origin.

Such forms and meanings of words, as do not belong to the text, are not inserted in the Vocabulary.

VOCABULARY.

ăb (ā), prep. gov. abl.: **1.** Locally: *From, away from.*—**2.** Of descent or birth: *From.*—**3.** To form an adverbial expression: ab alto, *on high, aloft* [akin to Gr. ἀπ-ό, Sans. *ap-a*].

ab-dūco, duxi, ductum, dūcĕre, 3. v. a. [ăb, "away"; dūco, "to lead"] ("To lead away"; hence) *To draw back or away; to withdraw.*

abduxi, perf. ind. of abdūco.

ăb-ĕo, ivi *or* ii, ĭtum, ire, v. n. [ăb, "away"; ĕo, "to go"] *To go away, depart.*

ăbĭbo, fut. ind. of ăbĕo.

ăbĭes, ĕtis (Abl. abiete as trisyll., viz. abjete, v. 663), f. *A fir-tree, pine-tree; a fir, pine;* —at v. 663 the abl. abiete is used for ex abiete, and denotes "the material": abiete puppes, *poops of fir, fir-poops.*

ăbĭs, ăbĭt, 2. and 3. pers. sing. pres. ind. of ăbĕo.

ăbĭto, 3. pers. sing. fut. imperat. of ăbĕo.

ab-nŭo, nŭi, nŭĭtum *or* nūtum, nŭĕre, 3. v. a. [ăb, "away"; nŭo, "to nod"] ("To nod away" from one; hence) *To decline, refuse, reject.*

ab-scindo, scidi, scissum, scindĕre, 3. v. a. [ăb, "away"; scindo, "to rend"] *To rend,* or *tear, away;*—at v. 686 abscindere is the Historic Inf. [§ 140, 2].

ac; see atque.

Ăcarnān, ānis, m. *A man of Acarnania* (now *Carnia*, a country of ancient N. Greece), *an Acarnian* [Gr. Ἀκαρνάν].

accēde, sing. pres. imperat. of accēdo.

ac-cēdo, cessi, cessum, cēdĕre, 3. v. n. [for ad-cēdo; fr. ăd, "to"; cēdo, "to go"] *To go to, approach;*—at vv. 732, 813 folld. by Acc. dependent on prep. in verb.

ac-cĕlĕro, cĕlĕrāvi, cĕlĕrātum, cĕlĕrāre, 1. v. n. [for ad-cĕlĕro; fr. ăd, in "intensive" force; cĕlĕro, "to make haste"] *To make haste, to hasten.*

accendĕrim, perf. subj. of accendo.

ac-cen-do, di, sum, dĕre, 3. v. a.: **1.** *To kindle, light up.* —**2.** Figuratively of hope: *To kindle, raise up,* etc.—Pass.:

ac-cendor, census sum, cendi [for ad-can-do; fr. ad, in "augmentative" force; root CAN, akin to Gr. κά-ω, καί-ω, "to light, kindle"].

accēpi, perf. ind. of accĭpĭo.

ac-cĭpĭo, cēpi, ceptum, cĭpĕre, 3. v. a. [for ad-căpĭo; fr. ăd, "to"; căpĭo, "to take"] ("To take to" one's self; hence) *To receive.*

D

ăc-curro, curri and cŭ-curri, cursum, currĕre, 3. v. n. [for ad-curro; fr. ăd, "to"; curro, "to run"] *To run to,* or *up to,* a person; *to run up.*

ă-cer, cris, cre, adj. [for ac-cer; fr. ᴀᴄ, root of ăc-ŭo, "to sharpen"] ("Sharp"; hence) *Bold, active, spirited, zealous.* ☞ Comp.: ăcr-ior.

ăc-erbus, erba, erbum, adj. [root ᴀᴄ, whence ăc-ŭo, "to make pointed *or* sharp"] ("Pointed, sharp"; hence) **1.** Of the mind, feelings, *etc.*: *Bitter.—***2.** *Bitter, grievous.*

ăcer-ra, ræ, f. [prob. for ăcer-na; fr. ăcer, ăcer-is, "maple"] ("A maple-thing"; hence) *An incense-box;* or, acc. to some, *an incense-pan, a censer.*

Ăcesta, æ, f. *Acesta* (earlier *Egesta,* later *Segesta,* now ruins near the modern *Calatafimi*), a town of Sicily, taking its name from king Acestes; see Acestes.

Ăcestes, æ (Acc. Acesten, v. 30), m. *Acestes;* a king in Sicily, son of the Sicilian river-god Crimisus and of Egesta, a Trojan woman;— at v. 498 Acestes = the name of *Acestes* [Gr. Ἀκέστης, "Healer"].

Ăchăī-cus, ca, cum, adj. [Achāi-a, "Achaia," a country of ancient S. Greece or the Peloponnēsus (now the Morēa) ("Of, *or* belonging to, Achaia; Achæan"; hence) *Grecian, Greek.*

Ăchĕron, ontis, m. ("Stream of pain *or* grief") *Acheron;* (a river of the lower world; hence) *the lower world* [Gr. Ἀχέρων].

Ăchilles, is, m. *Achilles;* a Greek hero in the Trojan war, son of Peleus, king of Thessaly, *and of the sea-*goddess Thetis [Gr. Ἀχιλλεύς].

Ăchīvi, ōrum, m. plur. [Achiv-us, "Greek, Grecian"] *The Greeks.*

ăc-ies, iēi, f. [ᴀᴄ, root of ăc-ŭo, "to sharpen"] ("An edge *or* sharp edge"; hence) Milit. t. t.: *An army, host, body of troops* in battle array.

ācrior, us; see ăcer.

acta, æ, f. *The sea-shore, beach* [Gr. ἀκτή].

actus, a, um, P. perf. pass. of ăgo.

ăcū-tus, ta, tum, adj. [ăcŭ-o, "to sharpen"] ("Sharpened"; hence) *Pointed, sharp.*

ăd, prep. gov. acc.: **1.** *To, towards.*—**2.** *To, up to.*—**3.** *At, near.*—**4.** *According to, in accordance with, after.*

ad-do, dĭdi, dĭtum, dăre, 3. v. a. [ăd, "to"; do, "to put"] **1.** *To put to,* or *on to.*—**2.** *To add.*—Pass.: **ad-dor,** dĭtus sum, di.

ad-dūco, duxi, ductum, dūcĕre, 3. v. a. [ăd, "to"; dūco, "to lead"] ("To lead to"; hence) *To draw, or pull, towards* one.—Pass.: **ad-dūcor,** ductus sum, dūci.

adductus, a, um, P. perf. pass. of addūco.

1. **ăd-ĕo,** adv. [prob. for ăd-ĕom; fr. ăd, "to *or* up to"; ĕom (= ĕum), old acc. of pron. is, "this"] ("To, *or* up to, this") Used with adverbs to give emphasis to the expression: *Indeed:*—jamque adeo, *and now indeed,* v. 864.

2. **ăd-ĕo,** ivi *or* ii, itum, ire, v. n. [ăd, "to"; ĕo, "to go"] *To go to, approach.*

ăděram, imperf. ind. of adsum.

ădest, 3. pers. sing. pres. ind. of adsum.

ăd-hĭbĕo, hĭbŭi, hĭbĭtum, hĭbēre, 2. v. a. [for ăd-hăbĕo; fr. ăd, "to"; hăbĕo, "to hold"]

VOCABULARY. 35

("To hold to, or towards; to direct towards"; hence, "to bring" a person "to" a place; hence) With Acc. of person and Dat. of feast, *etc.*: *To invite to.*

ăd-hūc, adv. [ăd, "up to"; huc (old form of hoc), "this"] Of time: *Up to this time, hitherto.*

ădīre, pres. inf. of 2. ădĕo.

ădĭ-tus, tūs, m. [ădĕo, "to go to," through root ADI (*i. e.* ăd; ĭ, root of ĕo)] ("A going to"; hence) *An approach.*

ad-jŭvo, jŭvi, jūtum, jŭvāre, 1. v. n. [ăd, "without force"; jŭvo, "to assist"] *To assist, help, aid.*

ad-nītor, nisus and nixus sum, niti, 3. v. dep. [ăd, "against"; nitor, "to lean"] ("To lean against"; hence) *To exert one's self, strive, etc.; to put forth efforts, etc.*

adnixus, a, um, P. perf. of adnitor.

adsim, pres. subj. of adsum;—at vv. 70, 364 adsint and adsit are used in the force of the Greek Optative, *i. e.* to express a wish.

ad-sum, af-fŭi, ăd-esse, v. n. [ăd, "at"; sum, "to be"] ("To be at" a place, *etc.*; hence) **1.** *To be present.*—**2.** Of things as Subject: *To be present, to be at hand, to arrive.*

advectus, a, um, P. perf. pass. of advĕho;—at v. 86½ advecta (supply ea = classis) is folld. by Acc. of place, viz. scopulos [§ 101].

ad-vĕho, vexi, vectum, vĕhĕre, 3. v. a. [ăd, "to"; vĕho, "to carry"] **1.** *To carry to a place, etc.*—**2.** Pass. in reflexive force: ("To carry one's self to"; *i. e.*) *To arrive at a place; see* advectus.

ad-vēlo, vēlāvi, vēlātum,

vēlāre, 1. v. a. [ăd, "without force"; vēlo, "to co\er, wrap," *etc.*] *To cover, encircle, surround.*

adven-to, tāvi, tātum, tāre, 1. v. n. intens. [advĕn-io, "to come to"] *To come to or towards; to proceed or come onwards; to draw near.*

adven-tus, tūs, m. [advĕnio, "to come to"] ("A coming to" a person or thing; hence, the act being regarded as complete) *Arrival.*

adver-sus, sa, sum, adj. [for advert-sus; fr. advert-o, "to turn towards"] ("Turned towards" an object; hence) **1.** *Opposite, in front.*—**2.** *Confronting* one another, *etc.*

advertīte, plur. pres. imperat. of adverto.

ad-verto, verti, versum, vertĕre, 3. v. a. [fr. ăd, "to"; verto, "to turn"] ("To turn to or towards"; hence) **1.** Pass. in reflexive force: *To turn one's, etc., self,* or *direct one's, etc., way to.*—**2.** *To direct* the mind, *etc.*;—at v. 304 supply eis or ad ea, as referring to preceding hæc.—Pass.: **ad-vertor,** versus sum, verti.

ad-vŏco, vŏcāvi, vŏcātum, vŏcāre, 1. v. a. [ăd, "to"; vŏco, "to call"] *To call to* one, *to summon, etc.*

ădўtum, i. n.: **1.** *The sanctuary or innermost part of a temple,* which none but priests or priestesses were allowed to enter.—**2.** *The interior,* or *innermost recess* of a tomb;—at v. 84 in plur. [ἄδυτον, "not to be entered"].

æger, gra, grum, adj. *Sick, feeble, etc.*:—æger anhelitus, *feeble breathing,* i. e. shortness of breath.

æmŭl-a, æ, f. [æmŭl-us, "striving, etc., with another"] ("She who strives, or vies,

D 2

with another; hence) Of a ship: A rival, competitor.

aem-ŭlus, ŭla, ŭlum, adj. [akin to ĭm-ĭtor, "to imitate"] ("Imitating"; hence, "emulating"; hence) In a bad sense: *Envious*.

Ænĕădēs, ārum; see Ænĕas.

Ænĕas, æ, m. *Æneas*; the mythic son of Anchises and the goddess Venus, and ancestor of the Romans. After death he was worshipped under the title of Jupiter Indiges.—Hence, **1. Ænĕădēs**, ārum, m. plur. (*The followers* or *countrymen of Æneas*; i. e.) *Trojans*. — **2. Ænēis**, ĭdos, f. *The Æneid*, an epic poem by Virgil, of which Æneas is the hero [Gr. Αἰνειάς].

Ænēis, ĭdos; see Ænĕas.

ăēnum, i; see ăēnus.

ăē-nus, na, num, adj. [for ær-nĕus; fr. æs, ær-is, "bronze"] ("Pertaining to *æs*"; hence) *Of copper* or *bronze*; *brazen*.—As Subst.: **ăēnum**, i, n. *A* bronze-*caldron* or -*pot* for boiling food.

Æŏl-ĭus, ĭa, ĭum, adj. [Æŏlus, "Æolus," the god of the winds] *Of*, or *belonging to*, *Æolus*:—Æoliæ procellæ, *the tempests of Æolus* (v. 791), i. e. the tempest which Æolus raised at the request of Juno, as mentioned by Virgil, Æn. 1, 81 *sq*.

æqu-æv-us, a, um, adj. [æqu-us, "equal"; æv-um, "age"] *Of equal*, or *the like, age*.

æqu-ālis, āle, adj. [æqu-(a)-o, "to equal"] ("That equals"; hence, "equal in age"; hence, as Subst.:) **æquālis**, is, m. *An equal in age, a comrade*.

æquātus, a, um, P. perf. pass. of æquo.

æqu-o, āvi, ātum, āre, 1. v. a. [æqu-us] **1.** [æquus, "even, level"] *To make even* or *level* with something: — æquāta rostra, *beaks made level*, i. e. *in a line with each other* or *abreast*.—**2.** [æquus, "equal"] *To make equal, to equalize*.—Pass.: *To be made*, or *become, equal*;—æquātæ auræ, *the breezes having* (or *that have*) *become equal*, i. e. *blowing with equal force*, not in gusts, etc.

æqu-or, ōris, n. [æqu-o, "to make level"] ("That which is made level"; hence, "a level surface") **1.** *A level plain*; v. 456.—**2.** ("The smooth surface of the sea" when calm; hence) Sing. and Plur.: *The waters* of the sea; *the sea* in any condition.

æqu-us, a, um, adj. ("Of one uniform nature" throughout; hence, "level, even"; hence) *Equal* [akin to Sans. *ek-as*, "one"].

āēr, āĕris, m.: **1.** *The air*.— **2.** *Cloud, mist, vapour* [Gr. ἀήρ].

ær-ĕus, ĕa, ĕum, adj. [æs, ær-is, "bronze"] ("Provided with *æs*"; hence) **1.** *Made of bronze, bronze-*.—**2.** Of ships: *With a beak of bronze; brazen-beaked*.

āĕr-ĭus, ĭa, ĭum, adj. [āēr, āĕr-is, "the air"] ("Of, or belonging to, the air"; hence) *Rising aloft in the air, high, lofty*.

æs, æris, n. *Bronze, copper* [akin to Sans. *ayas*, "iron"].

æs-tas, tātis, f. ("The burning season"; hence) *Summer* [prob. akin to Gr. αἴθω, "to burn *or* be hot"].

æther, ĕris (Acc. æthera, v. 13), m. ("The burning, *or* shining, thing"; hence) **1.** *The upper air* or *ether*; *the sky*.—**2.** *Heaven* [Gr. αἰθήρ].

æthĕr-ĭus, ĭa, ĭum, adj. [æther, æthĕr-is, "the ether *or*

VOCABULARY.   37

upper air"] ("Pertaining to æther"; hence) **1.** *Pertaining to the upper air* or *sky.*—**2.** *Of,* or *pertaining to, the sky* or *heavens; heavenly, celestial.*

ævum, i, n. *Life-time, life, age* [akin to Gr. αἰϝών; Sans. âyus, "life"].

af-fĕro, at-tŭli, al-lātum, af-ferre, 3. v. a. [for ad-fĕro; fr. ăd, "to"; fĕro, "to bring"] With Dat. [§ 106, a]: *To bring to.*

affixus, a, um, adj. [for affig-sus; fr. affīg-o, "to fasten on to" a thing] ("Fastened on to, attached to"; hence) *Holding fast, laying fast hold.*

af-flo, flāvi, flātum, flāre, 1. v. a. [for ad-flo; fr. ăd, "upon"; flo, "to blow or breathe"] *To blow* or *breathe upon* an object.

ăge; see **ăgo.**

agger, ĕris, m. [aggĕr-o, "to bring to" a place] ("That which is brought to" a place; hence, "materials" for forming an elevation; hence) **1.** *A mound.*—**2.** Of a road: *The raised track, causeway,* etc.

ăgĭte; see **ăgo.**

ag-men, mĭnis, n. [ăg-o, "to put in motion"] ("That which is put in motion"; hence) **1.** *A line* of persons or things.—**2.** Of oars: *The stroke.*—**3.** *A band, troop, company,* etc.—**4.** Plur.: *Troops, host,* etc.

agn-a, æ, f. [agn-us, "a lamb"] *A ewe-lamb.*

a-gnosco, gnōvi, gnĭtum, gnoscĕre, 3. v.a. [for ad-gnosco; fr. ăd, "in relation to"; gnosco (old form of nosco), "to know"] ("To know in relation to" one's self; hence) *To recognize.*

ăgo, ēgi, actum, ăgĕre, 3. v. a. ("To put, *or* set, in motion"; hence) **1.** *To lead.*—**2.** Of ships: *To urge,* or *impel, onwards;* to drive forwards by oars, etc.—**3.** *To drive before* one; *to chase, pursue.* — **4.** Mentally: *To urge on, stir up, rouse,* etc.—**5.** Of actions: *To do,* etc.—**6.** Imperat. as adv.: **ăge, ăgĭte,** *come on! come!*—**7.** Of time: *To pass, spend.*—Pass.: **ăgor,** actus sum, ăgi [Gr. ἄγω].

agr-estis, este, adj. [ăger, agr-i, "a field"; plur., "the fields, country"] *Of,* or *belonging to, the fields* or *country; country-, rustic.*

ăio, v. defect. *To say, speak* [akin to Sans. root ʌʜ, for ʌɢʜ, "to say, speak"].

āla, æ, f. *A wing.*

ălăcer, cris, cre, adj. *Quick, eager.*

Alb-a, æ, f. [alb-us, "white"] ("The white" city) *Alba;* the mother city of Rome, built by Ascanius, the son of Æneas, upon the broad rocky margin between the Alban lake (now Lago di Castello Grandolfo) and Mount Albanus (now Monte Cavo). From its length it obtained the designation of Alba Longa, *i. e.* "Long Alba."—Hence, (**Alb-ānus,** āna, ānum, adj. "Of, or belonging to, Alba; Alban." — As Subst.:) **Albāni,** ōrum, m. plur. *The people of Alba; the Albans.*

Albāni, ōrum; see Alba.

albus, a, um, adj. *White* [akin to Gr. ἀλφός].

Alcīdes, æ, m. *Alcides* ("Descendant of Alceus," the father of Amphitryon; hence, as being the supposed son of Amphitryon) *Hercules* [Gr. Ἀλκείδης].

āl-es, ălĭtis, adj. [for al-i-(t)-s; fr. āl-a, "a wing"; ɪ, root of ĕo, "to go"; (t) epenthetic letter] ("Wing-going";

hence) *With wings, winged.*—As Subst. comm. gen. *A bird.*

ăl-ĭter, adv. [ăl-ĭus, old form of ăl-ĭus, "another"] *In another manner, otherwise:*—haud ăliter, *not otherwise; i. e. just so; in this, or the like, way,* v. 592.

ăl-ĭus, ĭa, ĭud (Gen. ălĭus; Dat. ălĭi), adj. : **1.** *Another, other* of many.—As Subst.: **a.** Sing.: **ălĭus,** ĭus, m. *Another person, another.* — **b.** Plur.: **ălĭī,** ōrum, m. (a) *Others.*—(b) *The others, the rest.*—**2.** Repeated, whether in the same or in different cases: *One . . . another* [akin to Gr. ἄλ-λος, "another"].

al-lŏquor, lŏquūtus sum, lŏqui, 3. v. dep. [for ad-lŏquor; fr. ăd, "to"; lŏquor, "to speak"] *To speak to, address.*

al-nus, ma, mum, adj. [ăl-o, "to nourish"] ("Nourishing"; hence) *Propitious, favourable.*

ăl-o, ŭi, tum and ĭtum, ĕre, 3. v. a. ("To nourish"; hence) In figurative force: *To support,* etc. [akin to Gr. ἀλ-θω].

alt-ārĭa, ārĭum, n. plur. [alt-um, "a high place"] ("Things pertaining to *altum*"; hence, "that which is placed upon an altar (*ara*) for the burning of the victim"; hence) *A high altar,* or *altars,* on which sacrifices were offered only to the superior deities;—at v. 93 altaria is put poetically for that which was on it.

alt-e, adv. [alt-us, "high"] *On high, aloft.*

al-ter, tĕra, tĕrum (Gen. al-tĕrīus; Dat. altĕri), adj.: **1.** *Another, the other* of two.—**2.** Repeated: alter . . . alter, *The one . . . the other.*—**3.** *The second, the next;*—at v. 311 supply victor with alter [akin to ăl-ĭus; see ălĭus.

alter-nus, na, num, adj. [alter, "another"] ("Pertaining to *alter*"; hence) *Alternate, one after the other, by turns.*

al-tus, ta, tum, adj. [ăl-o, "to nourish"] ("Nourished; grown great by nourishment"; hence) **1.** *High, lofty.* — As Subst.: **altum,** i, n. *A high,* or *lofty, place; a height;*—at v. 508 plur. for sing.: alta pĕtens, *aiming at the high place,* i. e. *aiming aloft.* — **2.** *Deep.*—As Subst.: **altum,** i, n. *The deep, the main, the open sea.*—**3.** Of descent or birth: **a.** *Ancient, old, remote.*—**b.** *Lofty, exalted, high.*

ămā, pres. imperat. of ămo.

Amāzŏn-ĭus, ĭa, ĭum, adj. [Amāzŏn-es, "the Amazons"; a community of warlike women on the banks of the Thermōdon (now Terma), a river of Pontus] *Of,* or *belonging to, the Amazons; Amazonian.*

amb-ĕdo, ēdi, ēsum, ĕdĕre, 3. v. a. [amb-i, "around"; ĕdo, "to eat"] ("To eat, *or* gnaw, around"; hence) *To devour, consume,* by fire.—Pass.: **ambĕdor,** ēsus sum, ĕdi.

ambēsus, a, um, P. perf. pass. of ambĕdo.

ambĭg-ŭus, ŭa, ŭum, adj. [ambĭg-o, "to doubt"] *Doubtful, in doubt;*—at v. 326 supply eum (= Helymum) with ambĭgŭum.

amb-o, æ, o, adj. *Both* [Gr. ἄμφω].

1. **ăm-īcus,** īca, īcum, adj. [ăm-o, "to love"] *Loving, friendly.* — As Subst.: **ămīcus,** i, m. *A friend.*

2. **ămīcus,** i; see 1. ămīcus.

āmissus, a, um, P. perf. pass. of āmitto.

ā-mitto, mīsi, missum,

VOCABULARY. 39

mittĕre, 3. v. a. [ă (= ăb), "from"; mitto, "to let go"] ("To let go from" one; hence) *To lose* in any way;—at v. 853 the last syllable of amittěbat is lengthened in arsis. — Pass.: **ā-mittor**, missus sum, mitti.

amnis, is, m. ("Water-conductor"; hence) *A stream, river* [akin to Sans. *apnas*; fr. *ap*, "water"; root NI, "to conduct"].

ăm-o, ăvi, ătum, āre, 1. v. a.: **1.** Of personal Objects: *To love.* —**2.** Of things as Object: *To love,* i. e. *to take pleasure or delight in, to be fond of:*—litus ămā, *(love the shore; i. e.) keep close to,* or *hug, the shore,* v. 163 [akin to Sans. root KAM, "to love"].

ăm-œnus, œna, œnum, adj. [prob. ăm-o, "to love"] Of places: *Lovely, delightful, agreeable pleasant.*

ăm-or, ōris, m. [ăm-o, "to love"] **1.** *Love, affection.* — **2.** *A beloved person, an object of affection.*—**3.** *Love of,* or *desire for,* something.—N.B. Amōres, v. 334, is variously referred to 1 and 2.

am-plec-tor, plexus sum, ti, 3. v. dep. [am (= ambi), "around"; root PLEC, "to twine," whence plec-to] ("To twine around"; hence) **1.** Of things as Object: *To encircle, encompass.*—**2.** Of personal Objects: *To embrace.*

amplexus, a, um, P. perf. of amplector.

amplĭ-us, comp. adv. [adverbial neut. of amplī-or; fr. amplus, "extensive"] ("More extensively"; hence) Of time: *Longer, further, more.*

Amycus, i, m. *Amycus;* a son of Neptune, and king of the Bebrycians [Gr. Ἀμύκος].

an, conj. [prob. a primitive word] **1.** *Whether.*—**2.** *Or:*—an...an, *whether...or whether.*

an-cep-s, cĭpĭt-is, adj. [for an-capit-s; fr. an (inseparable prefix), "on both sides"; căput, căpĭt-is, "a head"] ("That has a head on both sides; double-headed"; hence) **1.** *From,* or *on, both sides.*—**2.** *Uncertain, dubious, doubtful.*—**3.** *Hesitating, wavering.*—**4.** *Difficult, perilous, dangerous.*

Anchīses, æ (Acc. Anchisen, v. 614), m. *Anchises;* the father of Æneas.—Hence, a. **Anchīs-ĭădes**, ădæ, m. *Son of Anchises;* i. e. *Æneas;* v. 407.—b. **Anchīs-ēus**, ĕa, ĕum, adj. *Of,* or *belonging to, Anchises:*—v. 761, ending with Anchiseo, is a Spondaic line, i. e. it has a spondee for its fifth foot.

Anchīsēus, a, um; **An-chīsĭădes**, æ; see Anchises.

ancĭpĭtem, ancĭpĭtes; see anceps.

ang-uis (dissyll.), uis, m. and f. *A serpent; a snake* [ang-o, "to squeeze"; and so, "the squeezing one"; cf. Gr. ἔχ-ις: Sans. *ah-i*, fr. a lost verb ANGH = ango].

ănhēlans, ntis, P. pres. of ănhēlo.—As Subst. m. *One who pants* or *is* in the act of *panting.*

ănhēl-ĭtus, ĭtūs, m. [ănhēl-o, "to pant"] **1.** *A panting.* —**2.** *A breathing, breath.*

ăn-hēlo, hēlăvi, hēlātum, hēlāre, 1. v. n. *To draw up the breath with difficulty, to gasp, to pant* [for ăn-hălo; fr. ăn (= ἀν-ά), "up"; hălo, "to draw the breath"; hence, "to draw up the breath"; hence, with the accessory notion of difficulty, as given above].

ănhēl-us, a, um, adj. [ănhēl-o, "to pant"] *Panting.*

ăn-ĭma, ĭmæ, f. ("That which blows *or* breathes"; hence, "air"; hence, "the vital principle"; hence) **1.** *Life.*—**2.** ("A living creature *or* being"; hence) *A soul* separated from the body; *a spirit,* or *shade,* of a departed person;—at v. 81 in plur. [akin to Sans. root ᴀɴ, "to blow *or* breathe"; cf. ănĭmus].

ăn-ĭmus, ĭmi, m. ("That which blows *or* breathes"; hence) **1.** *The* (rational) *soul* in man; *mind.*—**2.** *Heart, courage, spirit.*—**3.** *Will, inclination.*—**4.** *A haughty spirit, haughtiness, pride;*—at v. 473 plur. for sing. [akin to Gr. ἄνεμος, "a stream of air"; Sans. root ᴀɴ, "to blow *or* breathe"; cf. ănĭma].

an-nus, ni, m. ("That which goes round, a circuit"; hence) Of time: **1.** *A year.*—**2.** *A season* of the year [akin to Sans. ᴀɴ, "to go"; *am-ati*, "time"; also to Gr. ἐν-ϝος = ἐνιαυτός, "a year"].

ann-ŭus, ŭa, ŭum, adj. [ann-us, "a year"] *Of,* or *belonging to, a year; annual, yearly.*

ante, adv. and prep.: **1.** Adv.: **a.** *Before, in front.*—**b.** *Before, previously.* - **c.** *First, in the first place.*—**2.** Prep. gov. Acc.: **a.** *Before.*—**b.** *In front of.*—**c.** *Above, beyond.*

ant-īquus, īqua, īquum, adj. [ant-e, "before"] ("Pertaining to *ante*"; hence) *Old, ancient, belonging to former times.*

ap-pell-o, āvi, ātum, āre [for ad-pell-o; fr. ad, "towards"; pell-o, "to bring"] 1. v. a. (In reflexive force: "To bring one's self to" a person in order to address him, *etc.*; hence) **1.** *To address, accost, speak to.*—**2.** With second Acc.

[§ 99]: *To name,* or *call,* a person, *or* thing, that which is denoted by second Acc.; *to proclaim* one, *etc., as* something, *etc.*

aprī-cus, ca, cum, adj. [contr. fr. ăpĕri-cus; fr. ăpĕri-o, "to uncover"] ("Uncovered"; hence, "exposed to the sun, sunny"; hence) Of gulls: *Fond of the sun, sunning themselves,* etc.

apt-o, āvi, ātum, āre, 1. v. a. [apt-us, "joined on"] ("To make *aptus*"; hence, "to fit, adapt," *etc.*; hence) *To get ready, prepare.*

ăp-ud, prep. gov. acc. [prob. obsol. ăp-o, ăp-ĭo, "to lay hold of"] **1.** *Among, with.*—**2.** *At, near.*

ăqu-a, æ, f.: **1.** *Water.*—**2.** *A stream.*—**3.** Sing. and Plur. = mare: *The sea.*—**4.** *Rain* [akin to Sans. *ap*, "water"].

Aqu-ĭlo, ĭlōnis, m. ("The swift-flying thing"; hence) *The North Wind; a northern blast* [root ᴀᴄ; akin to ὠκ-ύς, "swift"; Sans. *āsu*, "swiftly"].

ār-a, æ, f. (old form ăs-a) ("A seat *or* raised place"; hence, "an elevation *or* structure" of wood, stone, *etc.*; hence, with reference to purposes of worship) *An altar* [prps. akin to Sans. root ăs, "to sit"; *ăs-ana*, "a seat"].

ără-trum, tri, n. [ăr(a)-o, "to plough"] ("The ploughing thing"; hence) *A plough.*

arbor, ŏris, f. ("A tree"; hence, as being made from a tree, and either with or without māli—see mālus) *A mast* of a ship.

Arcădĭa, æ, f. *Arcadia;* a mountainous country in the centre of the Peloponnesus (now the Morĕa) in ancient Greece.

arc-ĕo, ŭi (obsol. sup.

ĭtum), ēre, 2. v. a. ("To shut up, enclose"; hence, "to prohibit access to"; hence) *To repel, keep off or at a distance, drive away* [prob. akin to Gr. εἴργω, "to enclose"; and in some meanings to ἀρκέω, "to ward off, defend"; also to Sans. root RAKSH, "to preserve"].

ar-ces-so, sīvi, sītum, sēre, 3. v. a. [for ar-ced-so; fr. ar = ad, "to"; ced-o, "to go"] (In causative force: "to cause to go, *or* come, to" one; hence) *To call, summon, send for,* etc.

arcus, ūs, m.: **1.** *A bow.*— **2.** *A rain-bow.*

ardens, ntis, P. pres. of ardĕo.

ardĕo, arsi, arsum, ardēre, 2. v. n.: **1.** *To be on fire; to burn, blaze.*—**2.** Of the eyes, or of persons with reference to the eyes: *To flash, glow, sparkle,* etc. —**3.** *To burn* with excitement, etc.; *to be inflamed* or *excited*.

arduus, a, um, adj. ("Steep"; hence) **1.** *High, lofty, aloft.*—Hence, **arduum,** i, n. *A lofty place, height, eminence.*—**2.** Of a horse: *High* [akin to Sans. ūrdva, Gr. ὀρθός, "erect"].

ārē-na, nae, f. [ārē-o, "to be dry"] ("The dried, or dry, thing"; hence) **1.** *Sand.*—**2.** *A sandy place.*—**3.** *The shore, sea-shore.*—**4.** *A place of combat,* as strewed with sand; *the arena.*

arg-entum, enti, n. *Silver* [akin to Sans. *raj-atam*, "silver," as "the shining thing"; fr. root RAJ, "to shine"; cf. ἀργυ-ρος].

Argīvi, ōrum; **Argīvum;** see Argivus.

Arg-ivus, iva, ivum, adj. [Arg-os, "Argos"; the capital of Argōlis, one of the states of ancient S. Greece in the Peloponnēsus (now the Morēa). Juno was its tutelary goddess, and was worshipped there with especial reverence] *Of,* or *belonging to, Argos; Argive.*—As Subst.: **Argīvi,** ōrum (Gen. Argivûm, v. 672), m. plur. ("The Argives"; hence) *The Greeks.*

Argōlĭcus, a, um, adj.: **1.** *Of,* or *belonging to, Argolis,* the territory of Argos in the Peloponnēsus (now the Morēa); *Argolic:*—Argōlĭcum māre = Argōlĭcus sinus, *the sea,* or *bay, of Argolis* (now *the Gulf of Nauplia*).—**2.** *Greek, Grecian* [Gr. Ἀργολικός].

ār-ĭdus, ĭda, ĭdum, adj. [ār-ĕo, "to be dry"].

ar-ma, mōrum, n. plur. ("Things adapted" to any purpose"; hence) **1.** *Arms, weapons.* —**2.** *Armour.*—**3.** Of a ship: *The sails, tackling,* etc. [akin to Gr. ἄρ-ω, "to adapt"].

arm-ĭ-ger, gĕra, gĕrum, adj. [arm-a, "arms"; (i) connecting vowel; gĕr-o, "to bear"] *Arm-bearing* or *-carrying.* —As Subst.: **armĭger,** ĕri, m. *An armour-bearer:*—Jovis armiger, *i. e.* the eagle.

arrectus, a, um, P. perf. pass. of arrĭgo;—at v. 643 supply sunt with arrectæ.

ar-rīgo, rexi, rectum, rĭgĕre, 3. v. a. [for ad-rĕgo; fr. ăd, "up, upwards"; rĕgo, "to keep straight"] ("To keep straight up"; hence) **1.** *To lift,* or *raise, up.*—**2.** Mentally: *To rouse, excite.*—Pass.: **ar-rĭg-or,** rectus sum, rĭgi.

ar-s, tis, f.: **1.** *Art, skill.*— **2.** *A work* of art;—at v. 359 plur. for sing.—**3.** *Artifice, stratagem* [either akin to ἄρ-ω, "to join," and so, "a joining"; or fr.

ăr-o, "to plough," and so "a ploughing," as the earliest and most important act of skill].

arsi, perf. ind. of ardĕo.

ar-tus, tūs, m. ("A fitting on"; "that which fits on"; hence) *A joint; a limb* [Gr. ἀρ-ω, "to fit"].

ăr-und-o, ĭnis, f. [prob. ăr (=ăd), "at"; und-a, "water"] ("That which is at, or grows near, the water"; hence, "a reed"; hence, as made from a reed) *An arrow*.

arvum, i; see arvus.

(arv-us, a, um, adj. [ăr-o, "to plough"] *Ploughed*, but not yet sown.—As Subst.:) **arvum**, i, n. ("The ploughed thing"; *i. e.* "ploughed land, an arable field"; hence) **1.** Plur.: *Fields, plains*, etc.—**2.** *A region, country, district*.

Ascănĭus, ĭi, m. *Ascanius* (called also *Iŭlus*), son of Æneas and Crĕūsa.

aspec-to, tāvi, tātum, tāre, 1. v. a. intens. [aspĭcĭo, "to look at, see," through true root ASPEC] *To look at attentively; to keep looking at*.

asper, ĕra, ĕrum, adj.: **1.** *Rough*.—**2.** Of habits, etc.: *Rugged;*—at v. 730 folld. by Abl. of Respect [§ 116].—**3.** Of the sea or things connected with it: *Stormy, rough, tempestuous*.

a-spĭcĭo, spexi, spectum, spĭcĕre, 3. v. a. [for ad-spĕcĭo; fr. ăd, "on *or* upon"; spĕcĭo, "to look"] **1.** *To look upon, behold, see*.—**2.** Mentally: *To consider, regard*.

aspīrans, ntis, P. pres. of aspiro.

a-spīro, spīrāvi, spīrātum, spīrāre, 1. v. a. and n. [for ad-spiro; fr. ăd, "upon"; spiro, "to breathe"] **1.** Act.: With Dat. [§ 106, *a*]: *To breathe, or blow, something upon* one.—**2.** Neut.: ("To breathe upon"; hence) *To be favourable*, etc.

assĭd-ŭus, ŭa, ŭum, adj. [assĭd-ĕo, "to sit down, *i. e.* to continue *or* remain constantly" in a place] ("Sitting down, *i. e.* continuing, *etc.*, constantly" in a place; hence) With reference to time: *Constant, continual, unceasing*.

as-suesco (in poetstrisyll.), suēvi, suētum, suescĕre, 3. v. a. [for ad-suesco; fr. ăd, "to"; suesco, "to accustom"] With Dat. [§ 106, *a*]: *To accustom*, or *habituate, to*.—Pass.: **as-suescor**, suētus sum, suesci.

assuētus (trisyll.), a, um, P. perf. pass. of assuesco.

assul-tus, tūs, m. [for assult-tus; fr. assult-o, "to bound upon" in order to make an attack] ("A bounding upon"; hence) *A forward bound or spring; an assault*.

ast; see at.

astĭti, perf. ind. of asto.

a-sto, stĭti, stătum, stāre, 1. v. n. [for ad-sto; fr. ăd, "near"; sto, "to stand"] *To stand near, at hand*, or *close by*.

astrum, i, n. *A star* [Gr. ἄστρον].

at (ast), conj. *But* [akin to Sans. *atha*; Gr. ἀτ-άρ, "but"].

āter, tra, trum, adj. *Black, dark*, in colour.

at-que (contr. **ac**), conj. [for ad-que; fr. ăd, denoting "addition"; que, "and"] *And also, and besides, moreover, and*.

at-tingo, tigi, tactum, tingĕre, 3. v. a. [for ad-tango; fr. ăd, "against"; tango, "to touch"] ("To touch against, or come in contact with," something; hence) *To reach, arrive at* a place.

attollens, ntis, P. pres. of attollo.

at-tollo, no perf. nor sup.,

tollĕre, 3. v. a. [for ad-tollo; fr. ad, "up, upwards"; tollo, "to lift"] **1.** *To lift*, or *raise*, *up.*— **2.** Of a rock: Pass. in reflexive force: *To lift*, or *raise*, *itself up; to rise up.*—Pass.: **at-tollor**, no perf., tolli.

attŏn-ĭtus, ĭta, ĭtum, adj. [attŏn-o, "to thunder at"; hence, "to confound, amaze"] *Confounded, amazed, astonished, thunderstruck.*

attŭli, perf. ind. of affĕro.

Attus, i, m. *Attus;* a Roman house, or clan, which claimed descent from Atys, the youthful friend of Ascanius. Amongst its members was Attus Navius, the augur, who is said to have cut a whetstone in two in the presence of Tarquinius Priscus, the fifth king of Rome.—Plur.: *The Atti.*

Atȳs, ўos, m. *Atys;* a Trojan boy, the youthful friend of Iūlus or Ascanius; v. 569.

auc-tor, tōris, m. [for augtor; fr. aug-ĕo, "to produce"] ("He who produces" something; hence, "a father," etc.; hence) *An adviser, counsellor.*

auctūrus, a, um, P. fut. of augĕo.

aud-ax, ācis, adj. [aud-ĕo, "to dare"] *Daring, bold, courageous, spirited.*

audĕo, ausus sum, audēre, 2. v. semi-dep.: **1.** With Inf.: *To dare*, or *venture, to do something.*—**2.** With Acc. of thing: *To dare, venture upon, something;* v. 792.

audĭi, perf. ind. of audĭo.

aud-ĭo, īvi or ĭi, itum, ire, 4. v. a. *To hear.*—Pass.: **aud-ĭor**, audītus sum, audīri [akin to αὖς (= οὖς), αὐτ-ός, "an ear"].

audītus, a, um, P. perf. pass. of audĭo.

aug-ĕo, auxi, auctum, augere, 2. v. a. *To increase, augment* [akin to Gr. αὐξάνω = αὐγσάνω].

augŭr-ĭum, ĭi, n. [augŭror, "to augur"] **1.** *Augury.*—**2.** *An omen, sign, token, prognostic.*

aura, æ, f.: **1.** *The air; a breath of air.*—**2.** *A breeze.*—**3.** *The upper air; the heaven, sky* [Gr. αὐ.α].

aur-ātus, āta, ātum, adj. [aur-um, "gold"] ("Provided with *aurum*"; hence) Of a garment: *Embroidered with gold.*

aur-ĕus, ĕa, ĕum, adj. [id.] (Of, or belonging to, *aurum*; hence, "golden"; hence) *Gilded, gilt;*—at v. 352 aureis is to be pronounced as a dissyllable, by the figure synæresis.

aurīga, æ, m. *A charioteer, driver.*

aur-is, is, f. [for aud-is; fr. aud-ĭo, "to hear"] ("The hearing thing"; hence) *The ear.*

Aurōra, æ, f. ("The dawn, day-break"; hence, personified) *Aurōra*, the goddess of the dawn [akin to Gr. αὐ-ώς: = ἠ-ώς; Sans. *ush-as*, "the early morn"; fr. root USH, "to burn," and so "to shine," etc.].

aur-um, i, n. ("The burning thing"; i. e. "the glittering or shining metal") **1.** *Gold*, as a metal.—**2.** At v. 817, as being made of gold: either **a.** *A yoke of gold;* or **b.** *A golden car* [akin to Sans. root USH, "to burn"; Gr. αὖρ-ον].

Ausŏn-ĭus, ĭa, ĭum, adj. [Ausŏn-es, "the Ausones"; a very ancient, and perhaps Greek, name of the primitive inhabitants of Middle and Lower Italy] *Of, or belonging to, the Ausŏnes; Ausonian; Italian.*

auspĭc-ĭum, ĭi, n. [auspex,

44 VOCABULARY.

auspĭc-is, "a bird-inspector," *i. e.* one who marks the flight and cries of birds, and thence makes predictions] ("A thing pertaining to an *auspex*"; hence, "augury" from birds, auspices; hence) *A sign, omen, divine token.*

Au-ster, stri, m. ("The drier") *The South wind;*—at v. 850 in plur. [Gr. αὔ-ω, "to dry"].

ausus, a, um, P. perf. of audĕo;—at v. 792 supply est with ausa.

aut, conj. *Or:*—aut . . . aut, *either . . . or.*

aut-em, conj. *But, however* [akin to αὐτ-άρ, "but"].

auxĭl-ĭum, ĭi, n. [prob. fr. obsol. adj. auxĭl-is (= aug-sĭl-is, fr. aug-ĕo, "to increase"), "increasing"] ("The quality, *or* state, of the *auxilis*"; hence) *Aid, help, assistance;*—at v. 222 in plur.

Averna, ōrum; see Avernus.

Avernus, i, m. : **1.** *Avernus* (now *Lago d'Averno*); a lake in the neighbourhood of Cumæ almost entirely surrounded by wooded hills. Its exhalations were said to have been so deadly, as to kill birds which flew over it. In its neighbourhood was the fabled entrance to the lower world.—**2.** *Avernus; the lower world.*—Hence, (**Avern-us,** a, um, adj. "Of, or belonging to, Avernus *or* the lower world."—As Subst. :) **Averna,** ōrum, n. plur. (*sc.* loca) *Avernus,* or *the lower world.*

ă-vĭ-s, ăvĭs, f. *A bird* [akin to Sans. *vi*, "a bird"; the a is a prefix.

ăvus, i, m. *A grandfather.*

ax-is, is, m. ("An axle-tree"; hence, "the axis" of the earth; hence, "the pole" hence) *The heaves or beams* [akin to Sans. *aksh-a*, "the axle" of a wheel; Gr. ἄξ-ων].

Bacchus, i, m. : **1.** *Bacchus,* son of Jupiter and Semele, and god of wine and poets.—**2.** *Wine*—merō Bacchō, *of pure wine;* v. 77; Abl. of quality [§ 128, α] [Βάκχος].

baltĕus, ĕi, m. *A belt,* or *band, for carrying a quiver.*

Bēbrўcĭ-us, a, um [Bēbryc-s, "Bebrycia"; afterwards called Bithynia, a country of Asia Minor] (*Of,* or *belonging to, Bebrycia; Bebrycian, Bithynian.*

b-ellum, elli, n. [old form dŭ-ellum; fr. dŭ-o, "two"] ("A thing pertaining to two"; *i. e.* a contest between two parties; hence) *War, warfare.*

Bĕrŏe, ĕs, f. *Beroë,* the wife of Doryclus, whose form was assumed by Iris, when that goddess instigated the Trojan women to burn their ships [Gr. Βερόη].

bĭ-cŏlor, cŏlōris, adj. [bi (= bis), "twice"; color, "colour"] ("Having twice a colour"; hence) *Of two colours.*

bĭdens, ntis, f. [bĭdens (adj.), "with two teeth"] ("An animal with two rows of teeth, complete"; esp.) *A sheep.*

bīgæ, ārum, f. plur. (contr. fr. bijŭg-æ; see bijŭgus]) "The double-yoked" ones; hence, "a pair of horses"; hence) *A chariot,* or *car, drawn by two horses;* a *two-horse-chariot.*

bĭ-jŭg-us, a, um, adj. [bi (= bis), "twice"; jŭg-um, "a yoke"] ("Twice-yoked"; hence, "double-yoked"; hence) *Yoked two together;*—at v. 184 bijŭgum certamine means *the contest of the bigæ in the public games.*

bī-nī, næ, na, num. distribu-

VOCABULARY. 45

tive adj. plur. [bi=bis, "twice"]
("Pertaining to *bis*"; hence) **1.**
Two distributively; i. e. *two a-
piece.*—**2.** *Two.*
bi-penn-is, is, f. [bĭpenn-
is, "double-edged"] *A double-
edged,* or *two-edged, axe ; a battle-
axe.*
bis, num. adv. [for dŭ-is; fr.
dŭ-o, "two"] *Twice.*
blandus, a, um, adj. Of
things : *Pleasing, acceptable,
welcome.*
bŏnus, a, um, adj. *Good* in
the widest acceptation of the
term; *excellent.* ☞ Comp. :
mĕlĭor ; Sup. : optĭmus.
bos, bŏvis (Plur. **bŏves,**
bŏum), comm. gen. (" The low-
ing *or* bellowing one"; hence)
A cow or *ox* ;—Plur. : *Cattle*
[akin to Gr. βοῦς].
brāchĭum, ĭi, n. *An arm ;*
—Plur. : *The sail-yards* of a vessel [akin to Gr. βραχιών].
brĕvis, e, adj. (" Short ";
hence) In depth : *Shallow.* ☞
(Comp. : brĕv-ĭor) ; Sup. : brĕv-
issĭmus [akin to Gr. βραχύς,
"short"].
Būtōs, æ (Acc. Buten,
v. 372), m. *Butes,* a son of
Amȳcus king of the Bebrycians,
killed by Dares in a boxing encounter at the tomb of Hector
[Gr. Βούτης].

cæcus, a, um, adj. ("Blind";
hence) **1.** *Hidden, unseen.*—**2.**
*Where nothing can be seen;
dark.*
cædo, cĕcĭdi, cæsum, cæd-
ĕre, 3. v. a. [akin to cădo, "to
fall"] (In causative force : " To
cause to fall"; hence) **1.** *To
kill, slay, slaughter.*—**2.** *To offer,
sacrifice,* by killing victims.—
Pass. : **cædor,** cæsus sum,
cædi.
cælātus, a, um, P. perf.
pass. of cælo.

cæl-o, āvi, ātum, āre, 1. v. a.
[cæl-um, "a graver"] *To en-
grave in relief,* or *make raised
work,* on metals ; *to chase.*—
Pass. : **cæl-or,** ātus sum, āri.
cærŭlĕus, a, um, adj. : **1.**
Dark-coloured, dark.—**2.** *Dark-
blue, azure.*
cæstus, tūs, m. [for cæd-
tus; fr. cæd-o, "to strike"]
(" The striking thing"; hence)
A cæstus, gauntlet, boxing-glove,
for pugilists, formed of a strap
of bull's hide with balls of lead
or iron sewed into it.
cæsus, a, um, P. perf. pass.
of cædo.
calx, calcis, f. (sts. m.) *A
heel.*
campus, i, m. : **1.** *A field*
or *plain.*—**2.** Of a rock, *etc.* : *A
level surface* [prob. akin to κῆπος,
" a garden "].
candens, ntis, P. pres. of
candĕo.
candĕo, ŭi, no sup., ēre, 2.
v. n. *To be of a glistening white-
ness; to be brilliantly white* [prob.
fr. same root as cānus].
cand-ĭdus, ĭda, ĭdum, adj.
[cand-ĕo, "to be brilliantly
white"] (" Brilliantly white";
hence) *Fair, lovely, beautiful.*
căn-ĕo, ŭi, no sup., ēre, 2.
v. n. [căn-us, "grey"] *To be
grey* or *hoary* ; v. 416.
căn-is, is, comm. gen. *A
dog, hound* [akin to Gr. κύων,
κυν-ός ; German *hund* ; English
hound ; Sans. çvan].
căno, cĕcĭni, no sup., cănĕre,
3. v. a. (" To sing"; hence) **1.**
As the ancient oracles were
often given in verse : *To foretell,
forebode,* etc.—**2.** With Objective clause : *To give the signal,*
or *to announce,* that, *etc.* [akin to
Sans. root çaṅs, " to praise, to
relate "].
cā-nus, na, num, adj.
(" Burned "; hence) **1.** *Grey,*

VOCABULARY.

hoary.—**2.** *Ancient, venerable* [akin to Gr. κα-ίω, " to burn "].

căp-esso, essīvi *or* essīī, essītum, essĕre, 3. v. a. desid. [căp-ĭo, " to take "] (" To desire to take "; hence, "to seize, *or* catch at, eagerly "; hence) Of a place: *To repair,* or *resort, to; to betake one's self to, try to reach.*

căpĭo, cēpi, captum, căpĕre, 3. v. a.: **1.** *To take.*—**2.** *To get* or *obtain; to receive.*—**3.** *To take possession of, seize.*

căp-ut, ĭtis, n. : **1.** *The head.*—**2.** Of animals : *A head;* i. e. one of the particular sort of animals specified by the writer [akin to Sans. *kapâla;* Gr. κεφαλή].

carcer, ĕris, m. (" An enclosure *or* enclosed place; hence) Of a race-course : *A barrier, a starting-place.*—In front of the carcer, in the Roman circus, were two small statues of Mercury (*Hermŭli*) supporting a chain to keep in the horses. Sometimes a white line, or a furrow filled with chalk, supplied the place of the chain; and at the spot thus marked, the horses were kept back by the public officers denoted *Moratores* (i. e. " Hinderers *or* Delayers ") till the signal for starting was given [Sicilian κάρκαρ-ον].

carchēsĭum, ĭi, n. *A cup,* or *goblet,* contracted in the middle [Gr. καρχήσιον].

căr-ĕo, ŭi, ĭtum, ēre, 2 v. n. (" To shear *or* be shorn "; hence) With Abl. [§ 119, 1] : *To be without* or *free from; to be destitute* or *devoid of* [akin to καρ, a root of κείρ-ω, " to shear "].

cărīna, æ, f. : **1.** *The keel,* or *bottom,* of a vessel.—**2.** *A vessel, skin.*

Carpăth-ĭus, ĭa, ĭum, adj. [Carpăthus, " Carpathus" (now Scarpanto), an island in the Ægean Sea.] *Of, or belonging to, Carpathus; Carpathian.*

că-rus, ra, rum, adj. *Beloved, dear* [for cam-rus ; akin to Sans. root ΚΑΜ, " to love "].

Cassandra, æ, f. *Cassandra,* a daughter of Priam and Hecuba. Apollo bestowed upon her the gift of prophecy, but caused that none of her predictions should be believed [Gr. Κασσάνδρα].

castel-lum, li, n. dim. [for caster-lum ; fr. castrum, cast(e)r-i, " a fort "] *A small fort; a castle, citadel, fortress, stronghold.*

castīgo, āvi, ātum, āre, 1. v. a. *To reprove, chide, find fault with.*

(**cas-trum,** tri, n. " The covering thing "; hence) Plur. : **castra,** ōrum, *A camp* or *encampment,* as containing several tents or huts [prob. for skad-trum; akin to Sans. root ΣΚΑD, " to cover "].

cas-tus, ta, tum, adj. : **1.** *Chaste, pure.*—**2.** In a religious sense : *Holy, sacred, pious* [akin to Gr. καθ-αρός, " pure "].

că-sus, sūs, m. [for cad-sus ; fr. căd-o, " to fall "] **1.** *A falling, fall.* — **2.** *Chance, accident, event.* — **3.** *Misfortune, calamity.*

căterva, æ, f. *A troop, band, company.*

causa, æ, f. *A cause, reason.*

cau-tes, tis, f. (" A sharpened thing "; hence) *A sharp rock* [akin to Sans. root ço, " to sharpen "].

căv-ĕa, æ, f. [căv-us, " hollow "] (" A hollow place "; hence) Of a theatre : *The circular part,* where the spectators sat; *the spectators' seats* or *benches.*

căvus, a, um, adj. *Hollow.*

VOCABULARY. 47

cĕcĭni, perf. ind. of cāno.
cēdo, cessi, cessum, cēdĕre, 3. v. n.: **1.** *To go away, withdraw, draw back.*—**2.** *To yield; to give way* or *place; to resign the contest* [akin to Gr. χάζομαι (= χάσσομαι), "to retire"].
cĕlĕbrātus, a, um, P. perf. pass. of cĕlebro.
cĕlĕbr-o, āvi, ātum, āre, 1. v. a. [cĕlĕber, cĕlebr-is, "much frequented"; hence, of a religious ceremony, etc., to which great numbers of persons resort, "solemn, festive"] **1.** *To keep festive* or *festal.*—**2.** *To solemnize, celebrate:* — for *celebremus*, 1. pers. plur. subj. pres., consult *vertamus* in verto. — Pass.: **cĕlĕbr-or**, ātus sum, āri.
cĕl-er, ĕris, ĕre, adj. [CEL, root of cel-lo, "to urge on"] ("Urged on"; hence) *Swift, rapid, fleet.*
cĕlĕrans, ntis, P. pres. of cĕlĕro.
cĕlĕr-o, āvi, ātum, āre, 1. v. a. [cĕler, "swift"] ("To make *celer*"; hence) *To quicken; to hasten*, or *speed, on* or *onwards; to accelerate.*
cel-sus, sa, sum, adj. [cello, "to urge along"] ("Urged along"; hence) *High, lofty.*
Centaurus, i (m. *A Centaur.* The Centaurs were fabled monsters of antiquity, half man and half horse, that were said to have sprung from Ixion and a Cloud. They were, however, a Thessalian people, who were the first to break in horses, and who derived their name either from fighting on horseback with lances or from their pursuit of wild cattle), f. As the name of a ship: *The Centaur* [Κένταυρος, "Piercer, Lancer"; — or "Bull-piercer, Bull-goader"].

cēpi, perf. ind. of căpĭo.
cēpissem, pluperf. subj. of căpĭo.
cĕr-ebrum, ebri, n. ("That which is carried in the head or skull"; hence) *The brain,*—at vv. 413, 480 the second e is long [akin to Gr. κάρ-α, "the head"].
cerno, crēvi. crētum, cerněre, 3. v. a. ("To separate or sift"; hence) *To perceive, discern, see,* whether by the eye or the mind [root CER or CRE, akin to Gr. κρί-νω; Sans. root κρι, "to separate"].
certā-men, minis, n. [cert-(a)-o, "to contend"] ("That which contends"; hence) **1.** *A contest, struggle,* in games, *etc.* —**2.** *Emulation, zeal, eagerness,* etc.; v. 197.—**3.** *A fight, contest, engagement.*
certā-tim, adv. [id.] ("By a contending"; hence) *Eagerly.*
cer-to, tāvi, tātum, tāre, 1. v. n. intens. [CER, root of cerno, "to fight"] ("To fight"; hence) **1.** *To contend* in games, *etc.*—**2.** With Inf.: *To strive, earnestly endeavour, to do, etc.*
cer-tus, ta, tum, adj. [CER, root of cer-no, "to decide"] ("Decided"; hence) **1.** Of persons: *Certain, sure,* with respect to something.—**2.** Of things: *Fixed, settled, sure, certain.*
cer-vus, vi, m. ("The horned one") *A deer, stag* [akin to Gr. κέρ-ας, "a horn"].
cessi, perf. ind. of cēdo.
cēte; see cētus.
cētĕrus, a, um (rare in sing.), adj. *The other; the remaining; the rest of.*
cētus, i, m. (in plur. frequently **cētē**, n., in accordance with its Gr. origin; see below) *A sea-monster* of any kind; *e. g.* a whale, a shark, *etc.* [Gr. κῆτος].

ceu, adv. *As, like as.*
Chimaera, ae, f. *Chimaera* (a fabled monster in Lycia, with the fore part of a lion, the middle of a goat, the hinder part of a dragon. It was said to vomit forth fire. After it was named) one of the ships of Æneas [Gr. χίμαιρα, "a goat"].
chlămys, y̆dis, f. *A cloak, mantle* [Gr. χλαμύς].
chŏrus, i, m. ("A dance in a ring, a choral dance"; hence, "a dancing *or* singing band, a choir"; hence) *A band, troop, crowd,* etc., of any kind; see Phorcus [Gr. χορός].
cĭĕo, civi, citum, cĭēre, 2. v. a. ("To make to go"; hence) *To cause, produce,* etc. :—ciēre simulācra pugnae, *(to produce semblances of a fight;* i. e.) *to engage in sham-fights,* v. 585 [akin to Gr. κίω, "to go"].
cingĭte, plur. pres. imperat. of cingo.
cingo, cinxi, cinctum, cingĕre, 3. v. a. *To surround, encircle.*
cĭnis, ĕris, m. *Ashes;*—at vv. 55 and 81 in plur., of the ashes of the dead [akin to Gr. κόνις].
cinxi, perf. ind. of cingo.
circ-ŭlus, ŭli, m. [either akin to circus; or fr. circ-o, "to go round"] ("That which goes round"; hence, "a circle"; hence) *A ring, chain,* in a circular form; *a circlet.*
circum, adv. and prep. [prob. adverbial acc. of circus, "a ring"] ("In a ring"; hence) **1.** Adv. : *Around, round about, all round.*—**2.** Prep. with Acc. : *Around,* etc.
circum-flecto, flexi, flexum, flectĕre, 3. v. a. [circum, "around"; flecto, "to bend"] *To bend, or turn, round.*
circus, i, m. ("A ring, circle"; hence, "The Circus" or race-course at Rome; hence) *A natural circus or race-course; an open space* for games [Gr. κίρκος].
Cisseus, ĕi, m. *Cisseus;* a king of Thrace, father of Hecŭba, the wife of Priam, king of Troy [Κισσεύς, "Ivy-man"; i. e. "one crowned with ivy"].
cĭtĭus; see cito.
cĭt-o, adv. [cĭt-us, "swift"] *Swiftly, rapidly, quickly.* Comp. : cĭt-ĭus.
cĭ-tus, ta, tum, adj. [cĭ-ĕo, "to put in motion"] ("Put in motion"; hence) **1.** *Swift, rapid.*—**2.** In adverbial force: *Swiftly, rapidly.*
cīvis, is, comm. gen. ("A dweller"; hence) *A citizen,* whether man or woman, as a dweller in a city;—at v. 671 cives (fem.) may be rendered "country-women" [akin to Sans. root xshi, "to dwell"].
clăm-or, ōris, m. [clăm-o, "to cry out"] *Outcry, clamour; a shout.*
clārissĭmus, a, um; see clārus.
clā-rus, ra, rum, adj. ("Heard"; hence) **1.** *Clear* in sound; *loud,* etc.—**2.** *Clear, bright, shining.*—**3.** Of distinguished persons: *Renowned, illustrious, famous, celebrated.* (Comp. : clār-ior); Sup. : clār-issimus [prob. akin to Sans. root çru; Gr. κλύ-ω; Lat. clŭ-ĕo, "to hear"].
classis, is, f. : **1.** Of persons summoned for sea service : *A fleet* comprising the ships as well as the men serving in them. —**2.** *A fleet* of ships, alone [κλᾶσις = κλῆσις, "a calling"].
claudus, a, um, adj. *Limping, halting, lame* [akin to Sans. khóla, "crippled"; Gr. χωλός, "lame"].

VOCABULARY. 49

clāvus, i, m. ("The closing or fastening thing"; hence, "a peg"; hence, "the handle" of a rudder, "the tiller"; hence) *A rudder, helm* [akin to κλείω, "to close," etc.].

Clŏanthus, i, m. *Cloanthus;* a Trojan, one of the followers of Æneas. The Roman family, or house, of the Cluentii are said by Virgil to have been descended from him [Χλόανθ-ος].

Cluentĭus, ii, m. (Voc. Cluenti, v. 123), m. *Cluentius;* the name of a Roman family or house; see Clŏanthus.

clypĕus, i, m. ("That which covers"; hence) *A shield,* as covering or sheltering the body of the person carrying it [akin to Gr. καλύπ-τω, "to cover"].

coelum, i, n.: 1. *Heaven.*—2. *The heavens, the sky* [akin to Gr. κοῖλος, "hollow"].

coe-tus, tūs, m. [another form of cŏi-tus; fr. cŏĕo, "to come together," through root COI] ("A coming together"; hence) Of persons: *A meeting, company,* etc.; *an assembly, assemblage.*

cognoscĭte, plur. pres. imperat. of cognosco.

co-gnosco, gnōvi, gnĭtum, gnoscĕre, 3. v. a. [co (= cum), in "augmentative" force; gnosco (= nosco), "to become acquainted with"] ("To become acquainted with on all sides"; hence) 1. *To become acquainted with, learn, note.*—2. In perf. tenses: *To have knowledge of, to know.*

cō-go, cŏ-ēgi, cŏ-actum, cō-gĕre, 3. v. a. [contr. fr. co-ăgo; fr. co (= cum), "together"; ăgo, "to drive"] ("To drive together"; hence) 1. *To gather together, collect,* etc.—2. *To* ..., *compel.*—Pass.: **cō-gor,** actus sum, gi.

col-lĭgo, lēgi, lectum, lĭg-ĕre, 3. v. a. [for con-lĕgo; fr. con (= cum), "together"; lĕgo, "to gather"] ("To gather together, to collect"; hence) Of sails as Object: *To furl.*

collis, is, m. *A hill* [akin to Gr. κολώνη].

col-lūcĕo, no perf. nor sup., lūcēre, 2. v. n. [for con-lūcĕo; fr. con (= cum), in "augmentative" force; lūcĕo, "to give light"] ("To give light in a great degree"; hence) *To shine brightly, to be brightly illuminated.*

collum, i, n. *The neck.*

cŏlo, cŏlŭi, cultum, cŏlĕre, 3. v. a.: 1. *To dwell in, inhabit.*—2. *To worship, venerate,* etc. [akin to Sans. root KSHI, "to dwell"].

cŏlor, ōris, m. *Colour, hue.*

cŏlumba, æ, f. *A dove, pigeon.*

cŏma, æ, f. *The hair* [Gr. κόμη].

cŏm-e-s, cŏmĭtis, comm. gen. [for com-i-t-s; fr. com (= cum), "together"; I, root of ĕo, "to go"; (t) epenthetic] ("One who goes with" another; hence) *A companion; attendant.*

cŏmĭtans, ntis, P. pres. of cŏmĭtor.

cŏmĭtes, um, plur. of cŏmes.

cŏmĭt-or, ātus sum, āri, 1. v. dep. [cŏmes, cŏmĭt-is, "a companion"] *To be a companion to; to accompany, attend.*

com-mendo, mendāvi, mendātum, mendāre, 1. v. a. [for com-mando; fr. com (= cum), in "augmentative" force; mando, "to commit"] With Dat. of person [§ 106, a]: *To commit to the charge of; to*

E

confide, or *entrust, to* for protection.
commissus, a, um, P. perf. pass. of committo.
com-mitto, misi, missum, mittĕre, 3. v. a. [com (= cum), "together"; mitto, "to cause to go"] ("To cause to go together"; hence) **1.** Of a fight, *etc.*, as Object: *To engage in.*—**2.** Of games, *etc.*: Pass.: *To be engaged in*; i. e. *to have commenced* or *begun, to be beginning.*—Pass.: **com-mittor,** missus sum, mitti.
commōtus, a, um, P. perf. pass. of commŏvĕo.
com-mŏvĕo, mōvi, mōtum, mŏvēre, 2. v. a. [com (= cum), in "intensive" force; mŏvĕo] **1.** [mŏvĕo, "to move"] ("To move greatly"; hence) Of the wings of a bird: *To move,* or *fly, with force* or *rapidity.*—**2.** [mŏvĕo, "to remove"] ("To remove greatly"; hence) *To drive out,* etc.—Pass.: **com-mŏvĕor,** mōtus sum, mŏvēri.
compello, āvi, ātum, āre, 1. v. a. [compello (3. v. a.) in reflexive force, "to bring one's self" to a person in order to address him; hence) **1.** *To address, speak to, accost.*—**2.** *To address reproachfully,* etc.; *to chide, rebuke, take to task.*
com-plector, plexus sum, plecti, 3. v. dep. [com (= cum), "with"; plecto, "to entwine"] ("To entwine one's self with " some person or thing; hence) *To embrace, clasp.*
com-plĕo, plēvi, plētum, plēre, 2. v. a. [com (= cum), in "augmentative" force; plĕo, "to fill"] **1.** *To fill entirely* or *completely; to fill up, fill;*—at v. 107 with Abl. [§ 119, *b*].—**2.** Of time: *To finish, complete.*—Pass.: **com-plĕor,** plētus sum, plēri.

complērant, for complēvĕrant, 3. pers. plur. pluperf. ind. of complĕo.
1. **complexus,** a, um, P. perf. of complector.
2. **complexus,** ūs, m. [for complect-sus; fr. complect-or, "to embrace"] *An embracing, an embrace.*
compressi, perf. ind. of comprimo.
com-prĭmo, pressi, pressum, prĭmĕre, 3. v. a. [for comprĕmo; fr. com (= cum), "together"; prĕmo, "to press"] ("To press together"; hence) *To check, restrain, suppress.*
con-căvus, căva, căvum, adj. [con (= cum), in "intensive" force; căvus, "hollow"] *Completely hollow, hollowed out, worn hollow.*
con-cēdo, cessi, cessum, cēdĕre, 3. v. a. [con (= cum), in "augmentative" force; cēdo, "to yield"] *To grant, allow, yield, concede.*—Pass.: **concēdor,** cessus sum, cēdi.
conceptus, a, um, P. perf. pass. of concĭpio.
concessus, a, um, P. perf. pass. of concēdo.—As Subst.: **concessa,** ōrum, n. plur. *Things that are allowed; lawful, or allowable, things.*
con-cĭdo, cĭdi, no sup., cĭdĕre, 3. v. n. [for con-cădo; fr. con (= cum), in "augmentative" force; cădo, "to fall"] ("To fall utterly"; hence) *To fall,* or *tumble, down.*
con-cĭl-ĭum, ĭi, n. [for con-căl-ĭum; fr. con (= cum), "together"; căl-o, "to call"] ("A calling together"; hence) *A meeting, assembly* of persons.
con-cĭpĭo, cēpi, ceptum, cĭpĕre, 3. v. a. [for con-căpĭo; fr. con (= cum), in "intensive" force; căpĭo, "to take"] ("To take thoroughly"; hence)

Of a female: *To conceive;*—at v. 37 folld. by simple Abl. denoting the father, instead of Abl. with ex.—Pass.: **concĭpĭor**, ceptus sum, cĭpi.

con-clāmo, clāmāvi, clāmātum, clāmāre, 1. v. a. [con (= cum), in "intensive" force; clamo, "to cry out"] *To cry out aloud; to shout out*, etc.

concur-sus, sūs, m. [for concurr-sus; fr. concurr-o, "to run together"] ("A running together"; hence) *Assemblage, crowd, concourse.*

concussi, perf. ind. of concŭtio.

concussus, a, um, P. perf. pass. of concŭtio;—at v. 205 supply sunt with concussæ.

con-cŭtĭo, cussi, cussum, cŭtĕre, 3. v. a. [for con-quătĭo; fr. con (= cum), in "intensive" force; quătĭo, "to shake"] **1.** *To shake violently.*—**2.** Of persons, their feelings, etc.: *To agitate, alarm, trouble*, etc.— Pass.: **con-cŭtĭor**, cussus sum, cŭti.

condĭdi, perf. ind. of condo.

con-do, dĭdi, dĭtum, dĕre, 3. v. a. [con (= cum), "together"; do, "to put"] ("To put together"; hence) *To store or lay up;*—condere terrā, *to lay up in the earth;* i. e. *to bury, inter;* v. 48:—condĭdit se portu alto, *laid itself up in the deep (recess of the) harbour;* i. e. came to anchor in the harbour's deep recess; v. 243.—Pass.: **con-dor**, dĭtus sum, di.

confectus, a, um, P. perf. pass. of conficio;—at v. 362 supply sunt with confecti.

con-fĭcĭo, fēci, fectum, fĭcĕre, 3. v. a. [for con-făcio; fr. con (= cum), in "augmentative" force; făcĭo, "to do *or* make"] ("To do, *or* make, thoroughly"; hence) *To finish, complete, bring to an end.*—Pass.: **con-fĭcĭor**, fectus sum, fĭci.

con-fīdo, fīsus sum, fīdĕre, 3. v. n. semi-dep. [con (= cum), in "intensive" force; fīdo, "to trust"] With Dat. [§ 106, 3]: *To trust to, rely upon, put trust in, have confidence in.*

confīsus, a, um, P. perf. of confīdo.

con-fundo, fūdi, fūsum, fundĕre, 3. v. a. [con (= cum), "together"; fundo, "to pour"] ("To pour together"; hence, "to mingle, blend"; hence) With accessory notion of disorder, etc.: *To confuse, throw into confusion or disorder:*—confundere fœdus, *to throw a treaty into confusion*, i. e. *to violate*, or *break, it.*

con-grĕdĭor, gressus sum, grĕdi, 3. v. dep. [for con-grădĭor; fr. con (= cum), "together"; grădĭor, "to step"] ("To step together, plant foot to foot"; hence) With Dat. [§ 106, *a*]: *To fight, engage, contend with.*

1. **congressus**, a, um, P. perf. of congrĕdĭor.

2. **congres-sus**, sūs, m. [for congred-sus; fr. congrĕdĭor, "to meet" one] *A meeting, interview*, etc.;—v. 733 in plur.

con-jĭcĭo, jēci, jectum, jĭcĕre, 3. v. a. [for con-jăcio; fr. con (= cum), in "augmentative" force; jăcĭo, "to cast"] **1.** *To cast, throw, hurl.*—**2.** With Personal pron. in reflexive force: *To cast one's self*, etc.; i. e. *to betake one's self*, etc., *in haste.*

conjunge, sing. pres. imperat. of conjungo.

con-jungo, junxi, junctum, jungĕre, 3. v. a. [con (= cum), "together"; jungo, "to join"] *To join together, unite.*

conjux (old form **conjunx**), ŭgis, comm. gen. [for conjug-s; fr. CONJUGO, true root of conjungo, "to join together"] ("One joined together" with another; hence) ("A husband"; also) *A wife.*

con-nītor, nisus *or* nixus sum, nīti, 3. v. dep. [con (= cum), in "intensive" force; nītor, "to exert one's self"] *To exert one's self with all one's might, to strive eagerly.*

connixus, a, um, P. perf. of connitor.

1. con-sanguĭn-ĕus, ĕa, ĕum, adj. [con (= cum), denoting "correspondence"; sangu-is, sanguĭn-is, "blood"] ("Having the same blood"; hence) *Related by blood, akin.* — As Subst.: **consanguĭnĕus,** i, m. *A blood-relation, kinsman.*

2. consanguĭnĕus, i; see 1. consanguĭnĕus.

con-scĭ-us, a, um, adj. [con (= cum), "with"; sci-o, "to know"] ("Knowing" something "with" one's self; hence) *Self-conscious, conscious.*

consēdi, perf. ind. of con-sido.

con-sĕquor, sĕquūtus sum, sĕqui, 3. v. dep. [con (= cum), in "augmentative" force; sĕquor, "to follow"] **1.** *To follow after, come next to.*—**2.** *To come up with, overtake.*

con-sĕro, sĕrŭi, sertum, sĕrĕre, 3. v. a. [con (= cum), "together"; sero, "to join"] *To join,* or *fasten, together; to connect.*—Pass.: **con-sĕror,** sertus sum, sĕri.

consertus, a, um, P. perf. pass. of consĕro.

conses-sus, sûs, m. [for consed-sus; fr. consido, "to sit together," through a root CONSED] ("A sitting together"; hence) *A number of persons sitting together; an assembly.*

con-sīdo, sēdi, sessum, sīdĕre, 3. v. n. [con (= cum), "together"; sīdo, "to sit down"] **1.** Of a number of persons: *To sit down together* with others; *to seat one's self, sit down.*—**2.** Of a single pers n: *To sit down, take one's seat.*

consĭlĭum, ĭi, n. *Deliberation, consultation, counsel.*

con-sisto, stĭti, stĭtum, sistĕre, 3. v. n. [con (= cum), in "augmentative" force; sisto, "to stand"] *To stand, take one's stand.*

con-sŏno, sŏnŭi, no sup. sŏnāre, 1. v. n. [con (= cum), "together, at the same time"; sŏno, "to sound"] *To sound together* or *at the same time; to resound.*

con-spĭcĭo, spexi, spectum, spĭcĕre, 3. v. a. [for con-spĕcio; fr. con (= cum), in "augmentative" force; spĕcio, "to see"] *To see, behold, espy, descry.*

constĭti, perf. ind. of con-sisto.

constĭtŭam, fut. ind. of constĭtŭo.

con-stĭtŭo, stĭtŭi, stĭtūtum, stĭtŭĕre, 3. v. a. [for con-stătŭo; fr. con (= cum), in "augmentative" force; stătŭo, "to place or set"] **1.** *To place, set.*—**2.** *To erect, set up.*

con-sto, stĭti, stătum, stāre, 1. v. n. [con (= cum), in "strengthening" force; sto, "to stand"] ("To stand firm"; hence) *To be fixed, determined on,* or *settled* in the mind, *etc.*

con-sūmo, sumpsi, sumptum, sūmĕre, 3. v. a. [con (= cum), in "intensive" force; sūmo, "to take"] ("To take

VOCABULARY. 53

wholly"; hence, "to consume" food; hence) Of things in general: *To consume, destroy*, etc.—Pass.: **con-sūmor**, sumptus sum, sūmi.

consumptus, a, um, P. perf. pass. of consūmo.

con-surgo, surrexi, surrectum, surgěre, 3. v. n. [con (= cum), in "strengthening" force; surgo, "to rise"] **1.** *To rise, arise.*—**2.** Of the wind: *To spring up.*

con-tendo, tendi, tentum, tenděre, 3. v. a. and n. [con (= cum), in "augmentative" force; tendo, "to stretch"] **1.** Act.: **a.** *To stretch, or bend, with all one's,* etc., *might.*—**b.** *To draw tight, strain.*—**c.** With cursum: *To bend, direct, or shape, one's,* etc., *course.*—**d.** Of an arrow: *To launch, shoot.*—**2.** Neut.: ("To exert one's self"; hence) *To strive, contend.*

1. **contentus**, a, um, P. perf. pass. of contendo.

2. **conten-tus**, ta, tum, adj. [contĭněo, in force of "to curb or restrain," through root CONTEN (= CON; TEN, root of tĕněo)] ("Curbing, or restraining," one's self; hence) *Contented, satisfied, content.*

contĭgěram, pluperf. ind. of contingo.

con-tingo, tĭgi, tactum, tingěre, 3. v. a. [for con-tango; fr. con (= cum), in "augmentative" force; tango, "to touch"] ("To touch on all sides"; hence) **1.** *To come to, arrive at, reach* a place.—**2.** *To reach* with a weapon, *to hit.*

contĭnŭ-o, adv. [contĭnŭus, "holding together" in its parts; hence, "uninterrupted"] ("After the manner of the *continuus*"; i. e. "in uninterrupted succession"; hence) *Immediately, forthwith.*

con-torquĕo, torsi, tortum, torquēre, 2. v. a. [con (= cum), "in augmentative" force; torquĕo, "to twist"] ("To twist round"; hence, "to launch, hurl" a missile; hence) Of an arrow: *To shoot.*

contorsi, perf. ind. of contorqueo.

contrā, adv. and prep.: **1.** Adv.: **a.** *Over against, on the opposite side, opposite.*—**b.** *In opposition.*—**2.** Prep. gov. Acc.: **a.** *Against.*—**b.** *Over against, opposite.*

contus, i, m. *A pole* [Gr. κοντός].

con-vello, velli *or* vulsi, vulsum, vellěre, 3. v. a. [con (= cum), in "augmentative" force; vellu, "to pluck"] ("To pluck violently"; hence, "to tear, or rend, into small pieces"; hence) Of the sea: *To tear up,* etc., with oars.—Pass.: **con-vellor**, vulsus sum, velli.

convēni, perf. ind. of convěnio.

con-věnio, vēni, ventum, věnire, 4. v. n. [con (= cum), "together"; věnio, "to come"] *To come together, assemble.*

conversus, a, um, P. perf. pass. of converto.

con-verto, verti, versum, vertěre, 3. v. a. [con (= cum), in "augmentative" force; verto, "to turn"] **1.** *To turn, turn round.*—**2.** *To change, alter.*—**3.** *To change, or alter,* in feeling, *etc.; to estrange.*—Pass.: **con-vertor**, versus sum, verti.

convulsus, a, um, P. perf. pass. of convello.

cō-p-ĭa, ĭæ, f. [contr. fr. co-ŏp-ĭa; fr. co (= cum), in "intensive" force; ops, ŏp-is, "means" of any kind] *Means, power, ability,* etc.

cor, cordis, n. *The heart* [akin to Gr. κῆρ; Sans. hṛid].

corn-ĕus, ĕa, ĕum, adj. [corn-us, "a cornel-tree"] ("Of, or belonging to, *cornus*"; hence) *Of, or made of, the wood of the cornel-tree; cornel-*.

cor-nu, nûs, n.: **1.** *A horn of animals.*—**2.** *The extremity, or end, of t e sail-yards* of a ship [akin to Gr. κέρ-ας].

cŏrōna, æ, f. *A wreath, garland, crown, chaplet* [κορώνη, "a crow"; hence, "anything curved or bent like a crow's bill"; hence, "a garland," *etc.*].

corp-us, ŏris, n. ("That which is made or formed"; hence) **1.** *The body*;—at v. 683 applied to the hull of a vessel. —**2.** *A person* [akin to Sans. root KLIP, "to make"].

cor-rĭpĭo, rĭpŭi, reptum, rĭpĕre, 3. v. a. [for con-răpio; fr. con (= cum), "together"; răpio, "to drag or draw"] ("To d: ag, or draw, together"; hence) **1.** *To seize, snatch, snatch up.*— **2.** Of space traversed: *To hasten through* or *along; to pass*, or *dash, rapidly over*;—at v. 145 the perf. corripuēre is used in a force of the Gr. aorist; viz. to denote a customary action: *are wont to dash rapidly over*.

corrĭpŭi, perf. ind. of corrĭpio.

Cōrus, i, m. *The North-west wind*;—at v. 126 in plur.

cŏrusco, āvi, ātum, āre, 1. v. a. *To move quickly hither and thither; to brandish, wave*, etc.; —at v. 642 supply eum (= ignem) after cōruscat.

crassus, a, um, adj. *Thick*: —crassus cruor, *thick blood*, i. e. *clotted gore*, v. 469.

crātēr, ēris, m. *A bowl* for mixing wine; *a goblet* [κρατήρ].

crē-ber, bra, brum, adj. [cresco, "to increase"; through root CRE] ("Made to increase"; hence, "numerous"; hence) **1.** *Frequent, repeated*:—crebra mănus, *the frequent*—i. e. *rapidly plied—hand*, v. 436.—**2.** With Abl. [§ 119, b]: *Abounding in*: —creber ictibus, *abounding in blows*, i. e. plying blows rapidly or in quick succession.

crē-do, dĭdi, dĭtum, dĕre, 3. v. a. ("To put faith, *or* trust," in some person or thing; hence) *To trust, entrust, commit* [akin to Sans. prefix *çrat*, "faith"; do, "to put"].

crĕpĭtans, ntis, P. pres. of crĕpĭto.

crĕp-ĭto, no perf. nor sup., ĭtāre, 1. v. n. freq. [crĕp-o, "to rattle"] *To rattle loudly* or *fast; to keep rattling*.

crepo, ŭi, ĭtum, āre, 1. v. n. ("To rattle, clatter"; hence) *To break*, or *be broken, with a crash*.

crĕpŭi, perf. ind. of crĕpo.

Cressa, æ, f. *A woman of Crete, a Cretan woman* [Gr. Κρῆσσα].

Crēta, æ, f. *Crete* (now *Candia*); *an island in the S.E. of the Mediterranean* [Gr. Κρήτη].

Crīmīsus, i, m. *Crimisus; a river on the S.W. coast of Sicily*.

crī-nis, nis, m. [for crē-nis; fr. CRE, root of cre-sco, "to grow"] ("The growing thing"; hence) **1.** *The hair of the head*. —**2.** *The tail* of a comet [cf. Gr. θρίξ, τριχ-ός, akin to Sans. root DṚIH, "to grow"].

crūd-us, a, um, adj. ("Wrathful"; hence, "cruel, merciless"; hence) *Unprepared, raw*:—crudus cæstus, *a raw cæstus*, i.e. *a cæstus of raw hide* [akin to Sans. root KRUDH, "to be wrathful"].

crŭor, ōris, m. *Blood*.

cŭcurri, perf. ind. of curro.

VOCABULARY. 55

cuique, dat. sing. of quisque.

cul-men, mĭnis, n. ("The highest part" of a thing; hence) Of a building: *The roof.*

cul-tus, tūs, m. [for coltus; fr. cŏl-o, "to work *or* cultivate" the ground, *etc.*] ("A working, cultivation"; hence) *Mode,* or *manner, of living; habits.*

cum, prep. gov. abl. *With;* —written after personal pronouns, *e. g.* mecum for cum me [akin to Gr. ξύν (for κύν), σύν; Sans. *sam*].

cŭmŭl-o, ăvi, ătum, āre, 1. v. a. [cŭmŭl-us, "a heap"] ("To heap up"; hence, "to fill"; hence) With Abl.: *To load with* gifts, *etc.*

cunctans, ntis, P. pres. of cunctor.

cunc-tor, tătus sum, tări, 1. v. dep. ("To fluctuate"; hence) *To linger, delay* [akin to Sans. root ÇAŃK, "to fluctuate"].

cunctus, a, um (most frequently plur.), adj. [contr. from conjunctus, P. perf. pass. of conjungo, "to join *or* unite together"] ("United together"; hence) *All.*—As Subst.: **cuncti,** ōrum, m. plur. *All persons, all.*

cŭ-nĕus, nĕi, m. ("The sharpened thing"; hence, "a wedge"; hence) The wedgeform division of *a row of seats* in a theatre.

cŭpĕrem, imperf. subj. of cŭpĭo.

cŭp-īdo, ĭdĭnis, m. [cŭp-ĭo, "to desire"] *Desire.*

cŭp-ĭo, ivi *or* ii, ĭtum, ĕre, 3. v. a.: With Inf.: *To desire to* do, *etc.; to be desirous of* doing, *etc.* [akin to Sans. root KUP, "to desire"].

cūr-a, æ, f. [for cœr-a; fr. cœr-o, old form of quær-o, "to seek"] ("The seeking thing"; hence, with accessory notion of trouble) *Care, solicitude.*

curro, cŭcurri, cursum, currĕre, 3. v. n.: **1.** *To run.*—**2.** With Acc. of cognate Object: *To run over, to traverse rapidly.* —**3.** *To move quickly onwards, to make way,* etc., with oars; v. 222 [prob. akin to Sans. root ÇRI, "to go"].

curr-us, ūs, m. [curr-o, "to run"] ("A running; that which runs"; hence) *A chariot, car.*

cursus, sūs, m. [for currsus; fr. cur-ro, "to run"] ("A running"; hence, "quick motion" on foot, horseback, shipboard, *etc.;* hence) **1.** *A running.*—**2. a.** *A riding,* etc.—**b.** *An evolution* on horseback.—**3.** *A course* at sea.—**4.** *The course* of the heavenly bodies, *etc.*—**5.** Of troops: *An advance, charge,* etc.

cur-vus, va, vum, adj. *Bent, curved, winding* [akin to Gr. κυρ-τός, "curved"].

cuspis, ĭdis, f. *A point;*—at v. 208 acūtā cuspide is Abl. of quality [§ 115] [akin to Sans. root ço, "to sharpen"].

cust-os, ōdis, comm. gen. ("One who covers"; hence) *A guardian, governor,* to whose keeping youths were committed; see măgister [akin to Gr. κευθ-ω, "to cover"].

Cyclōpes, um; see Cyclops.

Cyclops, ōpis (Plur.: **Cyclōpes,** um), m. *A Cyclops;* one of a savage race of people on the coast of Sicily, who were fabled to have had but one eye, which was placed in the middle of the forehead, and to have been Vulcan's workmen [Gr. Κύκλωψ, "One with a round eye"].

cymbĭum, ĭi, n. *A small*

drinking-vessel; a cup or *tankard* [Gr. κυμβίον].

Cymŏdŏcē, ēs, f. *Cymodocē;* a sea-nymph, one of Neptune's attendants [Gr. Κυμοδόκη, " Wave-receiver "].

Cўthĕrēa, æ; see Cўthĕrēus.

(Cўthĕr-ēus, ēa, ēum, adj. [Cyther-a, "Cythera" (now "Cerigo"); an island in the Ægean Sea, celebrated for the worship of Venus] *Of Cythera; Cytherean.* — As Subst. :) **Cўthĕrēa,** æ, f. *Cytherea,* a name of Venus, who, according to some accounts, was sprung from the foam of the sea.—To this Virgil makes Neptune to allude at v. 80).

dă, pres. imperat. of do.

Dănă-i, ōrum, m. plur. [Dănă-us, "of, or belonging to, Danaus" (the brother of Ægyptus), who settled in Greece; hence, "Greek, Grecian"] *The Greeks.*

dăpes, plur. of daps.

dap-s, is (Gen. Plur. seems not to occur), f. ("A sacrificial feast"; hence) *A rich feast, a banquet* [akin to δαπ, root of Gr. δάπ-τω, "to devour," and δαπάνη, "expense"].

Dardănĭdæ, ārum, plur. of Dardănĭdes; see Dardănus, no. c.

Dardănĭdŭm for Dardănĭdārum; **Dardănĭus,** ĭa, ĭum; see Dardănus.

Dardănus, i, m. *Dardanus;* a son of Jupiter and Electra, and an ancestor of the royal house of Troy. — Hence, **a. Dardăn-us,** a, um, adj. ("Of, *or* belonging to, Dardanus"; hence) *Trojan.* — **b. Dardăn-ĭus,** ĭa, ĭum, adj. = Dardănus, no. a, above;—at *v. 30* Acestes is called Dardanius, as his mother was a Trojan woman; see Acestes.- **c. D.ırdăn-ĭdes,** æ (Gen. Plur. Dardănĭdŭm for Dardănĭdārum, v. 622), m. "A descendant of Dardanus"; hence) Plur. : *The Trojans.*

Dăres, is and ĕtis (Aco. Dăren, v. 456 ; Dărĕta, vv. 460, 463, 476), m. *Dares;* a Trojan, who prior to the destruction of Troy was accustomed to engage Paris with the cæstus. He was signally defeated in a pugilistic encounter with Entellus at the funeral games held in honour of Anchises [Gr. Δάρης, "Flayer"].

dē, prep. gov. abl. : **1.** Locally: **a.** *From, down from.*—**b.** *Out of, from.*—**2.** To denote descent: *From, of.*—**3.** *According to, in accordance with, after :* —dē mōre, *according to custom,* v. 96.

dĕa, æ, f. [akin to dĕus; see dĕus] *A goddess;*—at v. 657 dĕa = Iris; at vv. 383, 474, 709 = Venus.

dēbellandus, a, um, Gerundive of dēbello;—at v. 731 follld. by Dat. [§ 107, *d*].

dē-bello, bellāvi, bellātum, bellāre, 1. v. a. [dē, denoting "completeness"; bello, "to war"] ("To war completely"; hence) *To vanquish, utterly subdue.*

dē-bĭlis, bĭle, adj. [contr. fr. dē-hăbĭlis; fr. dē, in "negative" force; hăbĭlis, "handy"] ("Unhandy"; hence) *Feeble, weak, weakened, disabled.*

dē-cēdo, cessi, cessum, cēdĕre, 3. v. n. [dē, "away"; cēdo, "to go"] *To go away, depart.*

dĕc-et, ŭit, no sup., ēre, 2. v. n. (only in third person and Inf. : never with personal subject) *Is,* etc., *becoming* or *proper.*

VOCABULARY.

dēceptus, a, um, P. perf. pass. of dēcĭpĭo.

dē-cĭdo, cĭdi, no sup., cĭdĕre, 3. v. n. [for dē-cădo; fr. dē, "down"; cădo, "to fall"] *To fall down.*

dē-cĭpĭo, cēpi, ceptum, cĭpĕre, 3. v. a. [for dē-căpĭo; fr. dē, in "intensive" force; căpĭo, "to take"] ("To take thoroughly"; hence) *To beguile, deceive.*—Pass.: **dē-cĭpĭor,** ceptus sum, cĭpi.

dē-clāro, clārāvi, clārātum, clārāre, 1. v. a. [dē, denoting "completeness"; clāro, "to make clear"] ("To make a thing quite clear"; hence) With second Acc.: *To proclaim, announce, declare* an object as being that which is denoted by the second Acc.

dĕc-or, ōris, m. [dĕc-et, "(it) is becoming"] ("That which is becoming"; hence) *Comeliness, gracefulness, beauty.*

dĕcōr-us, a, um, adj. [dĕc-or, dĕcōr-is, "gracefulness, beauty," etc.] ("Having *decor*"; hence) **1.** *Becoming, suitable, proper,* etc.—**2.** *Graceful.*—**3.** *Decorated, adorned,* etc.

dē-curro, cŭcurri or curri, cursum, currĕre, 3. v. n. [dē, "down"; curro, "to run"] **1.** *To run down.*—**2.** *To sail down.*

dĕc-us, ŏris, n. [dĕc-et, "(it) is becoming"] ("That which is becoming," etc.; hence) **1.** *Ornament, decoration.* —**2.** *Dignity, honour.*

dĕdĕram, pluperf. ind. of do.

dĕdi, perf. ind. of do.

dēfer, pres. imperat. of dēfĕro.

dē-fĕro, tŭli, lātum, ferre, v. a. irreg. [dē, "down"; fĕro, "to bring"] *To bring down* to a place.

dē-hinc (in poets mostly as monosyll., but at v. 722 dissyll.), adv. [dē, "from"; hinc, "hence"] ("From hence"; hence) Of time: *After this, afterwards, next, then.*

dē-hisco, hīvi, no sup., hiscĕre, 3. v. n. [dē, "asunder"; hisco, "to yawn"] *To yawn,* or *gape, asunder.*

dē-inde (in poets mostly dissyll.), adv. [dē, "from"; inde, "thence"] ("From thence"; hence) *Afterwards, then, in the next place.*

dējēci, perf. ind. of dējĭcĭo.

dējectus, a, um, P. perf. pass. of dējĭcĭo.

dē-jĭcĭo, jēci, jectum, jĭcĕre, 3. v. a. [for dē-jăcĭo; fr. dē, "down"; jăcĭo, "to cast"] **1.** *To cast,* or *throw, down.*—**2.** *To bring down dead* by an arrow, etc.—Pass.: **dē-jĭcĭor,** jectus sum, jĭci.

dē-lābor, lapsus sum, lābi, 3. v. dep. [dē, "down"; lābor, "to glide"] *To glide down.*

dēlapsus, a, um, P. perf. of dēlābor.

dēlātus, a, um, P. perf. pass. of dēfĕro.

dēlectus, a, um, P. perf. pass. of dēlĭgo.

dēlēgi, perf. ind. of dēlĭgo.

dē-lĭgo, lēgi, lectum, lĭgĕre, 3. v. a. [for dē-lĕgo; fr. dē, "out or out from"; lĕgo, "to choose"] *To choose,* or *pick, out* from a number; *to select.*— Pass.: **dē-lĭgor,** lectus sum, lĭgi.

delphin, īnis (Gen. Plur. delphīnum, v. 594), m. *A dolphin* [Gr. δελφίν].

dēment-ia, iae, f. [dēmens, dēment-is, "out of one's mind, mad"] ("The state, or condition, of the *demens*"; hence) *Madness, folly.*

dēmitte, sing. pres. imperat. of dēmitto.

dē-mitto, misi, missum, mittĕre, 3. v. a. [dē, "down"; mitto, "to send"] *To send down.*

Dēmŏlĕus, ĕi, m. *Demolĕus;* a Greek slain by Æneas during the Trojan war [Δημόλεος, "Destroyer of the people"].

dens, dentis, m. *A tooth* [akin to Sans. *dant-as;* Gr. ὀδούς, ὀ-δόντ-ος].

densus, a, um, adj.: **1.** *Thick, dense.*—**2.** *Close, compact.*—**3.** *Frequent, oft-repeated.*

dē-pasco, pāvi, pastum, pascĕre, 3. v. a. [dē, "down"; pasco, "to feed"] ("To feed down, feed off"; hence) Of animals: *To feed upon, eat up, consume.*

dēpastus, a, um, P. perf. pass. of dēpasco.

dē-pello, pŭli, pulsum, pellĕre, 3. v. a. [dē, "away"; pello, "to drive"] *To drive away.*

dē-pōno, pŏsŭi, pŏsĭtum, pōnĕre, 3. v. a. [dē, "down"; pono, "to put"] ("To put down"; hence) *To place,* or *deposit,* for safe keeping.

dē-prendo, prendi, prensum, prendĕre, 3. v. a. [dē, "away from"; prendo, in force of "to snatch"] ("To snatch away from"; hence, "to seize"; hence) *To overtake, catch.*—Pass.: **dē-prendor,** prensus sum, prendi.

dēprensus, a, um, P. perf. pass. of dēprendo.

dē-prōmo, prompsi, promptum, prōmĕre, 3. v. a. [dē, "out of"; promo, "to bring forth"] ("To bring forth out of" something; hence) With Abl. dependent on prep. in verb [§ 122, *a*]: *To draw out from.*

dēpŭli, perf. ind. of dēpello.

dē-scendo, scendi, scensum, scendĕre, 3. v. n. [for dēscando; fr. dē, "down"; scando, "to climb"] ("T) climb down"; hence) **1.** *To go down* or *downwards; to descend.*—**2.** With *in* c. Acc.: *To lower one's self* or *descend to; to have recourse to.*

dē-sĕro, sĕrŭi, sertum, sĕrĕre, 3. v. a. [dē, in "negative" force; sĕro, "to join"] ("To disjoin; to undo *or* sever" one's connexion with some object; hence) *To forsake, abandon, desert.*—Pass.: **dēsĕror,** sertus sum, sĕri.

dēsertus, a, um, P. perf. pass. of dēsĕro.

dē-signo, signāvi, signātum, signāre, 1. v. a. [dē, "out"; signo, "to mark"] *To mark,* or *trace, out.*

dē-torquĕo, torsi, tortum, torquēre, 2. v. a. [dē, "away"; torquĕo, "to twist"] ("To twist away"; hence) *To turn forcibly aside* or *away.*

dē-trăho, traxi, tractum, trăhĕre, 3. v. a. [dē, "away from"; trăho, "to draw or drag"] ("To draw *or* drag away from"; hence) With Acc. of thing and Dat. of person: *To strip* something *off from* one; *to despoil* one *of* something.

dētraxĕram, pluperf. ind. of dētrăho.

dē-turbo, turbāvi, turbātum, turbāre, 1. v. a. [dē, "down"; turbo, "to move violently"] ("To move violently down"; hence) *To throw, cast,* or *hurl down.*

dĕus, i (Nom. Plur., di, v. 50; Gen. Plur., deûm, v. 707), m. *A god;*—at v. 391 the term is applied to Eryx as an appellation of honour [akin to Sans. *deva;* Gr. θεός].

dex-ter, tĕra *or* tra, tĕrum

VOCABULARY. 59

or **trum**, adj. *To*, or *on, the right hand* or *side; right* as opp. to "*left.*"—As Subst.: **dextĕra (dextra)**, æ, f. *The right hand* whether of the body or to denote direction.

dextĕra, æ; **dextra**, æ; see dexter.

dī, dīs, for dei, deis; see **dĕus**.

dīc, pres. imperat. of 1. dico.

dīcātus, a, um, P. perf. pass. of 2. dico.

dīcentur, 3. pers. plur. fut. ind. of 1. dico.

1. **dīco**, dixi, dictum, dicĕre, 3. v. a. ("To show, *or* point out," by speaking; hence) **1.** *To say, speak, tell.*—**2.** Without nearer Object: *To speak:*—dixit, (*he spoke;* i. e.) *he ceased to speak or finished speaking:*—dixĕrat, (*he had spoken;* i. e.) *he had ceased to speak* or *had finished speaking*.—**3.** *To state, mention, report.*—**4.** Pass.: *To be called something or by some name.*—Pass.: **dīcor**, dictus sum. dici [akin to Gr. δείκ-νυμι; Sans. root DIÇ, "to show"].

2. **dīc-o**, āvi, ātum, āre, 1. v. a. ("To proclaim *or* make known"; hence) *To dedicate*, or *consecrate*, to a deity.—Pass.: **dīc-or**, ātus sum, āri [akin to 1. dico].

dic-tum, ti, n. [dic-o, "to speak"] ("That which is spoken"; hence) *A word*.

dictus, a, um, P. perf. pass. of 1. dico.

Dīdo, ūs and ōnis, f. *Dido* (also called *Elissa*, v. 3), daughter of Belus, king of Tyre, and wife of Sichæus. When her husband was murdered by her brother Pygmalion, she fled with vast riches from her country to Africa, and there founded Carthage. Having hospitably entertained Æneas, when he fled from Troy, she became so devotedly attached to him, that on his leaving her she destroyed herself through grief (Gr. Ado; Hebrew *Didō*, "Lovely").

dī-dūco, duxi, ductum, ducĕre, 3. v. a. (di (= dis), "apart"; duco, "to draw") **1.** *To draw apart, separate*.—**2.** *To divide*.—Pass.: **dī-dūcor**, ductus sum, dūci.

Dīdȳmāon, ŏnis, m. *Didymaon;* an artist in metals; v. 259.

dĭes, ēi, m. (in sing. sometimes f.) *A day* [akin to Sans. *div*, "heaven; a day"].

dif-fĭcĭlis, fĭcĭle, adj. [for dis-facilis; fr. dis, in "negative" force; facilis, "easy"] ("Not easy"; hence) **1.** *Hard, difficult*.—**2.** *Dangerous*.

dif-fŭgĭo, fūgi, no sup. fŭgĕre, 3. v. n. [for dis-fugio; fr. dis, "in different directions"; fugio, "to flee"] Of several persons as Subject: *To flee in different directions; to scatter themselves, etc.; to scatter*.

dĭg-ĭtus, ĭti, m. ("The showing, *or* pointing, thing"; hence) **1.** *A finger*.—**2.** Of the feet: *A toe* [from same root as 1. dico].

dig-nus, na, num, adj. ("Shown, pointed out"; hence, "worthy"; hence) **1.** Of things: *Suitable, fit, becoming, proper*.—**2.** *That of which one, etc., is worthy; deserved, merited* (id.).

dī-grĕdior, gressus sum, grĕdi, 3. v. dep. (for di-gradior; fr. di (= dis), "apart"; gradior, "to step") ("To step apart" from others; hence) *To go away, depart*.

dīgressus, a, um, P. perf. of digredior.

dīlectus, a, um, P. perf. pass. of dīligo;—at v. 589 follid. by Dat. [§ 107, 4].

dī-līgo, lexi, lectum, līgĕre, 3. v. a. [for dī-lĕgo; fr. dī (= dis), "apart"; lĕgo, "to choose"] ("To choose, or select, apart" from others; hence) *To value,* or *esteem, highly; to love.*—Pass.: **dī-līgor,** lectus sum, līgi.

dī-mitto, misi, missum, mittĕre, 3. v. a. [dī (= dis), "apart"; mitto, "to send"] ("To send apart" from one; hence) Milit. t. t.: Of troops: *To disband, release from service,* etc.—It is probably in the foregoing meaning that *dimittere* is figuratively applied to *naves* at v. 29, and hence implies *to rest,* etc. The word is commonly said to be equivalent in this passage to *appellere,* "to bring to" a place. This view, however, is untenable, inasmuch as the place of arrival would have to be described; while, further, there is nothing in the word itself to countenance such an interpretation.

dī-mŏvĕo, mōvi, mōtum, mŏvēre, 2. v. a. [dī (= dis), "apart"; mŏvĕo, "to move"] *To move apart* or *asunder; to divide.*

Dīōres, is, m. *Diores;* a prince of the royal family of Troy; v. 297.

dīrēmi, perf. ind. of dirimo.

dīrĭge, sing. pres. imperat. of dirigo.

dī-rīgo, rexi, rectum, rĭgĕre, 3. v. a. [for dī-rĕgo; fr. dī (= dis), in "strengthening" force; rĕgo, "to keep, or lead, straight"] ("To keep, or lead, straight, *or* in a straight line"; hence) *To guide, direct.*

dĭr-ĭmo, ēmi, emptum, ĭmĕre, 3. v. a. [for dĭs-ĕmo; fr. dĭs, "apart"; ĕmo, "to take"] ("To take apart"; hence, "to separate"; hence) Of a fight, etc.: *To break off, to put an end to, stop.*

Dĭs, Dītis, m. [akin to dĕus; see dĕus] *Dis,* the Greek *Pluto;* the god of the lower world.

discens, ntis, P. pres. of disco.

disco, dĭdĭci, no sup., discĕre, 3. v. a. ("To be shown" how to do, *etc.,* something; hence) **1.** *To learn.*—**2.** With Inf.: *To learn how to do, etc.*—**3.** *To ascertain, find out, discover,* etc. [akin to δείκ-νῡμι, Sans. root DIÇ, "to show"; cf. 1. dico.

discrī-men, mĭnis, n. [for discrē-men; fr. discerno, "to separate," through root DISCER] ("That which separates" things from each other; hence) *An intervening space, interval, distance.*

discurrĕre, 3. pers. plur. perf. ind. of discurro.

dis-curro, cŭcurri and curri, cursum, currĕre, 3. v. n. [dis, "apart"; curro, "to run"] Of several persons as Subject: *To run apart* or *in different directions; to separate themselves,* etc.; *to break away.*

dis-pello, pŭli, pulsum, pellĕre, 3. v. a. [dis, "in different directions"; pello, "to drive"] *To drive in different directions; to disperse, scatter.*

dispŭli, perf. ind. of dispello.

dī-verbĕro, verbĕrāvi, verbĕrātum, verbĕrāre, 1. v. a. [dī (= dis), "asunder"; verbĕro, "to strike"] ("To strike asunder"; hence) Of the air as Object: *To cleave, divide, cut through.*

dīver-sus, sa, sum, adj. [for divert-sus; fr. divert-o, "to turn in a different direction"] **1.** *Turned in a different direction* or *away; away:*—quo diversus

VOCABULARY. 61

abis, *whither art thou going away out of thy course?* v. 166.—
2. *Opposite, in a contrary direction.*—**3.** *Remote, distant.*
dīv-īnus, īna, īnum, adj. [dīv-us, "a deity"] ("Of, or belonging to, a deity"; hence) *Divine, heavenly;*—at v. 47 divinus parens = Anchises.
dīvûm, for dīvōrum; see divus.
dīv-us, i (Gen. Plur. dīvûm, v. 45, *etc.*), m. [dīv-us, "divine"] ("A divine being"; hence) *A deity, god.*
dīxĕram, dīxī, pluperf. and perf. ind. of 1. dico.
dō, dědi, dătum, dăre, 1. v. a.: **1.** *To give* in the widest sense of the word.—**2.** Of words: *To give forth, utter, speak;* v. 852.—**3.** With Inf.: *To grant, concede,* etc., *to do,* etc.—**4.** Of sound as Object: *To give forth.*—Pass.: **dor,** dătus sum, dări [akin to Gr. δί-δω-μι; Sans. root pā].
dŏc-ĕo, ŭi, tum, ēre, 2. v. a. *To teach, instruct* [fr. same source as 1. dico; see 1. dico.
dŏcŭi, perf. ind. of dŏcĕo.
dŏl-or, ōris, m. [dŏl-ĕo, "to grieve"] *Grief, sorrow.*
dŏl-us, i, m. *Craft, fraud, guile, deceit* [Gr. δόλος].
dŏm-ĭtor, ĭtōris, m. [dŏmo, "to subdue"] *A subduer.*
dŏmus, i and ūs, f.: **1.** *A house, dwelling, home.*—**2.** *A house, family,* etc. [Gr. δόμος].
dōnātus, a, um, P. perf. pass. of dōno.
dōnec, conj.: **1.** *As long as, while.*—**2.** *Until.*
dōn-o, āvi, ātum, āre, 1. v. a. [dŏn-um, "a gift"] **1.** *To present with a gift.*—**2.** With Acc. of thing and Dat. of person: *To give, or present, something to one.*—**3.** *To reward.*—Pass.: **dōn-or,** ātus sum, ări.

dō-num, ni, n. [for dă-num; fr. da, root of do, "to give"] **1.** *A gift, present.*—**2.** *A votive gift,* or *offering,* to a deity.
Dōryclus, i (y̆, v. 620; y̆, v. 647), m. *Doryclus,* a Thracian; the husband of Bĕrŏĕ [Gr. Δόρυκλος].
dūco, duxi, ductum, dūcĕre, 3. v. a.: **1.** *To lead, conduct.*—**2.** *To draw after,* or *behind,* a person *or* thing.—**3.** Of troops, etc.: *To lead, command.*—**4.** *To lead, manage, conduct, direct,* etc.—**5.** *To lead off* or *away, to carry off,* a prize, *etc.*—**6.** Of origin, descent, etc.: *To derive, draw* [akin to Sans. root דυκ, "to draw out"].
duc-tor, tōris, m. [dūc-o, "to lead"] **1.** *A leader.*—**2.** *A commander,* military *leader.*—**3.** *A commander* of a vessel.
dūdum, adv. *A little while ago, not long since, lately, just now.*
dulc-is, e, adj. ("Sweet" in taste; hence) *Sweet,* or *delightful,* to the feelings, *etc.;* *beloved* [usually referred to Gr. γλυκ-ύς].
dum, adv. [prob. akin to obsol. dius = dies, "a day"] *While, whilst.*
dŭo, æ, o, num. adj. plur. *Two.*—As Subst. m.: *Two persons, two; the two* [Gr. δύο].
du-plex, plĭcis, adj. [for du-plic-s; fr. dŭ-o, "two"; plic-o, "to fold"] ("Twice-folded"; hence) *Two-fold, double.*
dūr-us, a, um, adj.: **1.** *Hard.*—**2.** Of persons: *Hardy.*—**3.** Of grief, etc.: *Severe, painful,* etc. [akin to Sans. druva, "firm"].

ē; see ex.
ĕa, nom. and acc. neut. plur. of is.
ĕădem, fem. nom. sing. of idem; v. 812.

VOCABULARY.

ec-ce, demonstr. particle [for ĕn-ce; fr. en, "lo!"; ce, demonstrative suffix] *Lo! behold! see!*

ēdĭdĕram, pluperf. ind. of 1. ĕdo.

ēdĭdi, perf. ind. of 1. ĕdo.

1. **ē-do,** dĭdi, dĭtum, dĕre, 3. v. a. [ĕ (= ex), "forth"; do, "to put"] ("To put forth"; hence) *To utter, declare,* etc.

2. **ĕdo,** ĕdi, ēsum *or* essum, ĕdĕre *or* esse, 3. v. a. ("To eat;" hence) Of things as Subject: *To eat up, devour, consume, destroy;* v. 633 [akin to Sans. root AD; Gr. ἔδω, "to eat"].

ē-dŏcĕo, dŏcŭi, doctum, dŏcēre, 2. v. a. [ĕ (= ex), "thoroughly"; dŏcĕo, "to teach"] *To teach,* or *show, thoroughly; to inform, apprise.*

effātus, P. perf. of effor;— at v. 633 supply est with effāta; and as the Subject illa = Bĕrŏē.

ef-fĕro, ex-tŭli, ē-lātum, efferre, v. a. [for ex, "out"; fĕro, "to bear"] **1.** *To bear, bring, carry out* or *forth.*—**2.** *To raise, uplift, elevate.*—Pass.: **ef-fĕror,** ē-lātus sum, ef-ferri.

ef-fēt-us, a, um, adj. [for ex-fēt-us; fr. ex, "forth"; fēt-o, "to lay eggs"] ("That has laid eggs; that has produced young"; hence, "exhausted by bearing"; hence) *Exhausted, worn out, enfeebled.*

ef-for, lātus sum, fāri, 1. v. dep. [for ex-for; fr. ex, "out"; for, "to speak"] ("To speak out"; hence) *To utter, speak,* etc.

effractus, a, um, P. perf. pass. of effringo.

ef-fringo, frēgi, fractum, fringĕre, 3. v. a. [for ex-frango; fr. ex, "out"; frango, "to break"] ("To break out, *or* open"; hence) *To dash out by a blow.*—Pass.: **ef-fringor,** fractus sum, fringi.

effūdi, perf. ind. of effundo.

ef-fŭgĭo, fūgi, fŭgĭtum, fŭgĕre, 3. v. n. [for ex-fŭgĭo; fr. ex, "away"; fŭgĭo, "to flee"] ("To flee away"; hence) Of a person in a foot-race: *To flee away from his competitors, to dart forwards.*

ef-fulgĕo, fulsi, no sup., fulgēre, 2. v. n. [for ex-fulgĕo; fr. ex, "forth"; fulgĕo, "to shine"] *To shine,* or *glitter, forth.*

effundens, ntis, P. pres. of effundo.

ef-fundo, fūdi, fūsum, fundĕre, 3. v. a. [for ex-fundo; fr. ex, "forth"; fundo, "to pour"] **1.** *To pour forth.*—**2.** Of words, complaints, etc.: *To pour forth, give vent to, utter.*—**3.** O.:reins: *To let loose, slacken,* etc.—**4.** Pass. in reflexive force: *To pour forth* as a stream would; *to rush forth, dart forward,* etc.; v. 145.—Pass.: **ef-fundor,** fūsus sum, fundi.

effūsus, a, um, P. perf. pass. of effundo.

ĕgens, ntis, P. pres. of ĕgĕo;—at v. 751 follд. by Gen. [§ 119. b].

ĕg-ĕo, ŭi, no sup., ēre, 2. v. n. ("To be needy"; hence) With Abl. or Gen. [§ 119. b]: *To be destitute* or *devoid of; to be without.*

ĕgo, pers. pron.: **1.** *I.*—**2.** Strengthened by suffix met: *I myself* [Gr. ἐγώ; Sans. *aham*].

ĕgŏmet; see ĕgo.

ē-grĕg-ĭus, ĭa, ĭum, adj. [ĕ (= ex), "out of"; grex, grĕg-is, "a flock"] ("That is out of the flock"; hence) *Noble, illustrious, distinguished,* etc.

ē-lābor, lapsus sum, lābi, 3. v. dep. [ē (= ex), "forth"; lābor, "to glide"] *To glide forth; to glide,* or *slip, away.*

VOCABULARY.

ēlapsus, a, um, P. perf. of ēlābor.

Elissa, æ, f. *Elissa;* a poetical name of Dido; see Dido [prob. Hebrew *Elishāh,* the name of a Western race of men on the coast of the Mediterranean (and of their country also), who seem to have been the descendants of Elishāh, the son of Javan, mentioned at Gen. x. 4. If so, the name appears equivalent to "Western Maiden *or* Woman"].

Elysium, ii, n. *Elysium;* in mythology, the abode of the blessed in the lower world ['Ηλύσιον (πεδίον)].

ēmensus, a, um, P. perf. of ēmētior.

ē-mētior, mensus sum, mētiri, 4. v. dep. [ē (= ex), "out"; mētior, "to measure"] ("To measure out"; hence) In space: *To traverse, pass over* or *through.*

ē-mico, micūi, no sup., micāre, 1. v. n. [ē (= ex), "forth"; mico, "to move quickly"] ("To move quickly forth"; hence) *To spring forth, dash forwards,* etc.

ēn, interj. *Lo! behold! see!* [Gr. ἤν].

ēnim, conj.: **1.** *Truly, certainly, indeed.*—**2.** *For.*

ensis, is, m. *A sword* [akin to Sans. *asi*].

Entellus, i, m. *Entellus;* a Sicilian pugilist, who signally defeated the Trojan Dares at the funeral games of Anchises.

ĕo, īvi or ii, ītum, īre, v. n. *To go;*—at v. 451 folld. by Dat. of place "whither" [Notes to Syntax, p. 136, *H*] [root I, akin to Sans. root I, Gr. *i-έναι*].

eōdem, masc. and neut. abl. sing. of idem.

ĕpŭlæ, ārum, f. plur. *A feast, banquet.*

ĕpŭlātus, a, um, P. perf. of ĕpŭlor.

ĕpŭl-or, ātus sum, āri, 1. v. dep. [ĕpŭl-um, "a feast"] *To feast, banquet,* etc.;—at v. 7 2 folld. by Acc. of "Duration of time" [§ 102, (1)].

Epytīdes, æ (Acc. Epytīdēn, v. 547), m. *The son of Epytus,* i. e. *Periphantes,* whose father Epytus was the herald of Anchises. Periphantes was entrusted by Æneas with the charge of Ascanius; v. 546 *sq.* ['Ηπυτίδης, "Son of Epytus"].

ĕqu-ĕs, ĭtis, m. [for equ-i-(t)s; fr. ĕqu-us; I, root of ĕo, "to go"] ("The horse-going one"; hence) *A horseman.*— Plur.: *Cavalry;*—at v. 560 applied to the mounted comrades of Ascanius.

ĕqu-estris, estre, adj. [ĕqu-us, "a horse"] *Pertaining to a horse; horse-, cavalry-.*

ē-quĭdem, adv. [for ecquidem; fr. demonstrative suffix ce, changed before the k sound into ec; quidem, "indeed"] *Indeed, verily, truly.*

ĕqu-us, i, m. *A horse* [akin to Gr. ἵκκ-ος = ἵππ-ος; Sans. *aç-va*].

ēreptus, a, um, P. perf. pass. of ēripio.

ergo, adv. *Therefore, accordingly.*

ē-rĭgo, rexi, rectum, rĭgĕre, 3. v. a. [for ē-rĕgo; fr. ē (= ex), "out of"; rĕgo, "to make straight"] ("To make straight out of" a place; hence) *To raise,* or *lift, up; to erect.*

ē-rĭpio, rĭpŭi, reptum, rĭpĕre, 3. v. a. [for ē-răpio; fr. ē (= ex), "away"; răpio, "to snatch"] **1.** *To snatch away.*— **2.** *To deliver, rescue, set free.*— Pass.: **ē-rĭpior,** reptus sum, rĭpi.

ērĭpŭi, perf. ind. of ērĭpio.

VOCABULARY.

ĕro, fut. ind. of sum.
erro, āvi, ātum, āre, 1. v. n.:
1. *To wander, rove, stray.*—**2.** Of a ship: *To wander from its course.*
err-or, ōris, m. [err-o, "to wander"] **1.** *A wandering, a straying about.*—**2.** *Error, mistake.*
ē-rŭ-o, rŭi, rŭtum, rŭĕre, 3. v. a. [ĕ (= ex), "out"; rŭo, "to cast down"] ("To cast down and out"; hence) Of a tree: *To tear up* from the roots.—Pass.: **ē-rŭor,** rŭtus sum, rŭi.
ērŭtus, a, um, P. perf. pass. of ērŭo.
Erўcīnus, a, um; see Eryx.
Erymanthus, i, m. *Erymanthus;* a mountain-chain in Arcadia, the central state of the Peloponnesus (now the Morĕa) [Gr. Ἐρύμανθος].
Eryx, ўcis, m. *Eryx:* **1.** A king in Sicily, the son of Butes and Venus, and so half-brother to Æneas; hence the expression *litora fraterna Erycis,* v. 24.—**2.** A high mountain (now *S. Giuliano*) with a city of the same name on the W. coast of Sicily, famed for its temple of Venus. — Hence, **Erўcīnus,** ina, inum, adj. *Of,* or *belonging to, Eryx* [Gr. Ἔρυξ].
1. **est,** 3. pers. sing. pres. ind. of sum.
2. **est** (= ĕdit), 3. pers. sing. pres. ind. of ĕdo; v. 683.
et, conj.: **1.** *And*—et... et, *both*... *and.*—**2.** *Also* [akin to Gr. ἔτι, "moreover"; Sans. *ati,* "much, exceedingly"].
ĕtĭam, conj. [akin to et] **1.** *And also, and furthermore; likewise, also, besides.*—**2.** *Even.*
Eumēlus, i, m. *Eumēlus;* a Trojan who conveyed to Æneas the tidings of the burning of the fleet [Gr. Εὔμηλος, "Rich in sheep"].
ĕuntem, masc. acc. sing. of iens.
ĕuntes, masc. acc. plur. of iens; v. 777.
Euryălus, i, m. *Euryalus;* the friend of Nisus, and victor in the foot-race at the funeral games of Anchises [Gr. Εὐρύαλος, "He with a broad threshing-floor"].
Eurўtĭon, ōnis, m. *Eurytion;* a brother of that Pandarus who hurled his spear at the Trojan horse, and a competitor in the archery contest at the funeral games of Anchises [Gr. Εὐρυτίων].
ē-vādo, vāsi, vāsum, vādĕre, 3. v. a. [ĕ (= ex), "out from"; vādo, "to go"] ("To go out from"; hence) *To escape from, escape.*
ē-vincĭo, vinxi, vinctum, vincīre, 4. v. a. [ĕ (= ex), "completely"; vincĭo, "to bind"] **1.** *To bind completely, bind round.*—**2.** *To enclose, envelope, tie up;*—at v. 364 of enclosing the hands in a cæstus.—Pass.: **ē-vincĭor,** vinctus sum, vincīri.
ēvinctus, a, um, P. perf. pass. of ēvincĭo;—at vv. 269, 774 folld. by Acc. of "Respect" [§ 101];—at v. 364 evinctis palmis is Abl. Abs. [§ 125].
ē-volvo, volvi, vŏlūtum, volvĕre, 3. v. a. [ĕ (= ex), "out"; volvo, "to roll"] With Personal pron. in reflexive force: Of a stream: *To roll itself forth; to roll forth, glide out,* etc.
ex (ē), prep. gov. abl.: **1.** *Out of* a place or number.—**2.** *Away from.*—**3.** *Down from.*—**4.** Of time: *From.*—**5.** To denote the material *of, with,* or *out of* which a thing is made:—ex

VOCABULARY.

ære, *of bronze*, v. 266.—**6.** *According to, in conformity or accordance with, after* [Gr. *ἐξ*].

exactus, a, um, P. perf. pass. of exigo.

exănĭmātus, a, um, P. perf. pass. of exănĭmo.

ex-ănĭm-is, e, adj. [ex, denoting "negation"; ănĭm-a, "life"] ("Lifeless, dead"; hence) *Lifeless*, or *dead, from fear* = English expression *terrified out of one's life.*—In this force rare, and never in form exănĭmus.

ex-ănĭm-o, āvi, ātum, āre, 1. v. a. [id.] ("To deprive of life"; hence) **1.** *To depr ve of spirit* or *courage, to terrify greatly.*—**2.** Pass.: *To be dead from fear,* etc.—Pass.: **ex-ănĭm-or**, ātus sum, āri.

ex-ardesco, arsi, arsum, ardescĕre, 3. v. n. [ex, "up"; ardesco, "to blaze"] ("To blaze up"; hence) Of grief: *To burst,* or *break, forth with violence.*

exarsi, perf. ind. of exardesco.

ex-cēdo, cessi, cessum, cēdĕre, 3. v. n. [ex, "out of, forth from"; cēdo, "to go"] ("To go out of, *or* forth from, a place; hence) Of a prize: *To withdraw,* or *retire from; i. e. to surrender all claim to.*

excel-sus, celsa, celsum, adj. [for excell-sus; fr. excell-o, "to raise up"] ("Raised up"; hence) *Elevated, lofty, high.*

excĭd-ĭum, ĭi, n. [for ex-scĭd-ĭum; fr. xxscɪᴅ (= ex; scɪᴅ, root of scindo), true root of exscindo, "to destroy"] *Destruction, overthrow.*

excĭĕram, pluperf. ind. of excĭo.

ex-cĭo, civi and cĭi, citum and cĭtum, cĭre, 4. v. a. [ex, "out"; cĭo, "to make to go"]

("To make to go out"; hence) **1.** *To call out* or *forth; to bring out*—**2.** *To rouse, excite.*—**3.** Of things as Object: *To raise up, produce.*

ex-cĭpĭo, cēpi, ceptum, cĭpĕre, 3. v. a. [for ex-căpĭo; fr. ex, "without force"; căpĭo, "to take"] ("To take"; hence) *To receive* a person in any way.

excussus, a, um, P. perf. pass. of excŭtĭo.

ex-cŭtĭo, cussi, cussum, cŭtĕre, 3. v. a. [for ex-quătĭo; fr. ex, "out"; quătĭo, "to shake"] *To shake,* or *cast, out* or *forth.*—Pass.: **ex-cŭtĭor**, cussus sum, cŭti.

exēdisse, perf. inf. of exēdo.

ex-ēdo, ēdi, ēsum, ĕdĕre, 3. v. a. [ex, denoting "completeness"; ĕdo, "to eat"] ("To eat completely, eat up"; hence) *To destroy, consume,* etc.

ex-ĕo, ĭvi *or* ĭi, ĭtum, ire, v. n. and a. [ex, "out"; ĕo, "to go"] **1.** Neut. : *To go,* or *come, out* or *forth* from a place, *etc.*—**2.** Act.: *To avoid, escape, elude, ward off;* v. 438.

ex-ercĕo, ercŭi, ercĭtum, ercēre, 2. v. a. [for ex-arcĕo; fr. ex, denoting "opposition"; arcĕo, "to enclose"] ("To drive out of the enclosure"; hence, "to drive on *or* about; to employ, exercise"; hence) Mentally: *To disturb, disquiet, agitate, vex,* etc.—Pass.: **ex-ercĕor**, ercĭtus sum, ercēri.

1. **exercĭtus**, a, um, P. perf. pass. of exercĕo.

2. **exerc-ĭtus**, ĭtūs, m. [exerc-ĕo, "to exercise"] ("Exercise"; hence, "an army," as a trained and disciplined body of men; hence) *A multitude, band, company;* see Phorcus.

ex-ĭgo, ēgi, actum, ĭgĕre,

F

3 v. a. [for ex-ăgo; fr. ex, "out"; ăgo, "to drive"] ("To drive out"; hence) *To bring to an end; to end, finish.*—Pass.:

ex-ĭgor, actus sum, ĭgi.

exĭgŭus, ŭa, ŭum, adj. In number: *Small, few;* v. 754.

exĭt, 3. pers. sing. pres. ind. of exĕo.

exĭ-tĭum, tĭi, n. [EXI, root of exĕo, "to go away"] ("A going away," *i. e.* to nought; hence) *Destruction, ruin.*

exĭ-tus, tūs, m. [exĕo, "to go out"; through true root EXI] ("A going out"; hence) Of circumstances, etc.: *An issue, result;*—at v. 5?3 exitus ingens is var'ously considered as having reference to the burning of the Trojan ships as mentioned at v. 659 *sqq.;* and as prefiguring the wars which in after ages were waged in Sicily between the Romans and the Sicilians aided by the Carthaginians.

ex-ŏrĭor, orsus sum, ŏrĭri 3. and 4. v. dep. [ex, "up"; ŏrĭor, "to rise"] ("To rise, or spring, up"; hence) Of lamentation, etc.: *To arise.*

ex-ō-sus, sa, sum, adj. [for ex-od-sus; fr. ex, in "intensive" force; ŏd-i, "to hate"] In active force, and folld. by Acc.: *Hating utterly* or *exceedingly;*—at v. 687 supply tu es with exōsus.

ex-pĕd-ĭo, ivi *or* ĭi, ĭtum, ĭre, 4. v. a. [ex, "out of"; pes, pĕd-is, "the foot"] ("To get the foot out of" a snare, etc.; hence, "to extricate"; hence) *To prepare, get ready, get out.*

exsātūrā-bĭlis, bĭle, adj. [exsātŭr(a)-o, "to satisfy fully"] *That can be satisfied fully, that can be satiated.*

exsĕquĕrer, imperf. subj. of exsĕquor.

ex-sĕquor, sĕquūtus sum, sĕqui, 3. v. dep. [ex, "to the end"; sĕquor, "to follow"] ("To follow to the end"; hence) Of vows, etc., as Object: *To follow up, carry out, accomplish, perform,* etc.;—at v. 54 exsĕquĕrer is used in zeugma with vota and pompas; with the latter word it is equivalent to dūcĕrem, "would lead."

ex-sors, sortis, adj. [ex, "without"; sors, "lot"] ("Without lot"; *i. e.*) *Independent of allotment.*

ex-specto, spectāvi, spectātum, spectāre, 1. v. a. [ex, "very much"; specto, "to look out"] ("To look out very much" for a thing; hence) **1.** *To wait for, await, wait to see; to wait until,* etc.—**2.** *To expect, look for.*—Pass.: **ex-spector**, spectātus sum, spectāri.

exstructus, a, um, P. perf. pass. of exstrŭo.—As Subst.: **exstructum**, i, n. *A mound,* or *heap of earth,* as that which has been piled up.

ex-strŭo, struxi, structum, strŭĕre, 3. v. a. [ex, in "augmentative" force; strŭo, "to pile, *or* heap, up"] *To pile,* or *heap, up.*—Pass.: **ex-strŭor**, structus sum, strŭi.

ex-sul, sŭlis, comm. gen. [for ex-sol; fr. ex, "out of"; sŏl-um, "land, country"] ("One who goes out of, *or* quits his land *or* country"; hence *An exile.*

exsultans, ntis, P. pres. of exsulto.

exsul-to, tāvi, tātum, tāre, 1. v. n. intens. [for exsalto; fr. EXSAL (*i. e.* ex; SAL, root of sălĭo), true root of exsĭlĭo, "to leap up"] ("To leap, *or* spring, up"; hence) *To rejoice exceedingly, to exult.*

exta, ōrum, n. plur. *The*

VOCABULARY. 67

higher *internal organs* of the body; *e.g.* the liver, heart, lungs, *etc.; the inwards.*
ex-templo, adv. [contr. fr. old ex-tempŭlo; fr. ex, "immediately after"; tempŭlum, a dimin. form of tempus, "time"] ("Immediately after the time"; hence) *Forthwith, at once, immediately.*
ex-tendo, tendi, tensum and tentum, tendĕre, 3. v. a. [ex, "out"; tendo, "to stretch"] Of a person as Object: *To stretch out* or *extend; to throw at full length;* v. 374.
ex-terrĕo, terrŭi, territum, terrēre, 2. v. a. [ex, in "augmentative" force; terrĕo, "to frighten"] *To frighten greatly; to alarm* or *terrify in a high degree.*—Pass.: **ex-terrĕor,** territus sum, terrēri.
exterrĭtus, a, um, P. perf. pass. of exterrĕo.
extrēmus, a, um, sup. adj. ("Outermost"; hence) **1.** *Last,* in the widest sense of the word. —**2.** *The last part,* or *end, of* that to which this adj. is in attribution.
extŭlĕrim, extŭli, perf. subj. and ind. of effĕro.
exŭe, pres. imperat. of exŭo.
exŭo, ŭi, ŭtum, ŭĕre, 3. v. a. *To put off* from one's self; *to lay aside.*
ex-ūro, ussi, ustum, ŭrĕre, 3. v. a. [ex, in "intensive" force; ŭro, "to burn"] *To burn up, destroy by fire.*
exussi, perf. ind. of exūro.

făces, acc. plur. of fax; v. 637.
făc-ĭes, ĭēi, f. [prob. fr. făcĭo] **1.** *Make, form, figure,* etc. —**2.** *Face.* — **3.** *Appearance, aspect.*
făcĭo, fēci, factum, făcĕre, 3. v. a. ("To cause to be";

hence) *To make,* in the widest sense of the term :—facere vela, *to make sail,* v. 281 :—for facere pedem see pes.—Pass. : **fīo,** factus sum, fĭĕri [akin to Sans. root भू, "to be"—in causative force].
factus, a, um, P. perf. pass. of făcĭo;—at v. 587 factă pace is Abl. Abs. [§ 125].
fall-ax, ācis, adj. [fall-o, "to deceive"] *Prone to deceive, deceitful.*
fallo, fĕfelli, falsum, fallĕre, 3. v. a. ("To cause to fall"; hence) **1.** *To deceive, confuse,* etc.—**2.** Pass. in reflexive force: *To deceive one's self, to be mistaken.*—Pass.: **fallor,** falsus sum, falli [akin to Gr. σφάλλω].
fāma, æ, f. ("That which is spoken or said"; hence) **1.** *Report, the common talk, rumour,* etc. — **2.** *Reputation, renown, fame* [Gr. φήμη].
fămŭlus, ŭli, m. *A servant, attendant.*
far, farris, n. ("Spelt," a species of grain; hence) *Meal, grits,* etc. :—far pium, at v. 745, has reference to the meal sprinkled on a victim's head previous to sacrifice.
fas, n. indecl. ("Divine law"; hence) *A right,* or *lawful, thing.*
făt-ālis, āle, adj. [făt-um, "fate"] ("Pertaining to *fatum*"; hence) *Given,* or *assigned, by fate; fated.*
fătīgo, āvi, ātum, āre, 1. v. a. ("To weary"; hence) *To harass, worry, worry out.*
fā-tum, ti, n. [FA, root of (for) fāri, "to speak"] ("That which is spoken"; hence) **1.** *Destiny, fate;*—sometimes in plur.—**2.** Plur.: Personified: *The Fates.*
fātus, a, um, P. perf. of for.
făvens, ntis (Gen. Plur.

F 2

făventûm for făventĭum, v. 148), P. pres. of făvĕo.

făvĕo, făvi, fautum, făvēre, 2. v. n.: **1.** *To be favourable, to favour.*—Phrase: Favete ore (*or* linguis), *Be favourable with your mouth* (*or tongues*); i. e. *use words of good omen; or be still or silent.* The foregoing formula was used before the commencement of any sacred ceremony by the officiating priest. At v. 71 Virgil puts it into the mouth of Æneas when about to begin the funeral-games in honour of his father, Anchises.—**2.** *To applaud.*

făvilla, æ, f. *Hot ashes, cinders, embers.*

făv-or, ōris, m. [făv-ĕo, in force of "to applaud"] *Applause, acclamation.*

fax, făcis, f. ("The shining thing"; hence) *A torch* [akin to Sans. root BHÂ, "to shine"].

fēci, perf. ind. of făcio.

fē-mĭna, mĭnæ, f. [fē-o, "to produce"] ("She that produces *or* brings forth"; hence) *A female, a woman.*

fĕre, adv. *Nearly, almost, for the most part.*

fĕrendo, Gerund in do fr. fĕro.

fĕrĭo, no perf. nor sup., ĭre, 4. v. a. *To strike.*

fĕr-o, tŭl-i, lā-tum, fer-re, v. a.: **1.** *To bear, carry, bring, convey:*—manum ferre in proelia, (*to carry the hand into battles;* i. e.) *to engage in pugilistic encounters,* v. 403:—ferre infesta tela, (*to carry hostile weapons;* i. e.) *to advance to the attack,* v. 582.—**2.** *To carry off, take away, remove,* etc.—**3.** Of a gift, prize, etc.: *To bear off or away; to receive, obtain, win,* etc.—**4.** *To bear, endure,* etc.—**5.** With Personal pron. in reflexive force: ("To bear one's self along"; *i. e.*) **a.** *To betake one's self, go,* etc.—**b.** With accessory notion of haste: *To hasten, speed, hurry onwards.*—**6.** *To report, relate,* etc.; v. 588.—Pass.: **fĕr-or,** lā-tus sum, fer-ri [akin to Gr. φέρ-ω, and Sans. root BHṚI; tŭl-i is formed fr. root TUL or TOL, whence tol-lo; lā-tum = tlā-tum, akin to τλά-ω].

ferr-ātus, āta, ātum, adj. [ferr-um, "iron"] ("Provided with *ferrum*"; hence) *Tipped,* or *pointed, with iron.*

ferrum, i, n.: **1.** *Iron.*—**2.** As made of iron: ("The head, *or* barb," of an arrow; hence) *An arrow.*

fĕr-us, a, um, adj. Of animals: *Wild.*—As Subst.: **fĕr-us,** i, m. *A wild animal;*—at v. 818 applied to the sea-horses that drew Neptune's car [akin to Gr. θήρ. in Æolic dialect φήρ, "a wild animal *or* beast"].

fessus, a, um, adj. *Wearied, weary.*

fīdens, ntis: **1.** P. pres. of fido.—**2.** Pa.: *Bold, confident,* etc.

fīd-es, ĕi, f. [fid-o, "to trust"] ("Trust"; hence, as producing trust, "a promise"; hence, "a promise of protection," etc.; hence) *Guardian care, protection,* etc.

fīd-o, fīsus sum, fīdĕre, 3. v. n. semi-dep. *To trust, be confident, feel confidence* [akin to πιθ, root of πείθω, "to persuade"; Pass.: "to believe *or* trust"].

fīd-us, a, um, adj. [fid-o, "to trust"] ("That is trusted *or* to be trusted"; hence) *Trusty, faithful.*

fīg-o, fixi, fixum, fīgĕre, 3. v. a.: **1.** *To fix, fasten.*—**2.** *To transfix, pierce.*—Pass.: **fīg-or,** fixus sum, figi [akin to Gr. σφίγ-γω, "to draw tight"].

fimus, i (only in sing.), m.:

VOCABULARY. 69

1. *Dung, excrement.*—**2.** *Mire, dirt.*

fī-nis, nis, m. and f. [prob. for fid-nis; fr. findo, "to divide," through root FID] ("The dividing thing"; hence, "a boundary or border"; hence) **1.** Of a race-course : *The end, goal.*—**2.** Of vessels competing in a race: *The starting-place, mooring.*—**3.** *Territory, land, country.*—**4.** *An end, termination,* etc.

fīn-ītĭmus, ĭtĭma, ĭtĭmum, adj. [fīn-is, "a border"] ("Pertaining to a *finis*"; hence) *Bordering upon, adjoining, neighbouring.*—As Subst.: **fīnītīmī,** ōrum, m. plur. *The neighbouring peoples.*

flō, factus sum, fiĕri, v. pass. irreg.; see fäcio: **1.** *To be made.*—**2.** *To become.*

fīxī, perf. ind. of fīgo.

fīxus, a, um, P. perf. pass. of fīgo.

flăgel-lum, li, n. dim. [for flager-lum; fr. flagrum, flag-(e)r-i, "a whip"] *A small whip.*

flāmen, mĭnis, n. [fl(a)-o, "to blow"] ("The blowing thing"; hence) *Of the air: A breeze, gale.*

flam-ma, mæ, f. ("The blazing thing"; hence) *A flame;* —at v. 689 sing. for plur.

flāvus, va, vum, adj. ("Burning"; hence, of colour) *Yellow* [akin to Sans. root BRÂJ, "to burn"].

flecte, pres. imperat. of flecto.

flecto, flexi, flexum, flect-ĕre, 3. v. a. *To bend, turn, turn round* [prob. akin to Gr. πλέκ-ω, "to plait or twist"].

flens, ntis, P. pres. of flĕo.

flĕo, flēvi, flētum, flēre, 2. v. n. and a.: **1.** Neut.: *To weep, shed tears.*—**2.** Act. : *To weep,* or *shed tears, for; to mourn for, bemoan,* etc. [akin to Gr. φλύ-ω, "to gush or overflow"].

flē-tus, tūs, m. [flĕ-o, "to weep"] *A weeping.*

flex-ĭlis, ĭle, adj. [flex-us, "a bending"] ("Pertaining to *flexus*"; hence) *Pliant flexible.*

flexus, a, um, P. perf. pass. of flecto.

flōs, flōris, m. ("That which expands or blossoms"; hence) *A flower* [akin to Sans. root PHAL, "to expand"; or Sans. root PHULL, "to blossom"].

flŭc-tus, tūs, m. [for flugv-tus; fr. flŭo, "to flow," through root FLUGV] ("A flowing—that which flows"; hence) *A billow, wave.*

flŭĭtans, ntis, P. pres. of flŭito.

flŭ-ĭto, ĭtāvi, ĭtātum. ĭtāre, 1. v. n. intens. [flŭ-o, "to flow"] ("To flow"; hence, "to swim, float"; hence) *To move unsteadily, to be tossing about.*

flū-men, mĭnis, n. [id.] ("That which flows"; hence) **1.** *A flood,* or *stream, of water.*—**2.** *A river.*

flŭo, fluxi, fluxum, flŭĕre, 3. v. n.: **1.** *To flow.*—**2.** *To run down, drip* with any fluid [akin to Sans. root PLU, "to flow, to swim"].

fŏc-us, i, m. ("The burning thing"; hence) *An altar* [akin to Sans. root DHUÇ, "to burn"].

fœd-e, adv. [fœd-us, "foul"] ("After the manner of the *fœdus*"; hence, "foully"; hence) *Basely, horribly, disgracefully, shamefully,* etc.

fœd-us, ĕris, n. [for fid-us; fr. fid-o, "to trust"] ("A trusting"; hence) *A league, covenant, agreement, treaty, compact.*

fŏl-ĭum, ĭi, n. *A leaf* [akin to Gr. φύλ-λον].

(**for**), fătus sum, fāri, 1. v. dep. *To speak, say* [akin to Gr. φά-ω, φη-μί, "to say"].

fōrem (= essem), imperf. subj. of sum.

for-ma, mæ, f. [for fer-ma; fr. fĕr-o, "to bear"] ("The thing that is borne"; hence) **1.** *Form, figure, shape.*—**2.** *A fine form, beauty.*

for-s, tis (only in Nom. and Abl. Sing.), f. [probably for fer-tis; fr. fĕr-o, "to bring"] ("A bringing"; "that which is brought"; hence) **1.** *Chance, hazard, accident.*—**2.** Adverbial expressions: **a.** Fors, (=fors sit, *chance may be;* i. e.) *Perchance, perhaps, peradventure.*—**b.** Forte (Abl.), *By chance, accidentally, by accident.*

forte; see fors.

for-tis, te, adj. *Brave, bold, courageous;*—at v. 389 the Sup. is folld. by Gen. of "thing distributed" [§ 130]. ☞ (Comp.: fort-ĭor;) Sup.: fort-issĭmus [for fer-tis; fr. fĕr-o; and so, "bearing, that bears"; hence, "strong"; hence, as a result, "brave," *etc.;* or akin to Sans. root DHṚISH, "to be courageous"].

fortissĭmus, a, um, sup. adj.; see fortis.

fort-ūna, ūnæ, f. [fors, fort-is, "chance"] ("That which belongs to *fors*"; hence) **1.** *Chance, hap, luck, fortune.*— **2.** *Good luck, good fortune, prosperity.*—**3.** Personified as a goddess: *Fortune.*

fŏr-um, i, n. ("An open space *or* area"; hence, "a forum *or* market-place"; hence, from justice being administered there) *The administration of justice* [usually considered akin to for-is, "a door," and so, "that which is out of doors";—but rather akin to Gr. root πορ,

whence πόρ-ος, "a passage"; πορ-εύομαι, "to go *or* pass"; and so, "that which is gone *or* passed through"].

fractus, a, um, P. perf. pass. of frango.

frăg-or, ōris, m. [frango, "to break," through root FRĀG] ("A breaking"; hence, "a crash" as when something is broken to pieces; hence) *A noise, din, shout;*—at v. 228 in plur.

frango, frēgi, fractum, frangĕre, 3. v. a. *To break, dash to pieces.*—Pass.: **frangor**, fractus sum, frangi [akin to Gr. ῥήγνυμι, and Sans. root BHAÑJ, "to split, break"].

frāter, tris, m. *A brother* [akin to Sans. *bhrā́tṛi*].

frāter-nus, na, num. adj. [frāter, frāt(e)r-is, "a brother"] *Of, or belonging to, a brother; a brother's;* see Eryx.

fraus, fraudis, f. *Deceit, fraud.*

frĕm-ĭtus, ĭtūs, m. [frĕm-o, "to roar"] Of persons: *A roaring, roar, shouting:*—fremitus secundus, (*favourable shouting;* i. e.) *acclamation,* v. 338.

frĕm-o, ŭi, ĭtum, ĕre, 3. v. n.: **1.** Of persons: *To make a low murmuring sound,* etc.; v. 555.— **2.** Of the wind: *To roar, rage* [Gr. βρέμ-ω].

frēnātus, a, um, P. perf. pass. of frēno.

frēn-o, āvi, ātum, āre, 1. v. a. [frēn-um, "a bridle"] *To provide, or furnish, with a bridle.*—Pass.: **frēn-or**, ātus sum, āri.

frē-num, ni, n. (in plur. m. and n. **frē-ni** and **frē-na**) ("The holding *or* restraining thing"; hence) *A bridle,* including bit, head-piece, and reins [akin to Sans. root DHṚI, "to hold"].

frĕtum, i, n.: **1.** *A strait,*

VOCABULARY. 71

frith.—**2.** (Sing, and) Plur.: *The sea.*

frē-tus, ta, tum, adj. ("Supported" by something; hence) With Abl. [§ 119, (a)]: *Relying, or depending, upon; trusting to* [akin to Sans. root DRBI, "to support"].

frīgĕo, frixi (only in old Grammarians), no sup., frigēre, 2. v. a. *To be cold, to be cold and stiff* [akin to ῥιγ, root of ῥιγ-έω, "to shiver with cold," with the digamma prefixed].

frīg-ĭdus, ĭda, ĭdum, adj. [frig-ĕo, "to be cold"] *Cold, chill.*

frondens, ntis, P. pres. of frondĕo.

frond-ĕo, no perf. nor sup., ēre, 2. v. n. [frons, frond-is, "a leaf"] *To have leaves, to be leafy.*

frond-ōsus, ōsa, ōsum, adj. [frons, frond-is, "a leaf"] *Full of, or abounding in, leaves; leafy.*

1. **frons,** frondis, f.: **1. a.** *A leaf.*—**b.** *Leaves, foliage, leafy branches.*—**2.** *A garland of leaves, a leafy garland.*

2. **frons,** frontis, f.: **1.** *The forehead* or *brow.*—**2.** Of a vessel: *The bow, prow;* v. 158 [akin to Sans. *bhrū;* Gr. ὀ-φρύ-ς; cf. English "brow"].

frustrā, adv. [akin to fraudo] ("In a deceived manner"; hence) *In vain, to no purpose:*—non frustra, (*not in vain, i. e.*) *effectually, with effect.*

fūdi, perf. ind. of fundo.

fūdissem, pluperf. subj. of fundo.

fŭĕram, pluperf. ind. of sum.

fŭĕrim, perf. subj of sum.

fŭg-a, æ, f. [fŭg-io, "to flee"] *A fleeing, flight.*

fŭgāram, for fŭgāvĕram, pluperf. ind. of fŭgo.

fūgi, perf. ind. of fŭgio.

fŭgiens, ntis, P. pres. of fŭgio.

fŭgio, fūgi, fŭgĭtum, fŭgĕre, 3. v. n. and a.: **1.** Neut.: **a.** *To flee, fly, take to flight.*—**b.** Of things: (a) *To pass rapidly, flee, speed its,* etc., *way.*—(b) *To flee away; to disappear* or *vanish; to recede from the sight.*—**2.** Act.: *To flee from* [akin to Gr. φυγ, root of φεύγ-ω, "to flee"; also to Sans. root BHUJ, "to bend"; Pass. in reflexive force, "to incline one's self"].

fŭg-o, āvi, ātum, āre, 1. v. a. [fŭg-a, "flight"] *To put to flight, make to flee, rout, drive* or *chase away.*—Pass.: **fŭg-or,** ātus sum, āri.

fuissem, pluperf. subj. of sum.

fulg-ĕo, fulsi, no sup., fulgēre, 2 v. n. *To shine, glitter, glisten* [akin to Sans. root RRÂJ, "to shine"].

fulg-or, ōris, m. [fulg-ĕo, "to flash"] ("The flashing thing"; hence, "a flash of lightning"; hence) *Glitter, gleam, brightness, glistening.*

ful-men, minis, n. [for fulg-men; fr. fulg-ĕo, "to flash"] ("The flashing thing"; hence) *A lightning-flash; a thunder-bolt.*

fulvus, a, um, adj. *Reddish yellow, gold-coloured.*

fū-mus, mi, m. ("The rushing, or shaken, thing"; hence) *Smoke* [akin to Gr. θύ-ω, "to rush"; also to Sans. root DHU or DHÛ, "to shake"; whence *dhú-ma,* "smoke"].

1. **fundo,** fūdi, fūsum, fundĕre, 3. v. a.: **1.** Of liquids: *To pour out* or *forth, to pour.*—**2.** Of speech, complaints, *etc.:* To *pour forth, utter.*—**3.** Of several living beings as Subject: *To stretch themselves,* etc., *out;* to

VOCABULARY.

stretch out their. etc., *limbs*; v. 837.—Pass.: **fundor,** fūsus sum, fundi [root FUD, akin to χύ-σις, "a pouring out"; χέ-ω, "to pour out"].

2. fund-o, āvi, ātum, āre, 1. v. a. [fund-us, "the bottom"] ("To lay the bottom of" a thing; hence) *To found.*—Pass.: **fund-or,** ātus sum, āri.

fund-us, i, m. *The bottom* of anything; — at v. 178 of the bottom of the sea [akin to βυθ-ός, "depth"; πυθ-μήν, "the bottom" of the sea].

fūn-is, is, m. ("The binding thing"; hence) **1.** *A cord, string.*—**2.** *A rope, cable* [akin to Sans. root BANDH, "to bind"].

fūrāre, pres. imperat. of 2. furor; v. 845.

fūrens, ntis, P. pres. of furo ;—at v. 202 foll. by "Respective Gen. [Notes to Syntax, p. 139, *E,* (2)].

fūr-o, ŭi, no sup., ĕre, 3. v. n. *To rage, rave, be furious* [akin to Sans. root BHUR, "to be active"].

1. fŭror, ōris, m. [fŭr-o, "to rage"] *Rage, madness, fury.*

2. fūr-or, ātus sum, āri, 1. v. dep. [fur, fūr-is, "a thief"] ("To act the part of a *fur*" in something; hence, "to steal"; hence) With Acc. of nearer Object, and Dat. of disadvantage [§ 107]: *To steal away,* or *withdraw,* something *from* something; v. 845.

fur-tim, adv. [fŭr-or, "to steal"] *By stealth, secretly, privily.*

fūsus, a, um, P. perf. pass. of 1. fundo.

fūtūrus, a, um, P. fut. of sum.

Gætūl-us, a, um, adj. [Gætūl-i, "The Gaetuli"; a people of that part of ancient Africa which is now Morocco] *Gætulian; African.*

gǎl-ĕa, ĕæ, f. ("The covering thing"; hence) *A helmet, headpiece* [akin to καλ-ύπτω, "to cover"].

gaudĕo, gāvīsus sum, gaudēre, 2. v. n. semi-dep. *To rejoice, delight* [akin to Gr. γηθέω].

gaud-ĭum, ĭi, n. [gaud-ĕo, "to rejoice"] ("A rejoicing"; hence) *Joy, gladness.*

gāza, æ, f. *Riches, wealth* [Gr. γάζα, said to be originally a Persian word].

gĕl-ĭdus, ĭda, ĭdum, adj. [gĕl-o, "to freeze"] ("Freezing"; hence) *Icy cold, cold.*

gĕmens, ntis, P. pres. of gemo.

gĕ-mĭnus, mĭna, mĭnum, adj. [prob. for gen-minus; fr. gĕn-o, "to bring forth"] ("Brought forth, *or* born," with another; hence) **1.** *Twin-born, twin.*—**2.** *Two-fold, double.*—**3.** *Two, both.*

gem-ma, mæ, f. [for gen-ma; fr. gĕn-o, "to bear"] ("The bearing thing"; hence, "the bud, *or* eye," of a plant; hence) *A precious stone, jewel, gem.*

gĕm-o, ŭi, ĭtum, ĕre, 3. v. a. and n.: **1.** Act.: *To mourn, lament, bewail, bemoan.*—**2.** Neut.: *To groan, moan,* etc.

gĕn-a, æ, f. *A cheek* [akin to Gr. γέν-υ, "the chin"].

gĕnĕrātus, a, um, P. perf. pass. of gĕnĕro.

gĕnĕr-o, āvi, ātum, āre, 1. v. a. [gĕnus, gĕnĕr-is, "a race *or* family"] ("To make a *genus*"; hence, "to procreate"; hence) Pass.: With Abl. of "origin" [§ 123]: *To spring,* or *descend, from.*—Pass.: **gĕnĕr-or,** ātus sum, āri.

gĕn-ĭtor, ĭtōris, m. [gĕn-o,

VOCABULARY. 73

"to beget"] ("A begetter"; hence) **1.** *A father;*—at v. 94 = Anchises.—**2.** As a term applied to the Dii Majōres: *The Father;*—at v. 817 = Neptune.

gĕn-ĭus, ĭi, m. [gĕn-o (= gigno), "to produce"] ("The producing one"; hence, "the one pertaining to existence"; hence) *The tutelary deity,* or *genius,* of a person or place;—at v. 96 genium is the Acc. of the complement after esse [§ 94, 2]. Supply eum (= serpentem) as the Subject of esse.

gen-s, tis, f. [gĕn-o, "to beget"] ("A begetting;—that which is begotten"; hence) **1.** *A clan, family.*—**2.** *A nation.*

gĕnu, us, n. *A knee;*—at v. 432 *genua* is to be pronounced as a dissyllable—*genva* [akin to Gr. γόνυ].

gĕnŭi, perf. ind. of gigno.

gĕnus, ĕris, n.: **1.** *Birth, descent, origin.*—**2.** Of persons: *A race, family* [akin to Gr. γένος].

gĕro, gessi, gestum, gĕrĕre, 3. v. a. *To bear, carry.*

gigno (old form **gĕno**), gĕnŭi, gĕnĭtum, gignĕre, 3. v. a. *To bring forth, bear, give birth to* [reduplicated fr. root GEN (akin to Sans. root JAN, "to bring forth," also "to be born"; whence also γεν), *e. g.* gen-gen-o, gĕ-gĕn-o, gĭ-gĕn-o, gĭ-gn-o; cf. γί-γν-ομαι, formed on the same principle].

Glaucus, i, m. *Glaucus;* a sea-god [Γλαῦκος, "Blue One"].

glōr-ĭa, Iæ, f. [akin to clā-rus, "bright"] *Glory, fame, renown.*

Gnōs-ĭus, ĭa, ĭum, adj. [Gnōs-us, "Gnosus"; the ancient capital of Crete ("Of, or belonging to, *Gnosus*"; hence) *Cretan.*

grāmĭn-ĕus, ĕa, ĕum, adj. [grāmen, grāmĭn-ĭs, "grass"] ("Of, or pertaining to, *gramen*"; hence) *Grassy, grass-covered.*

grando, ĭnis, f. *Hail, a hail-storm.*

grātĭor, us; **grātissĭmus,** a, um; see grātus.

grāt-or, ātus sum, āri,]. v. dep. [grāt-us, "pleasing"] ("To desire that which is pleasing" to some one; hence) With Objective clause: *To congratulate* one, *etc., that;* see rĕdux.

grātus, a, um, adj. *Delightful, pleasing, agreeable;*—at v. 128 folld. by Dat. [§ 106, (3)]. ☞ Comp.: grāt-ĭor; Sup.: grāt-issĭmus.

grăv-ĭs, e, adj.: **1.** *Heavy, ponderous;*—at v. 178 gravis refers to the weight of Menœtes, from his clothes having become thoroughly wet.—**2.** With respect to character: *Of weight or authority; venerable, etc.*—**3.** Of anger: *Heavy, severe* [akin to Gr. βαρ-ύς; Sans. *gur-u* for original *gar-u*].

grăv-ĭter, adv. [grăv-is, "heavy"] ("After the manner of the *gravis*"; hence) *Heavily.*

grĕmĭum, ĭi, n. *The lap, bosom;*—at v. 31 used figuratively with respect to the country in which the bones of Anchises were laid.

gres-sus, sūs, m. [for grad-sus; fr. grăd-ĭor, "to step"] **1.** *A stepping, step, gait.*—**2.** Of a ship: *The course.*

gŭbernā-clum, cli, n. [gŭbern(a)-o, "to steer"] ("That which serves for steering"; hence) *A helm, rudder.*

gŭbernā-tor, tōris, m. [id.] *A steersman, pilot.*

gur-ges, gĭtis, m.: **1.** *A whirlpool; an eddying stream.*—**2.** *Waters, stream, sea* [akin to Sans. *gar-gar-a,* "a whirlpool," as "the devouring thing," fr. root ωπι, "to devour"].

Gȳas, æ (Acc. Gȳan, vv. 18ϟ, 223), m. *Gyas*, a Trojan; one of the followers of Æneas, who commanded the Chimæra in the contest of the ships at the funeral games of Anchises.

gȳrus, i, m. Of a serpent: *A coil* [Gr. γύρος].

hăbē-na, næ, f. [hăbĕ-o, "to hold"] ("The holding thing," *i. e.* "that by which a thing is held"; hence) Plur.: Of horses: *The reins*.

hăbĕo, ŭi, ĭtum, ēre, 2. v. a.: **1.** *To have* in the widest acceptation of the term;—at v. 156 supply eum (= locum priŏrem) after hăbet.—**2.** *To hold, possess*. —**3.** With Part. perf. pass. in concord with the nearer Object of the verb, and forming a second predicate (a circumlocution for the perf. act. of the verb supplying such part.): *To have, hold,* or *possess* a thing as completed or finished, or a person in a certain state or condition:—si paratum Agmen habet, *if he has* (got) *the troop prepared* or *in a state of readiness*, v. 549; where paratum habet = paravit, and has instruxit joined to it by que.—**4.** With Adj. or Subst. as second Acc.: *To hold, account, deem, regard,* etc., some object to be, or as being, that which is denoted by such second Acc.; v. 50 [prob. akin to ἅπτομαι, "to lay hold of"; also to ἁρ-ιο, "to seize *or* grasp"].

hăbēto, 3. pers. sing. fut. imperat. of hăbĕo.

hac-tĕnus (in tmesis — hac celebrata tenus—v. 603), adv. [hac, fem. abl. sing. of hic, "this"; tĕnus, "up to"] (*"*Up to this"; hence) In time: *Up to this time* or *point; thus far*.

hæerens, ntis, P. pres. of hæreo.

hæerĕo, hæsi, hæsum, hærēre, 2. v. n.: **1.** *To be,* or *remain, fixed* or *fast* anywhere; *to cling.* **2.** *To be at a loss; to be perplexed* or *embarrassed*.

hæsi, perf. ind. of hæreo.

hāmus, i, m. ("A hook"; hence) *A hook-shaped link* of coats of mail [Gr. χαμός].

hast-īle, ilis, n. [hast-a, "a spear"] ("A thing belonging to a *hasta*"; hence, "the shaft, *or* handle, of a spear"; hence) *A spear, javelin*.

haud, adv. *Not at all, by no means, not*.

haurĭo, hausi, haustum, haurīre, 4. v. a. ("To draw" water; hence, "to drain, empty," a goblet, *etc.;* hence) *To exhaust,* etc. [akin to Gr. ἀρύω].

hĕbĕo, no perf. nor sup., ēre, 2. v. n. *To be slow, sluggish,* or *inactive*.

Hector, ŏris, m. *Hector;* the eldest son of Priam. He was slain by Achilles, who fastened his dead body to a war-chariot, and dragged it three times round the walls of Troy.—Hence, **Hectŏr-ĕus**, ĕa, ĕum, adj. *Of,* or *belonging to, Hector* [Gr. Ἕκτωρ, "Fast-holder," *i. e.* one who is the prop or stay of a place].

Hectŏrĕus, a, um; see Hector.

Hĕlȳmus, i, m. *Helymus;* a Sicilian, one of the attendants of Acestes.

herb-a, æ, f. ("That which feeds *or* is eaten"; hence) *Herbage, grass,* and all that is comprehended under the English expression of "green food" [akin to Gr. φέρβ-ω, "to feed" (whence φορβ-ή, "a pasture," as that which supplies food to

cattle), and Sans. root BHARB,
"to eat"; cf. grä-men, "grass"
(as "that which is eaten" by
cattle); akin to Gr. γράω, "to
eat"; γραίνω, "to gnaw"; and
Sans. root GRAS, "to eat").

Hercŭles, is, m. *Hercules,
son of Jupiter and Alcmēna,
celebrated more especially on
account of the twelve labours
imposed on him by Eurystheus,
king of Mycēnæ, whom he was
ordered by the Fates to serve
for twelve years. After death
he was deified as the god of
strength and the guardian of
riches* [Hercles—the Etruscan
form of Gr. Ἡρακλῆς—with **s**
inserted].

hērŏs, ōis, m. *A hero* [Gr.
ἥρως; Sans. vīr-a].

hērōum, gen. plur. of
hēros.

heu, interj. *Alas!*

hīb-ernus, erna, ernum,
adj. [for hĭem-ernus; fr. hĭems,
hĭem-is, "winter"] ("Of, or
belonging to, *hiems*;" hence) **1.**
Wintry, winter-.—**2.** *Stormy,
tempestuous.*

1. **hĭc,** hæc, hoc (Gen. hūjus;
Dat. huic), pron. dem *This
person or thing*: **1.** As Subst.:
a. Sing.: (a) **hĭc,** m. *This
man, he*.—(b) **hoc,** n. *This
thing, this*.—**b.** Plur.: (a) **hī,**
m. *These persons or men*:—hi ...
hi, *these* ... *those*.—(b) **hæc,**
n. *These things, these words*.—**2.**
hoc, adverbial Abl.: *On this
account, for this reason* [akin to
Sans. pronominal root i, aspir-
ated; with c (= ce), demonstrative suffix].

2. **hĭc,** adv. [1. hic, "this"]
1. *In this place, here*.-**2.** In
time: *Here.* — **3.** *Hereupon,
here.*

hĭem-s, is, f. ("The snowy
time"; hence) **1.** *Winter*.—**2.**
A storm, tempest akin to Sans.

him-a, "snow"; Gr. χειμ-ών,
"winter"; χεῖμα, "winter
weather").

h-in-c, adv. [for hi-im-c;
fr. hi, base of hi-c; locative
suffix im; c = demonstrative
suffix ce] ("From this very";
hence) **1.** *Locally: From this
place; hence*.—**2.** *Of origin:
Hence, from this source,* etc.

Hippŏcŏon, ontis, m.
*Hippocoon, son of Hyrtăcus,
who contended in the foot-race
at the funeral games of Anchises* [Gr. Ἱπποκόων, "One ob-
serving horses"].

hŏnor (hŏnōs), ōris, m.:
1. *Honour*.—**2.** As being a
mark of honour, *etc.*: **a.** *A reward, gift, prize,* etc.—**b.** *A
religious, or funeral, rite, ceremony,* etc., in honour of the
dead.—**c.** *A sacrifice,* or *offering,* to the gods.

hōra, æ, f.: **1.** *An hour, the
hour*.—**2.** *Time* [Gr. ὥρα].

horr-ĭdus, ĭda, ĭdum, adj.
[horr-ĕo, "to stand on end"]
("Standing on end"; hence)
Rough, presenting a rough or
terrible appearance, horrid.

hor-tor, tātus sum, tāri, 1.
v. dep. ("To instigate"; *i. e.*)
1. *To exhort, urge*.—**2.** *To en-
courage* [akin to Gr. ὄρ-νυμι, "to
rouse"].

hos-pes, pĭtis, m. ("The
one seeking to eat"; and in
Pass. force, "the one sought for
the purpose of eating *or* being
entertained"; hence) **1.** *A
visitor, guest*.—**2.** *An entertainer,
a host* [perhaps for hos-pit-s;
akin to Sans. root GHAS, "to
eat"; pět-o, "to seek"].

hos-tis, tis, comm. gen.
("The eating one"; hence, "a
stranger *or* foreigner" entertained as a guest; hence) **1.**
An enemy, or *foe,* of one's country.—**2.** In collective force:

The enemy [prob. akin to Sans. root GHAS, "to eat"].

hūc, adv. [for hoc, adverbial neut. acc. sing. of hic, "this"] *To this place, in this direction, hither;*—huc illuc, *hither and thither, in this direction and in that direction,* v. 408.

hūm-ānus, āna, ānum, adj. [contr. fr. hŏmĭn-ānus; fr. hŏmo, hŏmĭn-is, "a man"] *Of,* or *belonging to, man* or *men; human.*

hŭm-ĕrus, ĕri, m. *A shoulder* [akin to Gr. ὦμ-ος].

hūmī; see humus.

hūm-ĭdus, ĭda, ĭdum, adj. [hūm-ĕo, "to be moist"] *Moist, wet, damp,* etc.;—at v. 5ʄ4 as an epithet of the sea; so, Pindar has ὑγρὰ ἅλς, and ὑγρὸν πέλἄγος.

hŭm-us, i, f.: **1.** *The ground.*—**2.** Adverbial Gen. of place [§ 131, B, b]: **hūmī,** *On the ground* [akin to χαμ-αί, "on the ground"].

Hyrtăcīdes, æ, m. *Son of Hyrtacus,* i. e. Hippŏcŏon [Gr. Ὑρτᾰκίδης].

Iăsīdes, æ (Voc. Iăsīdē, v. 843), m. *Descendant of Iusius,* king of Argos, i. e. Palinūrus [Gr. Ἰασίδης].

Ibam, imperf. ind. of ĕo.

īc-tus, tūs, m. [ic-o, "to strike"] ("A striking"; hence) *A stroke, blow,* etc.

Ida, æ, f. *Ida;* a mountain of Phrygia, near Troy [Gr. Ἴδη].

Īdălĭ-us, a, um, adj. [Idăli-a or Idăli-um, "Idalia or Idalium," a mountain-city of Cyprus, sacred to Venus] *Of,* or *belonging to, Idalia* or *Idalium; Idalian.*

id-circ-o, adv. [id, neut. acc. sing. of is, "that"; circa, "around"; hence, "about, in respect to"] ("About, *or* in *respect to,* that"; hence) *On that account, for that reason, therefore.*

ī-dem, ĕădem, ĭ-dem (Gen. ejusdem; Dat. ĕidem), pron. dem. [pronominal root I, with demonstrative suffix dem] ("That very"; hence) **1.** *The same.*—**2.** When something new is added respecting a person or thing already named : *Likewise, also, moreover,* etc.

Ĭōns, euntis, P. pres. of eo.

ī-gnārus, gnāra, gnārum, adj. [for in-gnārus; fr. in, "not"; gnārus, "knowing"] ("Not knowing"; hence) *With Dess.* [§ 132] *or Gerund in di* [§ 141, 2]: *Ignorant of, unacquainted with, unversed in, not knowing.*

ignis, is, m.: **1.** *Fire.*—**2.** *Flame* [akin to Sans. agni, "fire"].

ī-gnō-ro, rāvi, rātum, rāre, 1. v. a. [for ĭn-gnā-ro; fr. in, "negative"; particle; root GNO; whence no-sco, old form gno-sco, "to know"] *Not to know, to be unacquainted with.*

ī-gnōtus, gnōta, gnōtum, adj. [for in-gnōtus; fr. in, "not"; gnōtus (= nōtus), "known"] *Not known, unknown.*

īlex, ilicis, m. *The holm-oak,* or *scarlet-oak.*

Īlĭăcus, ăca, ăcum; **Ilĭas,** ădis; see Ilium.

Īlĭum, ii, n. *Ilium;* another name for Troy;—at v. 261 the o of Īlĭō is not elided before the following vowel, but is made short in imitation of the Greek.—Hence, **a. Īlĭ-ăcus,** ăca, ăcum, adj. *Of,* or *belonging to, Troy; Trojan.*—**b. Īlĭ-as,** ădis, f. *A Trojan woman* [Gr. Ἴλιον, "the city of Ilus"—a son of Tros].

il-le, la, lud (Gen. illīus; Dat. illi), pron. adj. [for is-le;

VOCABULARY. 77

fr. is] *That.*—As Subst. of all genders and both numbers: *That person* or *thing; he, she, it; they,* etc.; at v. 394 supply dixit with ille.

il-līdo, līsi, līsum, līděre, 3. v. a. [for in-lædo; fr. in, "upon"; lædo, "to strike or dash"] *To strike, dash,* or *drive, upon* or *against;*—at v. 480 folld. by in c. Acc.;—at v. 206 supply Dat. ěi (= murīci) after illīsa [§ 106, *a*].

illīsī, perf. ind. of illīdo.

illīsus, a, um, P. perf. pass. of illīdo.

illūc, adv. [adverbial neut. of illic, "that" person *or* thing] **1.** *To that place, thither,* etc.— **2.** *In that direction,* etc.

im-āgo, ǎgǐnis, f. ("That which imitates"; hence) *A form, appearance, shade* of a deceased person; v. 636 [root IM, akin to Gr. μιμ-έομαι, "to imitate"].

imber, bris, m.: **1.** *A heavy rain; a pelting shower* or *storm.* —**2.** *A rain-cloud, storm-cloud* [akin to Gr. ὄμβρος].

im-mā-nis, ne. adj. ("Not to be measured"; hence) *Vast, huge, immense;*—at v. 372 immānī corpŏre is Abl. of quality [§ 115] [for in-mā-nis; fr. in, "not"; Sans. root MĀ, "to measure"].

im-memor, Gen. mĕmŏris, adj. [for in-mĕmor; fr. in, "not"; mĕmor, "mindful"] With Gen. [§ 133] *Unmindful* or *forgetful of; not remembering.*

im-mensus, mensa, mensum, adj. [for in-mensus; fr. in, "not"; mensus, "measured"] ("Unmeasured"; hence) *Vast, huge, immense.*

im-miscĕo, miscŭi, mistum *or* mixtum, miscēre, 2. v. a. [for in-miscĕo; fr. in, "in"; miscĕo, "to mix"] ("To mix in"; hence) With Acc. and Dat. [§§ 95; 106, *a*] *To intermingle* something *with* something else: —immiscēre mānus mānĭbus, (*to intermingle hands with hands;* i. e.) *to join in an encounter, hand to hand.*

immissus, a, um, P. perf. pass. of immitto.

im-mitto, mīsi, missum, mittĕre, 3. v. a. [for in-mitto; fr. in, "into"; mitto, "to send"] ("To send into *or* upon"; hence, with the notion of the place "whither," etc., to be mentally supplied) **1.** Of a pair of horses in a racing chariot: *To let loose* from the starting-post;—Pass.: Of the horses: *To be let loose; to have the head given; to dash onwards.* —**2.** Of reins: *To let loose* upon the horses' necks, *i. e.* to give horses their heads;—at v. 663 used figuratively of flames.— Pass.: **im-mittor,** missus sum, mitti.

im-mōtus, mōta, mōtum, adj. [for in-mōtus; fr. in, "not"; mōtus, "moved"] **1.** *Unmoved, immoveable, motionless.* —**2.** Of the sea: *Calm, still, unruffled, tranquil.*

im-mundus, munda, mundum, adj. [for in-mundus; fr. in, "not"; mundus, "clean"] ("Not *mundus*"; hence) *Unclean, foul, impure, filthy.*

im-pĕd-ǐo, īvi *or* ǐi, ītum, īre, 1. v. a. [for in-pĕd-ǐo; fr. in, "in"; pes, pĕd-is, "the foot"] ("To get the foot in" something; hence, "to shackle," etc.; hence) *To surround, encircle.*

im-pello, pǔli, pulsum, pellĕre, 3. v. a. [for in-pello; fr. in, "against"; pello, "to drive"] ("To drive, thrust," etc., something "against" an object; hence) With accessory notion of motion: *To drive* or *urge onwards; to impel.*

impĕr-ĭum, ĭi, n. [impĕro, "to command"] *A command, order.*

im-pingo, pēgi, pactum, pingĕre, 3. v. a. [for in-pango; fr. in, "against"; pango, in force of "to drive"] With Dat. [§ 106, *a*] : *To drive,* or *dash,* an object *against* something.

im-pĭus, pĭa, pĭum, adj. [for in-pĭus; fr. in, "not"; pĭus, "holy"] *Unholy, wicked.*

im-plĕo, plēvi, plētum, plēre, 2. v. a. [for in-plĕo; fr. in, in "augmentative" force; plĕo, "to fill"] **1.** *To fill completely* or *entirely.*—**2.** With Abl. [§ 119, 3] : *To fill up, make quite full* etc.—Pass. : **impleor,** plētus sum, plēri.

im-pōno, pŏsŭi, pŏsĭtum, pōnĕre, 3. v. a. [for in-pōno; fr. in, "upon"; pōno, "to put"] ("To place, or put, upon "; hence) *To set, assign,* or *put,* etc., *to:*—imponere finem pugnæ, *to put an end to the fight,* v. 463.

impŏsŭi, perf. ind. of impōno.

impressus, a, um, P. perf. pass. of imprĭmo.

im-prĭmo, pressi, pressum, prĭmĕre, 3. v. a. [for in-prĕmo; fr. in, "upon "; prĕmo, " to press"] ("To press upon "; hence) *To form,* or *make,* by pressing upon; *to mark, stamp, emboss,* etc. — Pass. : **imprīmor,** pressus sum, prīmi.

im-prŏbus, prŏba, prŏbum, adj. [for in-prŏbus; fr. in, "not"; prŏbus, " good "] ("Not good, bad "; hence) *Shameless, impudent, vile, base.*

im-pūbes, is and ĕris, adj. [for in-pūbes; fr. in, " not"; pūbes, " grown up, of ripe age"] ("Not *pūbes*"; hence) *Youthful, young.*

impŭli, perf. ind. of impello.

īmus, a, um, sup adj. : **1** *Lowest, deepest.*—Adverbial expression : ab imo, *from the bottom,* i. e. at v. 810, *from the very foundations.*—**2.** *Where the thing is lowest;* i. e. *the lower part,* or *bottom, of* that which is represented by the subst. to which it is in attribution. (☞ Pos. : infĕrus ; Comp. : infĕrior.)

In, prep. gov. abl. and acc. **1.** With Abl. : **a.** *In, within.*—**b.** *On, upon;* see vv. 180, 554, 578.—**c.** Of clothing, *or* anything, in which a person or thing is : *In, with;* vv. 37, 489 —**2.** With Acc. : **a.** *Into.*—**b** *On, upon.*—**c.** *Towards.*—**d.** *Of* custom, manner, etc. : *According to, after.*—**e.** Of the persons or things amongst whom anything is divided : *For, among.*—**f.** To denote purpose, *etc.* : *To* *for:*—in verbera, *for blows,* i. e. for the purpose of applying the lash more vigorously, v. 147.

Ĭnānis, e, adj. *Empty.*

incēdens, ntis, P. pres. of incēdo.

in-cēdo, cessi, cessum, cēdĕre, 3. v. n. [in, "in"; cēdo "to go"] (" To go in *or* along " hence) **1.** *To enter, advance in procession.*—**2.** *To walk, pace, pace about.*

incend-ĭum, ĭi, n. [incendo, "to burn"] *A burning, conflagration.*

in-cen-do, di, sum, dĕre 3. v. a. (" To put fire in *or* into" hence) **1.** *To set on fire, burn.*—**2.** Mentally : *To fire, rouse, excite, kindle, inflame.*—**3.** *To make bright* or *brilliant; to brighten, cause to glitter,* etc.— Pass. : **in-cen-dor,** sus sum di [for in-can-do; fr. in, "in or into"; root CAN; akin to κά·ω " to burn "].

incensus, a, um, P. perf

pass. of incendo;—at v. 665 supply esse with incensas.

incep-tum, ti, n. [for in-cap-tum; fr. incipio, "to begin," through true root INCAP] ("A beginning"; hence) **1.** *An undertaking, attempt.*—**2.** *A design, purpose.*

inceptus, a, um, P. perf. pass. of incipio.

in-certus, certa, certum, adj. [in, "not"; certus, "sure"] *Not sure, uncertain, doubtful.*

in-cipio, cepi, ceptum, cipere, 3. v. a. [for in-capio; fr. in, "in"; capio, "to take"] ("To take in" hand, etc.; hence) *To begin, commence, undertake, set about.*—Pass.: **in-cipior**, ceptus sum, cipi.

in-cludo, clusi, clusum, cludere, 3. v. a. [in, "in"; cludo (= claudo), "to shut"] *To shut in or up; to enclose.*—Pass.: **in-cludor**, clusus sum, cludi.

inclusus, a, um, P. perf. pass. of includo.

incumbens, ntis, P. pres. of incumbo.

in-cumbo, cubui, no sup., cumbere, 3. v. n. [in, "upon"; obsol. cumbo, "to lie down"] ("To lie down upon"; hence) With Dat. [§ 106, a]: *To lean upon:*—incumbere remis, *(to lean upon the oars;* i.e.) *to ply the oars vigorously or stoutly*, v. 15.

in-curvo, curvavi, curvatum, curvare, 1. v. a. [in, "without force"; curvo, "to bend"] *To bend.*

i-n-de, adv. [probably fr. pronominal root I. with n, epenthetic; de, suffix] ("From that" thing; hence) *In time: After that, after this, in the next place, then.*

in-deprensus, deprensa, deprensum, adj. [for in-deprend-sus; fr. in, "not"; de-

prend-o, "to discover, observe"] *Undiscovered, unobserved.*

in-dico, dixi, dictum, dicere, 3. v. a. [in, in "augmentative" force; dico, "to say"; hence, "to declare"] *To proclaim, announce, appoint.*

indignans, ntis, P. pres. of irdignor.

in-dignor, dignatus sum, dignari, 1. v. dep. [in, "not"; dignor, "to deem worthy"] ("To deem unworthy"; hence) **1.** *To be indignant or displeased; to be angry.*—**2.** Act.: *To disdain, despise, think lightly of.*

in-dom-itus, ita, itum, adj. [in, "not"; dom-o, "to tame"] ("Untamed"; hence) *That cannot be checked or restrained; ungovernable.*

in-duco, duxi, ductum, ducere, 3. v. a. [in; duco, "to lead"] **1.** [in, "into"] ("To lead into"; hence) Mentally: *To induce, persuade, move, etc.—* **2.** [in, "upon"] ("To lead upon"; hence) With Dat. [§ 106, a]: *To put something on the hands, etc.;* v. 379.

inductus, P. perf. pass. of induco.

in-duo, dui, dutum, duere, 3. v. a.: **1.** *To put into.*—**2.** Pass. in reflexive force: *To put one's self into,* i. e. *to put on, to clothe or arm one's self with.*—Pass.: **in-duor**, dutus sum, dui [akin to Gr. ἐν-δύω].

indutus, a, um, P. perf. pass. of induo.

in-eo, ivi or ii, itum, ire, v. a. [in, "into"; eo, "to go"] ("To go into"; hence) **1.** Of an employment, *etc.*: *To enter upon, undertake, discharge.*—**2.** *To enter into, take part in.*—**3.** *To enter upon, begin, commence.*

in-faustus, fausta, faustum, adj. [in, "not"; faustus,

"fortunate"] *Unfortunate, unlucky, ill-omened.*
infectus, a, um, P. perf. pass. of inficio.
in-fēlix, fēlicis, adj. [in, "not"; fēlix, "happy"] ("Not felix"; hence) *Unhappy, unfortunate, miserable.*—As Subst. m.: *An unhappy,* or *unfortunate, one* or *man*; v. 465.
in-fen-sus, sa, sum, adj. ("Striking or wounding"; hence) *Hostile, inimical* [for in-fend-sus; fr. in, in "augmentative" force; obsol. fend-o = Gr. θείν-ω; see infestus at end].
infer-nus, na, num, adj. [infer, "below"] ("That is, or lies, below"; hence) *Of,* or *belonging to, the lower world.*
in-fĕro, tŭli, (il)-lātum, ferre, v. a. [in, "in or into"; fero, "to bring"] ("To bring into" a place; hence) **1.** With Personal pron. in reflexive force: ("To bring one's self into"; *i. e.*) With accessory notion of haste: *To betake one's self,* etc., *in haste.*—**2.** *To give, pay, render, offer.*
inferrem, imperf. subj. of infero.
in-fes-tus, ta, tum, adj. ("Striking against"; hence) **1.** *Hostile:*—infesta tela, *hostile weapons,* i. e. couched lances, *or* lances in rest.—**2.** *Dangerous* [prob. for in-fe(n)d-tus; fr. in, "against"; obsolete fe(n)d-o, akin to Gr. θείν-ω, θείν-ω, "to strike"].
in-fĭcĭo, fēci, fectum, fĭcĕre, 3. v. a. [for in-făcio; fr. in, "in"; făcio, "to make"] ("To make" to be or go "in"; hence, "to dip in"; hence, as a result) *To dye, stain, tinge.*—Pass.: **in-fĭcĭor,** fectus sum, fĭci.
in-fīgo, fixi, fixum, fīgĕre, 3. v. a. [in, "into"; fīgo, "to fix"] *To fix,* or *drive, into; to remain,* or *stick, fast in.*—Pass.: **in-fīgor,** fixus sum, fīgi.
in-findo, fĭdi, fissum, findĕre, 3. v. a. [in, "without force"; findo, "to cleave"] ("To cleave, divide"; hence) *To make* by cleaving:—infindere sulcos, *to make,* or *plough up, furrows* in the sea, v. 142.
infit, v. def. *He,* etc., *begins.*
infractus, a, um, P. perf. pass. of infringo.
in-fringo, frēgi, fractum, fringĕre, 3. v. a. [for in-frango; fr. in, "without force"; frango, "to break"] ("To break"; hence) *To break, weaken, soften, turn,* etc., in purpose, *etc.*—Pass.: **in-fringor,** fractus sum, fringi.
in-fundo, fūdi, fūsum, fundĕre, 3. v. a. [in, "upon"; fundo, "to pour"] **1.** *To pour upon* or *on.*—**2.** *To spread over.*—Pass.: **in-fundor,** fūsus sum, fundi.
infūsus, a, um, P. perf. pass. of infundo.
ingĕmĭnans, ntis, P. pres. of ingemino.
in-gĕmĭno, gĕmĭnāvi, gĕmĭnātum, gĕmĭnāre, 1. v. a. and n. [in, in "augmentative" force; gemino, "to double"] **1.** Act.: *To redouble, repeat, reiterate.*—**2.** Neut.: *To be redoubled, to increase,* etc.
in-gens, gentis, adj. [in, "not"; gens, "a race or kind"] ("That is not of its race or kind"; hence) **1.** *Vast, immense, huge.*—**2.** *Great, mighty.*
in-grĕdĭor, gressus sum, grĕdi, 3. v. dep. [for in-grădior; fr. in, "without force"; grădior, "to step"] ("To step"; hence) *To advance; to go, walk,* or *move along.*
in-horrĕo, horrŭi, no sup., horrēre, 2. v. n. [in, "without

VOCABULARY. 81

force"; horrĕo, in force of "to tremble, shudder"] *To tremble or have a tremulous motion; to shudder, quiver.* etc.

ĭn-hospĭtus, hospĭta, hospĭtum, adj. [ĭn, "in-"; hospĭtus, "hospitable"] *Inhospitable.*

ĭnībo, fut. ind. of Ĭnĕo.

ĭn-ĭmīcus, ĭmīca, ĭmīcum, adj. [for in-ămīcus; fr. ĭn, "not"; ămīcus, "friendly"] *Unfriendly, hostile.*

ĭn-īquus, īqua, īquum, adj. [for in-æquus; fr. ĭn, "not"; æquus, "favourable"] *Unfavourable, adverse.*

ĭn-necto, nexŭi, nexum, nectĕre, 3. v. a. [ĭn, "without force"; necto, "to tie"] *To bind, tie, fasten;* - at v. 511 with Dat. [§ 106, *a*], and also with Acc. of "Respect" [§ 100] after P. perf. pass.—Pass.: **ĭn-nector,** nexus sum, necti.

innexŭi, perf. ind. of innecto.

innexus, a, um, P. perf. pass. of innecto.

ĭn-noxĭus, noxĭa, noxĭum, adj. [ĭn, "not"; noxĭus, "hurtful"] *Not hurtful, harmless.*

Īno, ūs, f. *Ino;* daughter of Cadmus, wife of Athāmas king of Thebes, mother of Lĕarchus and Melicerta. Being pursued by her husband, who had become raving mad, she threw herself with Melicerta into the sea, whereupon they were both changed into sea-deities. Melicerta was called by the Greeks Palæmon, by the Romans Portūnus.—Hence, **Īn-ōus,** ōa, ōum, adj. *Of,* or *belonging to, Ino.*

ĭn-ŏpīn-us, a, um, adj. [ĭn, "not"; ŏpīn-or, "to think"] ("Not thought of"; hence) *Unexpected.*

inquĭo (inquam), v. defect. *To say.*

ĭn-sĕquor, sĕqnūtus sum, sĕqui, 3. v. dep. [ĭn, "after, close upon"; sĕquor, "to follow"] **1.** With Dat. [§ 106, *a*]: *To follow after* or *close upon.*—**2.** With Acc.: With accessory notion of hostility: *To follow after, pursue.*

ĭn-sign-is, e, adj. [ĭn, "upon"; sign-um, "a mark"] ("That has a mark upon it"; hence) *Remarkable, distinguished,* etc.

ĭn-sŏno, sŏnŭi, no sup., sŏnāre, 1. v. n. [ĭn, in "augmentative" force; sŏno, "to sound"] ("To sound loudly or aloud"; hence) *To make a loud sound:*—insŏnāte flagello, *to make a loud sound with a whip,* i. e. *to crack a whip loudly.*

ĭn-sons, sontis, adj. [ĭn, "not"; sons, "guilty"] *Guiltless, innocent.*

insŏnŭi, perf. ind. of insŏno.

instans, ntis, P. pres. of insto.

ĭn-staur-o, āvi, ātum, āre, 1. v. a. ("To make to stand"; hence, "to repair"; hence) *Of religious rites,* etc.: *To renew, repeat, celebrate afresh, perform over again* [ĭn, "without force"; STAUR, akin to STA, root of sto, "to stand"; like Gr. σταυρ-ός, "a pale"; and Sans. *sthâur-a,* "fixed, stable," from root STHÂ].

ĭn-stīg-o, āvi, ātum, āre, 1. v. a. ("To prick, *or* goad"; hence) *To stir up, stimulate, urge on,* etc. [ĭn, "without force"; root STIG, akin to Gr. στίζω (= στιγ-σω), "to prick"].

ĭn-sto, no perf. nor sup., stāre, 1. v. n. [ĭn, "upon"; sto, "to stand"] ("To stand upon"; hence) With Dat. [§ 106, *a*]: *To press hard,* or *close, upon; to be very near to.*

G

in-strŭo, struxi, structum, strŭĕre, 3. v. a. [ĭn, "without force"; strŭ ɔ, "to build"] ("To build, erect"; hence) *To prepare, get ready.*
instruxi, perf. ind. of instrŭo.
in-sŭo, sŭi, sūtum, sŭĕre, 3. v. a. [ĭn, "into"; sŭo, "to sew"] *To sew into* something. —Pass.: in-sŭor, sūtus sum, sŭi.
insurgens, ntis, P. pres. of insurgo.
in-surgo, surrexi, surrectum, surgĕre, 3. v. n. [ĭn, "up"; surgo, "to rise"] 1. *To rise up, raise one's self up.*— 2. With Dat. [§ 106, a]: Of rowers: *To rise up* from their seat *to* the oars in order to give greater impetus to them; *to put forth the whole strength to, to ply vigorously.*
insūtus, a, um, P. perf. pass. of insŭo.
in-tendo, tendi, tentum and tensum, tendĕre, 3. v. a. [ĭn, "without force"; tendo, "to stretch or bend"] 1. *To stretch forth or out; to extend.*— 2. With Abl.: *To furnish, or provide,* with something by stretching out.—Pass.: in-tendor, tentus sum, tendi.
intentus, a, um: 1. P. perf. pass. of intendo.—2. Pa.: *Eager, intent, attentively watching.*
inter, prep. gov. acc.: 1. *Between.*—2. *Among, amidst, in the midst of.*—3. Of time: *During, in the course of.*—4. Of persons: *Among, with:*—inter se, *among themselves,* i.e. *one with another, mutually.*
interdum, adv. *Sometimes.*
intĕr-ĕā, adv. [for interĕam; fr. inter, "between"; eam, acc. sing. fem. of is, "*that*"] ("Between that" and something else; hence) *Of time: Meanwhile, in the mean time.*
intĕr-ĭor, ĭus, comp. adj. [obsol. intĕr-us, "within"] *Inner, on the inner side, nearer in.*
in-terr-ĭtus, ĭta, ĭtum, adj. [ĭn, "not"; terr-ĕo, "to frighten"] 1. *Not frightened, undismayed, undaunted.*—2. Of vessels: *Unobstructed, not hindered,* by accidents, *etc.*
inter-vall-um, i, n. [inter, "between"; vall-um, "the mound" of a camp] ("That which is between the *vallum*" and the soldiers' tents; hence) In space: *Space between, distance, interval;*—v. 320, ending with intervallo, is a Spondaic line, *i. e.* has a Spondee as the fifth foot.
in-texo, texŭi, textum, texĕre, 3. v. a. [ĭn, "into"; texo, "to weave"] ("To weave into, to interweave"; hence) *To embroider.*—Pass.: in-texor, textus sum, texi.
intextus, a, um, P. perf. pass. of intexo.
in-trĕmo, trĕmŭi, no sup., trĕmĕre, 3. v. n. [ĭn, "without force"; trĕmo, "to tremble"] *To tremble, quiver, shake.*
intrĕmŭi, perf. ind. of intrĕmo.
in-tr-o, āvi, ātum, āre, 1. v. a. ("To step within"; hence) *To enter* [prob. ĭn, "into, within"; root TRA, akin to root TRI, "to step beyond"].
in-vălĭdus, vălĭda, vălĭdum, adj. [ĭn, "not"; vălĭdus, "strong"] ("Not *validus*" hence) *Weak, feeble.*
invectus, a, um, P. perf. pass. of invĕho.
in-vĕho, vexi, vectum, vĕhĕre, 3. v. a. [ĭn, "upon"; vĕho, "to carry"] ("To carry

VOCABULARY. 83

upon"; hence) Pass.: With Abl.: **1.** *To be carried on board of a ship, to sail in.*—**2.** *To be carried, or ride, on a horse.*—Pass.: **in-vĕhor**, vectus sum, vĕhi.

in-vĭdĕo, vidi, visum, vidēre, 2. v. a. and n. [in, in "augmentative" force; vĭdĕo, "to look at"] ("To look at or towards"; hence, with accessory notion of malevolence, "to look maliciously at"; hence) With Dat.: *To envy, feel envy at, be envious of.*

invĭdi, perf. ind. of invĭdĕo.

invīto, āvi, ātum, āre, 1. v. a. ("To invite" a person to come to, or into, a place; hence) **1.** *To invite a person to do, etc., something.*—**2.** *To tempt, allure, attract*, etc., the mind.

Īŏn-ĭus, ĭa, ĭum, adj. [Iones, "The Iones," the early Greek inhabitants of the country on the shores of the Corinthian Gulf"] ("Of, or belonging to, the *Iones*"; hence) *Ionius:*—an epithet of the sea bathing the W. shores of Greece, and separating them from those of Sicily and S. Italy.

i-pse, psa, psum (Gen. ipsius; Dat. ipsi), pron. dem. [for is-pse; fr. is; suffix pse] ("The very person or thing mentioned; hence) *Self, very;*—at v. 323 ipse belongs to quo, and imparts to it greater emphasis or distinction.—As Subst. Masc. of all persons and both numbers: *I*, etc., *myself*.

Īra, æ, f. *Anger, wrath, rage.*
Īre, pres. inf. of ĕo.
Īris, Idis (Acc. Irim, v. 606), f. *Iris;* a daughter of Thaumas and Electra, the swift-footed messenger of the celestial deities, esp. of Juno [Gr. Ἶρις, "Speaker"].

ir-rĕmĕā-bĭlis, bīle,

adj. [for in-rĕmĕā-bĭlis; fr. in, "not"; rĕmĕ(a)-o, to return"] *From which one cannot return.*

ir-rīdĕo, rīsi, rīsum, ridēre, 2. v. a. [for in-rīdĕo; fr. in, "at"; rīdĕo, "to laugh"] *To laugh at, ridicule,* etc.—Pass.:

ir-rīdĕor, risus sum, rīdēri.

irrīsus, a, um, P. perf. pass. of irrīdĕo.

ir-rĭtus, rĭta, rĭtum, adj. [for in-rātus; fr. in, "not"; rātus, "ratified"] ("Not ratified"; hence, "of no effect"; hence) *Of persons: That does not effect, or attain, one's object; in vain, to no purpose.*

īs, ĕa, id, pron. dem. [pronominal root I] *This, that, person or thing just mentioned.*—As Subst.: **a.** Sing.: (a) Masc. *He.*—(b) Neut.: *It.*—**b.** Plur.: (a) Masc.: *Those just mentioned; they.*—(b) Neut.: *Those things* [akin to Sans. pronominal root I].

Ismăr-ĭus, ĭa, ĭum, adj. [Ismăr-us or Ismăr-a, "Ismarus or Ismara," a mountain of Thrace] ("Of, or belonging to, Ismarus; Ismarian"; hence) *Thracian.*

is-te, ta, tud (Gen. istius; Dat. isti), pron. dem. [is, "this, that"; demonstr. suffix te] *This, or that, person or thing.*

ĭt, 3. pers. sing. pres. ind. of ĕo.

ĭta, adv. *Thus, in this way or manner;*—at v. 382 = *as follows, in the following way,* etc. [akin to Sans. *iti*, "thus"].

Ĭtăl-ĭa, æ, f. *Italy;* a country of S. Europe.—Hence, **Ĭtăl-us**, a, um, adj. *Of, or belonging to, Italy; Italian.*—As Subst.: **Ĭtăli**, ōrum, m. plur. *The people of Italy, the Italians* [acc. to some fr. ἰταλός, "a bull," in reference to its breed of cattle, which was considered ex-

G 2

cellent; acc. to others fr. a man named Italus].

Ĭtălus, a, um; see Ĭtălĭa.

Ĭ-ter, ĭtĭnĕris, n. [ĕo, "to go," through root ɪ] ("The act of going"; hence) **1.** *A way, path, road,* etc.—**2.** *A course, voyage by sea.*—**3.** *Of birds: Course, flight, way through the air.*

Ĭtĕr-um, adv. ("Beyond this, further"; hence) *Anew, afresh, a second time, again* [akin to Sans. *itara,* "other"].

Ĭūlus, i, m. *Iulus;* another name for Ascănĭus, the son of Æneas. The Julian family at Rome claimed descent from him [Gr. 'Ιουλος, "Down"].

jă-cĕo, cŭi, cĭtum, cēre, 2. v. n. ("To be made to go"; hence, effect for cause) **1.** *To lie anywhere.*—**2.** *To lie prostrate or at one's length* [akin to Sans. root yâ, "to go"].

jăcĭo, jēci, jactum, jăcĕre, 3. v. a. [akin to jăcĕo] ("To cause to go"; hence) **1.** *To cast, throw.*—**2.** *Of walls: To build, erect,* etc.—Pass.: **jăcĭor**, jactus sum, jăci.

jactans, ntis, P. pres. of jacto.

jac-to, tāvi, tātum, tāre, 1. v. a. intens. [jăc-ĭo, "to throw"] *To keep throwing, to toss about,* etc.—Pass.: **jac-tor**, tātus sum, tāri.

jăcŭi, perf. ind. of jăcĕo.

jăcŭl-um, i, n. [jăcŭl-us, "cast"] ("The cast thing"; hence) *A javelin, dart, missile.*

jam, adv. [prob. = eam, acc. sing. fem. of is, "this, that"] **1.** *At this time, at present, now.*—**2.** *Already.*—**3.** With nec: *And no more, and no longer,* etc.

jam-dūdum, adv. [jam, "at that time"; dūdum, "some time since"] ("At that time some time since"; hence) **1.** *A long time since, ago,* or *previously.*—**2.** With pres. to indicate that the existing state, *etc.,* of the verb began long since: (*Is* and *has been*) *for this long time past.*

Jōvis, gen. of Jŭpĭter.

jŭbē, pres. imperat. of jŭbĕo.

jŭbĕo, jussi, jussum, jŭbēre, 2. v. a. *To order, command, bid.*—Pass.: **jŭbĕor**, jussus sum, jŭbēri.

jŭg-um, i, n. [jungo, "to join," through root ᴊᴜɢ.] ("The joining thing"; hence, "a yoke" for draught animals; hence) *A pair,* or *team, of horses,* etc., yoked together.

junctus, a, um, P. perf. pass. of jungo.

jungo, junxi, junctum, jungĕre, 3. v. a.: **1.** *To join, unite.*—**2.** *To bind, tie,* or *fasten together.* —**3. a.** *Of draught-animals: To yoke,* or *harness, together.*— **b.** *Of ships' prows:* ("To yoke together"; *i. e.*) *To make even* or *level* with each other:— junctis frontibus, *with prows abreast,* v. 157.—Pass.: **jungor**, junctus sum, jungi [akin to Gr. ζυγ, root of ζευγνυμι; and to Sans. root ʏᴜᴊ].

Jū-no, nōnis, f. *Juno;* the daughter of Saturn and wife of Jupiter. In the Trojan war she was a strong supporter of the Greeks [akin to Jŭpĭter].

Jū-pĭter, Gen. Jŏvis, m. ("Heaven's father") *Jupiter;* a son of Saturn, and mythic king of the heathen celestial deities [akin to Sans. *dyu*, "heaven"; Lat. păter, "father"].

jūra, plur. of jus.

jū-s, ris, n. ("That which binds" morally; hence) Plur.: *Laws, ordinances* [akin to Sans. root ʏᴜ, "to bind"].

jussi, perf. ind. of jŭbĕo see also jussus.

jus-sum, sī, n. [for jubsum; fr. jŭb-ĕo, "to order"] ("A thing ordered"; hence) *An order, command.*

jussus, a, um, P. perf. pass. of jŭbĕo;—at v. 834 supply sunt with jussi.

jŭvenc-us, i, m. [jŭvencus, "young"] Of cattle: *A young bullock, a steer.*

jŭven-īlis, īle, adj. [jŭvĕnis, "a youth"] *Of,* or *belonging to, a youth; youthful.*

1. **jŭvĕn-is,** is, adj. comm. gen. *Young, youthful.* — As Subst.: *A young person; young man* between seventeen and forty-five or forty-six years of age [akin to Sans. *yuvan,* "young"].

2. **jŭvĕnis,** is; see 1. jŭvĕnis.

jŭven-ta, tæ, f. [jŭvĕn-is, "young"] ("The state of the *juvenis*"; hence) *Youth.*

jŭven-tus, tūtis, f. [id.] ("The state of the *juvenis*"; hence) *Youth,* i. e. at vv. 134, 555, *young men, young persons.*

lābens, ntis, P. pres. of 2. lābor.

lăb-o, āvi, ātum, āre, 1. v. n. [akin to 2. lābor] *To totter, to be unsteady,* etc.

1. **lăb-or (lābos),** ōris, m. ("The act of acquiring *or* taking"; hence) **1.** *Labour, toil.*— **2.** *Hardship, fatigue,* etc. [akin to Sans. root LABH, "to acquire"; Gr. λαβ, root of λαμ(β)άνω, "to take"].

2. **lābor,** lapsus sum, lābi, 3. v. dep.: **1.** *To glide,* or *glide onwards.* — **2.** *To slip,* or *fall, down* on the ground, *etc.*;—at v. 329 applied to Nisus slipping and falling in the foot-race;—at v. 181 applied to Ænestes slipping from the deck and falling overboard [akin to Sans. root LAMB, "to fall"].

lăbyrinthus, i, m. ("A labyrinth"; i. e. a large building containing numerous chambers or compartments, each of which opened by several doors into different passages winding in all directions. It was constructed with the design of causing a person who had once entered it to wander backwards and forwards out of one compartment into another, and to become so involved in the intricate mazes of the place, as to have no probable chance of escape.—At v. 588 Virgil refers to) *The labyrinth* built by Dædalus for Minos, king of Crete, and in which the Minotaur, a mythic monster, half-man and half-bull, was confined [Gr. λαβύρινθος].

lac, lactis, n. *Milk;* as that which is drawn from the udder, *etc.,* by rubbing or stroking :— lacte novo, v. 77, Abl. of quality [§ 125, *a*] [akin to Sans. root MRIJ, "to stroke"; cf. Gr. γάλα, γά-λακτ-ος].

lăc-er, ĕra, ĕrum, adj. ("Bitten"; hence) *Torn, mangled, maimed, mutilated* [akin to Gr. δάκ-νω; Sans. root DAÇ, "to bite"].

lăcertus, i, m.: **1.** *The upper arm.*—**2.** *The arm* generally.

lăc-esso, essīvi *or* essĭi, essītum, essĕre, 3. v. a. ("To bite eagerly, to mangle"; hence, "to assault, assail"; hence) Of a fight as Object: *To provoke, urge on, engage in* [akin to Gr. δάκ-νω; Sans. root DAÇ; see lăcer].

lacrĭma, æ (old form dacrĭma), f. ("The biting thing"; hence) *A tear* [akin to Gr. δάκρ-

v. "a tear," and Sans. root DAÇ; see lăcer].
lacrĭmans, ntis, P. pres. of lacrĭmo.
lacrĭm-o, āvi, ātum, āre, 1. v. n. [lacrĭm-a, "a tear"] *To shed tears, weep*.
lætus, a, um, adj. *Joyful, joyous, rejoicing* [akin to Sans. root LAS, "to shine, delight"].
læva, æ; **læva**, ōrum; see lævus.
læv-us, a, um, adj. *Left*, i. e. *on the left side*.—As Subst.: a. **læva**, æ, f. *The left hand* or *side*.—b. **læva**, ōrum, n. plur. *The places on the left, the left-hand places* or *side;* v. 825.
lapsus, a, um, P. perf. of 2. lăbor.
Lar (old form **Las**), Lăris, m. ("The shining one") *A Lar;* i. e. a tutelary deity of a house or city [akin to Sans. root LAS, "to shine"].
lāt-e, adv. [lăt-us, "wide"] ("After the manner of the *lātus*"; hence) *Widely, far and wide, extensively*.
lătebr-ōsus, ōsa, ōsum, adj. [lătebr-a, "a hiding-place"] *Of* a rock: *Full of hiding-places; affording many a hiding-place*.
lăt-ĕo, ŭi, ĭtum, ēre, 2. v. n.: 1. *To be,* or *lie, hid; to be concealed*.—2. *To escape notice* or *observation; to be unknown* [akin to λαθ, root of λανθάνω].
Lătīni, ōrum; **Lătīnus**, a, um; see Lătĭum.
Lătĭum, ĭi, n. *Latium* (now Campagna di Roma, and a part of the *Terra di Lavoro*); a country of Italy, in which Rome was situate. — Hence, **Lătīnus** (contr. fr. Lătĭ-inus), ĭna, ĭnum, adj. *Of,* or *belonging to, Latium; Latin*. — As Subst.: **Lătīni**, ōrum, m. plur. *The Latins*.

lătrā-tus, tūs, m. [lătr(ā)-o, "to bark"] *A barking, bark*, of dogs.
1. **lātus**, a, um, adj. *Broad, wide* [akin to Gr. πλατύς; Sans. prĭthu].
2. **lătus**, ĕris, n. ("The extended thing"; hence) *A side* [prob. akin to 1. lātus].
Laurens, ntis, adj. [for Laurent-s; fr. Laurent-um, "Laurentum" (now "Torre di Paterno"); a maritime town of Latium between Ostia and Lavinium] *Of,* or *belonging to. Laurentum; Laurentian*.
laurus, i and ūs, f.: 1. *A laurel-tree, laurel*.—2. *A laurel-branch*.—3. *A laurel-wreath, a laurel-crown*.
laus, laudis, f.: 1. *Praise, commendation*. — 2. *A praiseworthy, glorious,* or *noble deed* [prob. akin to Gr. κλύ-ω; and to Sans. root ÇRU, "to hear"]; and so, "that which one hears" of one's self, in a good sense].
laxārant, for laxāvĕrant, 3. pers. plur. pluperf. ind. of laxo.
lax-o, āvi, ātum, āre, 1. v. a. [lax-us, "loose"] ("To loosen"; hence) 1. Of sleep as Subject: *To relax; to render weak, feeble,* or *powerless.* — 2. Of persons yielding to sleep as Subject: *To relax, unbend*.
lēbes, ētis (Acc. Plur. lĕbētas, v. 266), m. *A caldron,* or *pot,* for cooking [Gr. λέβης].
lectus, a, um: 1. P. perf. pass. of lĕgo.—2. Pa.: *Chosen, picked, select*.
lĕgo, lēgi, lectum, lĕgĕre, 3. v. a: 1. *To collect* or *gather.* —2. *To choose, select*.—Pass.: lĕgor, lectus sum, lĕgi [Gr. λέγ-ω].
len-tus, ta, tum, adj. ("Embracing"; hence) 1. *Tenacious, fast-holding.*—2. *Slow*

VOCABULARY. 87

[akin to Sans. root LIŃG, "to embrace"].

lĕo, ōnis, m. *A lion* [Gr. λέων].

Lēthæus, a, um; see Lēthē.

(**Lēthē**, es, f. *Lēthē*, a river of the lower world, the waters of which caused forgetfulness. — Hence) **Lēth-æus**, æa, æum, adj. "*Of, or belonging to, Lēthē*"; hence) *Producing forgetfulness or sleepiness; Lēthean* [Λήθη, "Forgetfulness, Oblivion"].

lē-tum (**-thum**), ti, n. ("That which melts or dissolves"; hence) *Dissolution, death* [akin to Gr. ὄ-λε-θρος, "destruction"; Sans. root LĪ, "to melt"].

lĕvātus, a, um, P. perf. pass. of levo.

1. **lĕv-is**, e, adj.: **1.** *Light, swift, fleet.*—**2.** Of sleep: *Light, mild, gentle* [akin to Gr. ἐ·λαχ-ύς; also to Sans. *laghu*].

2. **lēv-is**, e, adj.: **1.** *Smooth.*—**2.** *Polished.*—**3.** *Slippery* [Gr. λεῖ-ος].

lēv-o, āvi, ātum, āre, 1. v. a. [lēv-is, "smooth"] ("To make smooth"; hence) *To make bright, to polish*.—Pass.: **lēvor**, ātus sum, āri.

lībans, ntis, P. pres of lībo.

lībo, āvi, ātum, āre, 1. v. a. ("To take"; hence, with accessory notion of the purpose for which a thing is taken) **1.** Of wine, etc., for religious purposes: *To take and pour out in honour of a deity; to make a libation of.*—**2.** *To take a portion of, to taste*.

lībr-o, āvi, ātum, āre, 1. v. a. [lībr-a, "a balance"] ("To balance or poise"; hence, as that which is balanced, etc., is easily set in motion) *To dash, launch, hurl, etc.*

Lĭbў-cus, ca, cum, adj. [Libў-a, "Libya"; a country of Africa] *Of, or belonging to, Libya; Libyan; African.*

Lĭbystes, tdis, f. adj. *Of, or belonging to, Libya, a country of Africa; Libyan, African* [Gr. Λιβυστίς].

lĭcĕo, ŭi, ĭtum, ēre, 2. v. n. *To be allowed or permitted; to be allowable*.—Rarely found in any other form than 3rd pers. sing., and in impersonal construction; —at v. 82 the Subject of licŭit is the clause fines ... Tybrim [§ 157]; so, at v. 350 the Subject of licĕat is the clause me casūs misereri insontis amici; cf., also, vv. 796, 797.

lī-men, minis, n. [for ligmen; fr. līg-o, "to tie or bind"] ("That which ties or binds"; hence, "the connecting timber" of a door-way, whether above or below; hence) **1.** *A sill or threshold.*—**2.** *The barrier, or starting-place*, in a racecourse.

līn-ĕus, ĕa, ĕum, adj. [līnum, "flax"] ("*Of, or belonging to, linum*"; hence) *Made of flax or hemp; hempen*.

linquo, liqui, lictum, linquĕre, 3. v. a.: **1.** *To leave, quit.*—**2.** *To leave behind.*—**3.** *To abandon, forsake, desert* [akin to Sans. root RICH, and Gr. λείπω].

linquens, ntis, P. pres of linquo.

liquĕo, liqui or licŭi, no sup., liquēre, 2. v. n. *To be liquid or fluid;*—so, only in P. pres.

liqui, perf. ind. of linquo.

liqu-ĭdus, ĭda, ĭdum, adj. [liqu-ĕo, "to be fluid"] **1.** *Fluid, flowing, liquid.*—**2.** *Clear, bright, transparent, limpid.*

lī-tus, tŏris, n. [prob. LI, root of lī-no, "to overspread"]

("That which is overspread," esp. by the sea; hence) *The shore, sea-shore, beach, strand.*

lŏc-o, āvi, ātum, āre, 1. v. a. [loc-us, "a place"] *To place, set.*—Pass.: **lŏc-or**, ātus sum, āri.

lŏc-us, i, m. (plur. **lŏci**, m., and **lŏca**, n.) **1.** *A place, spot*, etc.—**2.** *A place, position* [prob. akin to Gr. root λεχ, "to put"].

long-aev-us, a, um, adj. [long-us, "long"; aev-um, "age"] ("Having long age"; hence) *Aged.*

long-e, adv. [long-us, "long"; hence, "far off"] ("After the manner of the *longus*"; hence) **1. a.** *Afar off, at a distance.*—**b.** *By far, by much, greatly, exceedingly.*—**c.** *Comp.*: *Farther, to a greater extent*, etc.—**2.** *To a distance, far away.* ¶ *Comp.*: longius; (Sup.: longissime).

longius; see *longe*.

long-us, a, um, adj. *Long, whether in extent or duration* [akin to Sans. dīrghá-s].

lŏqu-ēla, ēlae, f. [loqu-or, "to speak"] ("A speaking"; hence, "speech"; hence) *A word.*

lŏqu-or, quūtus sum, qui, 3. v. dep. *To speak, say* [akin to Sans. root λαχ, "to speak"].

lŏquūtus (trisyll.), a, um, P. perf. of *loquor*.

lōr-ica, icae, f. [lōr-um, "a thong"] ("A thing pertaining to—i.e. made of—thongs"; hence, "a corselet or breast-plate made of leathern thongs; a leathern cuirass"; hence) *A breastplate or cuirass in general*;—at v. 280, one made of steel links.

lō-rum, ri, n. ("That which is cut"; hence, "a thong"; hence) *Plur.: The reins* of horses [prob. akin to Sans. root lū, "to cut"].

lū-brĭcus, brica, bricum, adj. ("Belonging to that which is made loose"; hence) **1.** *Slippery.*—As *Subst.*: **lūbrĭcum**, i, n. *A slippery place*—at v. XIX in plur.—**2.** *Smooth, and so slippery, as easily eluding the grasp* [akin to Sans. root lu, "to loose"].

lūc-ĕo, luxi, no sup., lucēre, 2. v. n. ("To shine"; hence) *Of persons: To glitter, glisten*, etc.

lūc-ĭdus, ĭda, ĭdum, adj. [lūc-ĕo, "to shine"] *Of the sky: Shining, bright, brilliant, glittering.*

luctans, ntis, P. pres. of *luctor*.

luc-tor, tātus sum, tāri, 1. v. dep. ("To seize in the embrace"; hence, "to seize, grasp" in the arms; hence, "to wrestle"; hence) *To struggle, strive, labour, toil.*

lū-cus, ci, m. ("That which is cut; a cut place"; hence) **1.** *An open wood*; i. e. one in which the trees are not crowded together; *a wooded glade or grove, sacred to some deity.*—**2.** *A wood in general* (Gr. ἄλσος, "to cut").

lūd-o, lusi, lusum, lūdere, 3. v. n. [lud-us, "play"] *To play, sport.*

lū-dus, di, m.: **1.** *Play, sport.*—**2.** *Plur.: Public games.*

lū-men, mĭnis, n. [for luc-men; fr. lūc-ĕo, "to shine"] ("That which shines"; hence, "light"; hence) *An eye.*

lustrans, ntis, P. pres. of *lustro*.

lustr-o, āvi, ātum, āre, 1. v. a. [lustr-um, "an expiatory offering"] ("To make an expiatory offering for, to purify"; hence, from the priest going round those whom he purified, "to go around"; hence) *To pass in review*, or *to parade, before*.

lux, lūcis, f. [for luc-s; fr. lūc-ĕo, "to shine"] ("That which shines *or* is bright"; hence) **1.** *Light.*—**2.** *Life*.

mac-to, tāvi, tātum, tāre, 1. v. a. freq. ("To adore" a deity, *etc.*; hence) **1.** *To slaughter in sacrifice; to sacrifice, immolate.*—**2.** *To kill, slay* [prob. akin to Sans. root MAH, "to adore"].

măcŭla, æ, f. ("A spot, *or* stain," of filth, *etc.*; hence) *A spot, mark*, etc., of any kind [prob. akin to Sans. *mala*, "filth"].

măcŭl-ōsus, ōsa, ōsum, adj. [măcŭla, in force of "a spot, *or* mark"] *Full of spots, spotted, mottled*.

măd-ĕ-făcĭo, fēci, factum, făcĕre, 3. v. a. [măd-ĕo, "to be wet"; (e) connecting vowel; făcĭo, "to make"] *To make to be wet; to wet, soak, saturate*.

mădĕfēcĕram, plup. ind. of mădĕfăcĭo.

mădens, ntis, P. pres. of mădĕo.

măd-ĕo, ŭi, no sup., ēre, 2. v. n. *To be wet, moist, dripping*, etc. [akin to Gr. μαδ-άω; Sans. root MAD, "to be wet"].

mădē-sco, mădŭi, no sup., mădēscĕre, 3. v. n. inch. [măd-ĕo, "to be wet"] *To become wet or moist*.

măd-ĭdus, ĭda, ĭdum, adj. [măd-ĕo, "to be wet"] *Wet, dripping*.

Mæander (Mæandrŏs), dri, m. (The *Mæander* or *Mæandros*—now the *Meinder* or *Boyuk Meinder*—a river rising in Phrygia in Asia Minor, and remarkable for its many windings. Hence) *A border of a garment wrought with many windings* [Gr. Μαίανδρος].

măg-ĭs, comp. adv. [akin to mag-nus] *More, in a greater degree*.

măg-ister, istri, m. [root MAG; see magnus] ("He that is great *or* mighty"; hence, "a master"; hence) **1.** Of a vessel: *A pilot, steersman.*—**2.** *A guardian, master*, or *tutor; a* name given to those who had the charge of boys of high birth; v. 669;—at vv. 257, 546 the term *custos* is employed of the same class of persons.

magn-ănĭm-us, a, um, adj. [magn-us, "great"; ănĭm-us, "soul"] *Great-souled, magnanimous*.

mag-nus, na, num. adj.: **1.** *Great, large*, whether in extent, size, or degree.—**2.** *Great*, in rank, power, *etc., mighty, powerful.*—**3.** Of sound: *Great, powerful, loud.*—**4.** *Great, important, weighty*, *of weight.*—**5.** *Abundant, numerous.*—**6.** Of persons with respect to age: *Great, advanced*;—maxima nātu, (*most advanced with respect to birth*; i. o.) *the most advanced in years, the oldest*, v. 644, where natu is Abl. of "Respect" [§ 116]; see 3. nātus. ☞ Comp.: májor (i. e. mag-ĭor); Sup.: maximus (i. e. mag-simus) [root MAG, akin to Gr. μέγ-ας, Sans. *mah-a*, "great"; fr. root MAGH, "to be great; to be powerful"].

mā-la, læ, f. [for mand-la; fr. mand-o, "to eat"] ("The eating thing"; hence) *The cheek-bone, the jaw*.

Mălea, æ, f. *Malea* (now *Malia*); a promontory of the Pĕlŏponnēsus (now the Morĕa); —at v. 193 the e is short.

măl-ĭ-gn-us, a, um, adj. [contr. fr. măl-ĭ-gĕn-us; fr. măl-us, "bad"; (i) connecting vowel; GEN, root of gigno, " to produce"] (In pass. force: "Born bad"; hence) *Of an evil nature, ill-disposed, malignant.*

māl-us, i, f. (" An appletree"; hence) *A mast* of a ship. —Observe that at v. 511 mālo is Dat. dependent on innexa [§ 106, a]; and also that as the word is fem. alto is not in concord with it; see āb, no. 3 [Gr. μηλ-έα].

mān-ĕo, si, sum, ēre. 2. v. n.: **1.** *To stay, remain.*—**2.** Of life: *To remain, continue, last* [Gr. μέν-ω].

Mān-es, ium, m. plur. [obsol. mān-us, "good"] ("The good, *or* benevolent, ones") **1.** *The Manes;* the deified souls of the departed. They were of a benevolent nature; while the Larvæ and Lemures were malignant spirits.—**2.** *The ghost, spirit,* or *shade* of a (single) deceased person.

mā-nus, nūs, f. ("The measuring thing"; hence) **1.** *The hand.*—**2.** *A body, number, company, multitude* of persons [akin to Sans. root MĀ, "to measure"].

măre, is, n. *The sea;*—at v. 616 māris is Gen. of "thing measured" after tantum [§ 131] [akin to Sans. *vāri*, "water"].

Māro, ōnis, m. *Maro;* see Virgīlius.

mā-ter, tris, f. *A mother* [akin to Gr. μήτηρ; Sans. *mātṛi;* fr. Sans. root MĀ, in meaning of " to produce"; and so " the producer "].

māter-nus, na, num, adj. [māter, mātĕ)r-is, "a mother"] *Of,* or *belonging to, a mother; a mother's;*—at v. 72 materna = "of Venus," who was the mother of Æneas.

mātūrus, a, um, adj. (Of *fruits, etc.:* "Ripe"; hence) Of persons: With Respective Gen. [Notes to Syntax, p. 139, E, (z)] : *Ripe with respect to,* or *in :—* maturus ævi, *ripe in age,* i. e. *advanced in years, old, aged,* v. 73.

maxĭmus, a, um; see magnus.

mē, acc. and abl. sing. of ĕgo.

mēcum = cum me; see cum.

mĕd-ĭus, ĭa, ĭum, adj.: **1.** *That is in the middle* or *midst; middle,* etc. :—mĕdĭa vallis, *the valley in the midst* of the surrounding hills, *i. e.* the interjacent valley, v. 289.—As Subst.: **mĕdĭum**, ĭi, n. *The middle, the midst.*—**2.** *The middle of* that denoted by the subst. to which it is in attribution :— media inter cornua, (*between the middle of the horns;* i. e.) *in the middle between the horns,* v. 479 [akin to Sans. *madhyas;* Gr. μέσος].

Mĕlĭbœa, æ, f. *Melibœa;* a maritime town of Thessaly celebrated for the dye obtained from the purple-fish caught off its shores.—Hence, **Mĕlĭbœus**, a, um, adj. *Of,* or *belonging to, Melibœa; Melibœan* [Gr. Μελίβοια, " She who takes care of cattle "].

Mĕlĭbœus, a, um; see Mĕlĭbœa.

mĕlĭor, us; see bŏnus.

Mĕlĭte, ēs, f. *Melite;* a Nereid, one of Neptune's attendants; v. 825 [Gr. Μελίτη, " She with honey"].

membrum, i, n. *A limb, member.*

Memmĭ; see Memmĭus.

Memmĭus, ĭi (Gen, Memmi, v. 117), m. *A Roman house* or *family,* said by Virgil to be descended from Mnestheus; see Mnestheus.

měm-or, ōris, adj. [akin to měmĭni. "to remember"] *Remembering, bearing in mind, mindful.*

měmŏrans, ntis, P. pres. of měmŏro.

měmŏrātus, a, um, P. perf. pass. of měmŏro.

měmŏr-o, ăvi, ātum, āre, 1. v. a. [měmor, "mindful"] ("To make (another) mindful" of something; hence) **1.** *To relate, declare.*—**2. a.** With double Acc. [§ 99]: *To call an object something.*—**b.** Pass. folld. by Nom. [§ 87, *D, a*; Notes to Syntax, p. 134, III. *D*]: *To be called* something.

mēne = mē (acc. sing. of ěgo); ne, enclitic; vv. 843, 849; see 2. ne, no. 1.

Měnœtes, is, m *Menœtes;* a Trojan, the steersman of the ship commanded by Gyas at the funeral games in honour of Anchises [Gr. Μενοίτης].

men-s, tis, f. ("The thinking"; hence) **1.** *The mind,* as being the seat of thought.—**2.** *Mind, feeling,* etc.—**3.** *Intention, design, purpose* [Lat. root MEN; akin to Sans. *man-as,* "mind"; fr. root MAN, "to think"; cf. also Gr. μέν-ος].

men-sis, sis, m. [root MEN, whence men-sus, P. perf. of mētĭor, "to measure"] ("The measuring thing"; hence) *A month,* as a measure of time.

mēr-ěo, ŭi, ĭtum, ēre, 2. v. a., and **měr-ěor,** ĭtus sum, ēri, 2. v. dep. ("To obtain, *or* acquire, as a portion *or* allotment"; hence, "to get, obtain," *etc.*; hence) *To deserve, merit,* esp. *to deserve well,* etc. [akin to μερ or μορ, root of Gr. μείρομαι, "to obtain by lot"].

merg-us, i, m. [merg-o, "to plunge"] ("A plunger"; hence) *A diver* or *gull.*

měrĭtus, a, um, P. perf. pass. of měrěo.

měrŭi, perf. ind. of měrěo.

měrus, a, um, adj. Of wine: *Pure, unmixed* with water.

mēt-a, æ, f. [mět-ĭor, "to measure"] ("The measuring thing"; hence, "a pillar" for marking a measured space; hence) *The turning-point* or *goal* in a race-course, *etc.*;—at v. 171 for ships, and also plur. for sing.; cf. v. 130.

mětŭens, ntis: **1.** P. pres. of mětŭo.—**2.** Pa.: With Objective Gen. [§ 132]: *Fearful,* or *apprehensive, of; dreading.*

mětŭ-o, mětŭi, mětŭtum, mětŭěre, 3. v. a. [mětus, uncontr. gen. mětŭ-is, "fear"] *To fear, dread.*

mětus, ūs, m. *Fear, dread.*

mě-us, a, um, pron. poss. [mē, acc. sing. of ěgo, "I"] *Of,* or *belonging to, me; my, mine.*

mĭhi, dat. sing. of ěgo;—at v. 162 as *Dātĭvus Ethĭcus* [§ 107, *a*].

mill-e, num. adj. indecl. *A thousand.*—As Subst.: **millĭa,** ĭum, n. plur. *Thousands* [akin to Gr. χίλ-ιοι].

millĭa, ĭum; see mille.

Mĭn-erva, ervæ, f. ("The thinking one, the one having mind") *Minerva;* the goddess of wisdom, who was a strong partisan of the Greeks in the Trojan war. She presided over the arts generally, and amongst them over weaving and spinning; see v. 284 [akin to Sans. root MAN, "to think"; Gr. μέν-ος, "mind"; Lat. root MEN, as in mens, memini].

mĭnistr-o, ăvi, ātum, āre, 1. v. a. [minister, ministr-i, "a servant"] ("To act the part of a *minister* to" one; hence, "to wait upon"; hence) *To provide, furnish, supply.*

mĭnor, us; see parvus.
mīrātus, a, um, P. perf. of miror.
mī-ror, rātus sum, rāri, 1. v. dep. ("To smile upon" in token of approval, *etc.*; hence) **1.** *To admire.*—**2.** *To wonder*, or *marvel*, at [akin to Sans. root SMI, "to smile"].
miscĕo, miscŭi, mistum and mixtum, miscēre, 2. v. a.: **1.** *To mix, mingle:*—miscēre māria coelo, (*to mix the seas with the sky*; i. e.) *to raise a violent tempest*; v. 790.—**2.** Pass.: *To be intermingled* with others.—Pass.: **miscĕor**, mistus *or* mixtus sum, miscēri [akin to Gr. μίσγω, μίγνυμι, and to Sans. miçra, "mixed"].
miscŭi, perf. ind. of miscĕo.
mĭser, ĕra, ĕrum, adj.: **1.** *Wretched*, *miserable.*—**2.** Of things: *Sad, melancholy, wretched.*
mĭsĕrandus, a, nm: **1.** Gerundive of misĕror.—**2.** Adj.: Of persons: *To be pitied*.
mĭsĕrans, ntis, P. pres. of misĕror.
mĭsĕrātus, a, um, P. perf. of misĕror.
mĭsĕr-ĕo, ŭi, ĭtum, ēre, 2. v. n. [miser, "wretched"] ("To feel, *or* be, *miser*"; hence) **1.** Personal: *To feel pity or compassion.*—**2.** Impers.: **mĭsĕret**: With Acc. and Gen. [§ 134]: *It distresses* one, *etc., for*; one, etc., *feels pity or compassion for.*
mĭsĕr-ĕor, ĭtus sum, ēri, 2. v. dep. [id.] (id.) With Gen.: *To pity, compassionate, commiserate;* —at v. 350 casus is the Gen. dependent on misĕrēri [§ 135].
mĭsĕret; see misĕrĕo.
mĭsĕr-or, ātus sum, āri, 1. v. dep. [miser, "wretched"] ("To be wretched for," *or* on *account of*, "some person or thing"; hence) *To pity, compassionate, commiserate.*
mīsi, perf. ind. of mitto.
missus, a, um, P. perf. pass. of mitto.
mistus, a, um, P. perf. pass. of miscĕo.
mīt-ĭgo, ĭgāvi, ĭgātum, ĭgāre, 1. v. a. [mit-is, in force of "mild, gentle"] *To render mild* or *gentle; to pacify.*
mitto, misi, missum, mittĕre, 3. v. a.: **1.** *To allow to go.*—**2.** *To send.*—**3.** *To bring to a conclusion; to end.*—Pass.: **mittor**, missus sum, mitti.
Mnestheus (dissyll.), ĕi and ĕos (Dat. Mnesthei, dissyll., v. 184), m. *Mnestheus;* a Trojan, one of the followers of Æneas. At the funeral games in honour of Anchises he commanded the Pristis [Gr. Μνεσθεύς, shortened fr. Μενεσθεύς, "One who abides"].
1. **mŏdō**, adv.: **1.** *Only, merely.*—**2.** *Just now, a little while ago.*
2. **mŏdō**, abl. sing. of mŏdus.
mŏ-dus, di, m. ("A measure, or standard" by which anything is measured; hence) *A way, manner, method, mode* [akin to Sans. root MĀ, "to measure"; whence also μέτρον, "a measure"].
moen-ĭa, ĭum, n. plur. ("The things that ward off"; hence) Defensive *walls, fortifications* [akin to ἀ-μύν-ω, "to ward off"].
moes-tus, ta, tum, adj. [for moer-tus; fr. moer-ĕo, "to be sad"] **1.** *Sad, sorrowful, mournful.*—**2.** *Connected with mourning, indicating sorrow, sad, unhappy.*
mōles, is, f.: **1.** *An immense, or vast, mass; a huge bulk;*—at vv. 118, 223, ingenti mole is

VOCABULARY.   93

Abl. of quality [§ 115].—**2.** *A vir* military *engine* or *machine*; v. 439.

mōn-s, tis, m. [for min-s; fr. min-ĕo, "to project"] ("That which projects or juts forth"; hence) *A mountain, mount.*

mŏn-strum, stri, n. [mŏn-ĕo, "to warn"] ("That which warns"; hence, in a bad sense) **1.** *An evil omen, a prodigy.*—**2.** *A monstrous or fearful thing; a monster.*

mont-ānus, āna, ānum, adj. [mons, mont-is, "a mountain"] ("Of, or belonging to, a mons"; hence) *Situated, or being, in the mountains; mountain-.*

mŏn-ŭmentum, ŭmenti, n. [mŏn-ĕo, "to remind"] ("The thing serving to remind"; hence) *A token, record, or memorial of any kind.*

mŏra, æ, f. *Delay*;— at vv. 140, 388 used in the Subject of *est* to be supplied.

mŏrans, ntis, P. pres. of *mŏror.*

mŏrātus, a, um, P. perf. of *mŏror.*

mŏri-bundus, bunda, bundum, adj. [mŏr-or, "to die"] *Dying.*

mŏr-or, ātus sum, āri, 1. v. dep. [mŏr-a, "delay"] **1.** Neut.: *To delay, tarry, linger, etc.*—**2.** Act.: ("To delay" a person or thing; hence) *To care nothing about, to hold in light esteem, not to regard or value, to disregard, etc.*

mors, tis, f. [mŏr-ior, "to die"] ("A dying"; hence) *Death.*

mort-ālis, āle, adj. [mors, mortis, "death"] ("Of, or belonging to, mors"; hence) *Subject to death, mortal.*—As Subst.: **mortālis**, is, m. *A mortal being, a man.*

m-ōs, ōris, m. [for mŏd-os

fr. mŏd-o, "to go"] ("The going, the pursuing one's way"; hence) *Custom, wont, usage, etc.*—Plur.: *sine more*, (*without wont; i.e.*) *in an unwonted way; to an unusual measure.*

mō-tus, tūs, m. (for mov-tus; fr. mov-ĕo, "to move") *A moving, motion, movement.*

mŏvens, ntis, P. pres. of *mŏveo.*

mŏvĕo, mōvi, mōtum, mŏvēre, 2. v. a. ("To cause to go"; hence) **1.** *To move, set in motion.*—**2.** With Personal pron. in reflexive force: *To move one's self, etc.*; *to move along.*—**3.** *To oust, remove.*—**4.** Mentally: *To ponder, revolve, consider, turn over* [akin to Sans. root *si*, "to go"].

mox, adv.: **1.** *Soon, presently.*—**2.** *In the next place, afterwards.*

mulcens, ntis, P. pres. of *mulceō.*

mulc-ĕo, mulsi, mulsum or mulctum, mulcēre, 2. v. a. ("To stroke"; hence) *To soothe, etc.* [akin to Sans. root *mṛj*, "to rub or stroke"].

multi, ōrum; see *multus.*

mult-i-plex, plĭcis, adj. [for multi-plic-s; fr. mult-us, (plur.) "many" (i) connecting vowel; plic-o, "to fold"] **1.** *Having many folds.*—**2.** *Having many parts.*—**3.** *Manifold, many, numerous.*

mul-tus, ta, tum, adj.: **1.** Sing.: *Much*;—at v. 815 simply *copiōsus* with *multa.*—Neut. plur. as adv.: **multa**, *Much, greatly*; v. 869.—**2.** Plur.: *Many.*—As Subst.: **a.** *multi*, ōrum, m. plur. *Many persons, many.*—**b.** *multae*, ārum, f. plur. *Many women, many*; v. 641.—**c.** *multa*, ōrum, n. plur. *Many things.* Comp.: *plūs*; Sup.: *plūrĭmus* [perhaps akin to Gr. μαλα].

VOCABULARY.

mūnus, ĕris, n.: **1.** *An office, employment, duty.*—**2.** *A gift, present;*—at v. 337 mŭnĕre means "by the kindness or kind interposition" of his friend, who, as it were, gave him the victory.

mūrex, ĭcis, m. ("A murex," a species of fish furnished with sharp prickles; hence) *A pointed rock,* etc.

mur-mur, mŭris, n. *A low murmuring sound; a murmur.*

mūr-us, i, m. ("The encircling thing"; hence) *The wall of a city,* etc. [akin to Sans. root MUṚ, "to encircle"].

mūtātus, a, um, P. perf. pass. of mūto.

mū-to, tāvi, tātum, tāre, 1. v. a. freq. [for mov-to; fr. mŏv-ĕo, "to move"] ("To move much" from its place; hence) *To change, alter.*—Pass.: **mūtor,** tātus sum, tāri.

Mycēna, æ, f. (also, **Mycēnē,** ēs, f.; **Mycēnæ,** ārum, f. plur.) *Mycena* (*Mycenæ* and *Mycenæ*); a city of Argŏlis in the Peloponnēsus (now the Morĕa), of which Agămemnon was king.—N.B. When the name of a place is given with a case of urbs (also of oppĭdum, insŭla, or civĭtas), it is usually put in apposition; sometimes (as at v. 52), yet rarely, it is found as a dependent Genitive.

myrtus, i and ūs, f.: **1.** *A myrtle-tree, a myrtle.*—**2.** *A myrtle-branch.*—**3.** *A myrtle-wreath* or *-gurland* [Gr. μύρτος].

nam, conj. *For.*
nam-que, conj. [nam, "for"; suffix, que] *For.*
nando, Gerund in do fr. no.
nā-scor, tus sum, sci, 3. v. dep. [for gna-scor; fr. root GNA, another form of root GEN; see gigno] **1.** *To be born.*—**2.** With Abl. of Origin [§ 123]: *To be born of* or *sprung from.*

nātans, ntis, P. pres. of nāto.

nā-to, tāvi, tātum, tāre, 1. v. a. intens [ua(o), "to swim"] ("To swim, float"; hence) *Of* the eyes: *To swim,* i. e. *to be unsteady, to fail.*

1. **nātus,** a, um, P. perf. of nascor.

2. **nā-tus,** i, m. [nā-scor, "to be born"] ("He that is born"; hence) *A son;*—Plur.: *Children,* collectively, both male and female.

3. **nā-tus,** tūs (only in Abl. sing.), m. [id.] ("A being born"; hence) *Birth, age, years;* see magnus.

nauta, æ, m. *A sailor, seaman* [Gr. ναύτης].

Nautes, æ, m. *Nautes;* a Trojan soothsayer, who counselled Æneas to leave in Sicily such of his followers as were weary of their toils, together with the women and the old men [Ναύτης, "Sailor"].

nautĭcus, a, um, adj. *Of,* or *belonging to, a sailor* or *sailors* [Gr. ναυτικός].

nāv-ālis, āle, adj. [nāv-is, "a ship"] ("Of, or belonging to, a ship or ships"; hence) *Naval, sea-.*

nāvĭg-ĭum, ĭi, n. [nāvĭg-o, "to sail"] ("A sailing"; hence) *A vessel, ship, bark.*

nāvis, is, f. *A ship* [akin to Gr. ναῦς and Sans. nans].

1. **ne,** adv. and conj.: **1.** Adv.: *No, not.*—**2.** Conj.: *That not; lest* [prob. akin to Sans. na, "not"].

2. **ne,** enclitic and interrogative particle: **1.** In direct questions joined to the Indicative, it throws emphasis on the word to which it is attached, but is

without any English equivalent.
—**2.** In indirect questions with Subj.: *Whether:*—ne ... ne, *whether ... or whether.*

nec, necdum, necnon; see neque.

necto, nexŭi, nexum, nectĕre, 3. v. a. *To bind, fasten;*—at v. 309 nectentur (pass.) is folld. by Acc. of "Respect" [§ 100]. —Pass.: **nector,** nexus sum, necti [akin to Sans. root NAH, "to bind"].

nĕ-fa-ndus, nda, ndum, adj. [ne, "not"; f(a)-or, "to speak"] ("Not to be spoken or mentioned"; hence) *Impious, abominable, unhallowed, wicked.*

nĕ-fas, n. indecl. [ne, "not"; fas, "divine law"] ("That which is contrary to *fas*"; hence) *That which is unlawful or abominable; a dreadful, or horrible, thing.*

nē-mo, minis, comm. gen. [contr. fr. ne-homo; fr. ne, "not"; homo, "a person"] *No person, no one, nobody.*

nem-us, ŏris, n. ("The feeding thing"; hence) *A wood with much pasture land; a grove* [Gr. νέμ-ω, "to feed"].

Nept-ūnus, ūni, m. ("The B ther") *Neptune;* the mythic god of the sea and waters [Gr. νίπτ-ομαι, "to bathe"].

nĕ-que (contr. **nec),** conj. [ne, "not"; que, "and"] *And not, neither:* — neque (nec) ... neque (nec), *neither ... nor:*—nec-non, ("nor not"; *i.e.*) *and also, and besides, moreover, further:*—nec-dum, *and not yet, nor as yet.*

nĕ-quīquam, adv. [ne, "not"; quīquam, adverbial abl. of quisquam, "any"] ("Not in any" way; hence) *In vain, to no purpose.*

Nēr-ēis, ēĭdos, f. [Nēr-eus (dissyll.), "Nereus"; a sea-god, son of Oceanus and Tethys, and husband of Doris] *A daughter of Nereus, a Nereid or sea-nymph* [Gr. Νηρεύς, "Swimmer"].

nerv-us, i, m. ("A sinew, nerve"; hence) *Of a bow: A bow-string* [Gr. νεῦρ-ον].

Nēsaeē, ēs, f. *Nesaee;* a Nereid, one of Neptune's attendants [Gr. Νησαίη, "She of the island, Island-nymph"].

nexans, ntis, P. pres. of nexo.

nex-o, ŭi, no sup., āre, 1. v. a. [nex-us, "a tying or binding"] **1.** *To tie, bind, fasten together.*—**2.** With Personal pron. in reflexive force: *Of a snake: To tie, fasten, or twine itself;* v. 279, where se belongs to nexantem as well as to plicantem.

ni, conj. *If not, unless* [akin to 1. ne].

nīd-us, i, m. *A nest* [akin to Sans. *nīd-a,* "a nest"].

niger, gra, grum, adj. *Black, dark.* (Comp.: nigr-ior;) Sup.: niger-rimus.

nigrans, ntis: **1.** P. pres. of nigro.—**2.** Pa.: *Black, dark, dusky-coloured;*—at v. 97 folld. by Acc. of "Respect" [§ 100].

nigr-o, āvi, ātum, āre, 1. v. n. [nīger, nigr-i, "black"] *To be black.*

nĭ-hil (contr. **nīl),** n. indecl. [shortened by apocope fr. ni-hilum—for ne hilum (*i.e.* ne, "not"; hilum = filum, "a thread"); "not a thread"; hence] *Nothing.*—In adverbial force: *In no degree* or *respect; not at all.*

nil; see nihil.

nimb-us, i, m.: **1.** *A violent or pouring rain; a tempest.*—**2.** *A black rain-cloud, a thunder-cloud.*—**3.** *A cloud* of smoke, ashes, *etc.;* v. 666 [akin to νίφ-ω, "to snow," or νίπ-τω, "to wash"].

nĭmĭ-um, adv. [nĭmĭ-us, "beyond measure, too much"] *Too much, too.*

nĭ-sĭ, conj. [ni (= ne), "not"; si, "if"] *If not;* i. e. *unless, except.*

1. **nī-sus,** sūs, m. [for nit-sus; fr. nĭt-or, "to bear, or rest, upon"] ("A bearing, or resting, upon" something; hence, "a tread, step"; hence) *Posture, position.*

2. **Nīsus,** i, m. *Nisus;* the friend of Euryalus [Gr. Νίσος].

nĭte-sco, nĭtŭi, no sup., nĭtescĕre, 3. v. n. inch. [nĭtĕ-o, "to shine"] *To begin to shine* or *glisten; to shine, glisten.*

no, āvi, no sup., āre, 1. v. n. *To swim* [akin to Gr. νέω].

nōbīs, dat. and abl. plur. of ĕgo;—at v. 391 as Dātīvus Ethĭcus [§ 107, a].

nŏcendi, Gerund in di fr. nŏcĕo.

nŏc-ĕo, ŭi, ĭtum, ēre, 2. v. n. *To harm, hurt, injure,* etc. [akin to Sans. root NAÇ, "to perish"].

noct-urnus, urna, urnum, adj. [nox, noct-is, "night"] *Of,* or *belonging to, the night.*

nōd-us, i, m. ("The thing tied, or bound," together; hence) **1.** *A knot, fastening.*—**2.** Of a snake: *A knot, coil, fold* [prob. akin to Sans. root NH (old form NADH), "to tie or bind"].

nō-men, mĭnis, n. [no-sco, "to know"] ("That which serves for knowing" an object; hence) **1.** *A name.*—**2.** *Fame, reputation, renown.*

non, adv.: **1.** *Not.*—**2.** Imparting a contrary force to the word to which it is joined:—non immĕmor, *not unmindful,* i. e. *mindful,* v. 39; cf., also, v. 305 [akin to Sans. *no*].

non-dum, adv. [non, "not"; dum, "yet"] *Not yet, not as yet.*

nō-nus, na, num, adj. [for nov-nus; fr. nŏv-em, "nine"] ("Pertaining to *novem*"; hence) *Ninth.*

nos, nostrum or nostri, plur. of ĕgo;—at v. 21 nos (Nom.) is emphatic.

nos-ter, tra, trum, pron. poss. [nos, plur. of ĕgo, "I"] *Our.*

nō-ta, tæ, f. [no-sco, "to know"] ("That by which a person or thing is known"; hence) *A mark, spot,* etc.

nŏtāte, plur. pres. imperat. of nŏto.

nŏt-o, āvi, ātum, āre, 1. v. a. [nŏt-a, "a mark"] ("To mark, impress with a mark"; hence) Mentally: *To mark, remark, observe, note.*

1. **nō-tus,** ta, tum, adj. [no-sco, "to know"] *Known, well-known.*

2. **Nōtus,** i, m.: **1.** *Notus; the South Wind* personified.—**2.** *Wind* in general [Gr. Νότος].

nŏvem, num. adj. indecl. *Nine* [akin to Sans. *navan*].

nŏv-o, āvi, ātum, āre, 1. v. a. [nŏv-us, "new"] **1.** *To make new* or *anew; to renew.*—**2.** *To change, alter,* etc.

nŏvus, a, um, adj. *New, fresh* [akin to Gr. νέος, and Sans. *nava*].

nox, noctis, f.: **1.** *Night.*—**2.** Personified as a goddess: *Night.*—**3.** *Darkness, gloom, obscurity* [akin to Gr. νύξ, Sans. *nakta*].

nūb-es, is, f. *A cloud* [akin to Sans. *nabhas,* "sky, atmosphere"; Gr. νέφος].

nūbĭl-a, ōrum, n. plur. [nūbĭl-us, "cloudy"] ("The cloudy things"; hence) *The clouds.*

nūdātus, a, um, P. perf. pass. of nūdo.

nūd-o, āvi, ātum, āre, 1. v. a. [nūd-us, "naked"] **1.** *To make naked or bare, to strip of clothing.*—**2.** Milit. t. t.: *To leave uncovered or bare; to expose to the enemy.*—Pass.: **nūd-or**, ātus sum, āri.

nūd-us, a, um, adj. *Naked, bare;*—at v. 871 nudus means 'bare of earth,' *i. e.* "unburied."

nullāne = nulla, neut. nom. plur. of nullus; ne, enclitic; v. 633; see 2. ne.

n-ullus, ulla, ullum (Gen. nullīus; Dat. nulli), adj. [for ne-ullus; fr. ne, "not"; ullus, "any"] *Not any, none, no.*—As Subst. m. *No one, nobody.*

nū-men, mĭnis, n. [nū-o, "to nod"] ("A nodding" with the head; "a nod"; hence) **1.** *Of the gods: Divine will or power.*—**2.** *Godhead, divinity,* etc.—**3.** *A deity, whether a god or goddess.*

nŭm-ĕrus, ĕri, m. ("The distributed thing"; hence) **1.** *A number.*—**2.** *A collected body, or number, of persons, etc.* [Gr. νέμ-ω, "to distribute"].

nunc, adv. *Now, at this time:*—nunc... nunc, now... now, *at one time... at another time* [akin to Gr. νῦν (fr. Sans. *nu* or *nū*), with c (for ce), demonstrative suffix].

nuntĭ-us, ĭi, m. [perhaps contracted fr. nov-ven-tĭus; fr. nŏv-us, "new"; věn-ĭo, "to come"] ("A person, or thing, newly come"; hence) **1.** *A bearer of news or tidings; a messenger, courier,* etc.—**2.** *News, tidings, a message.*

nŭ-per, adv. [for nov-per; fr. nŏv-us, "new"] *Newly, lately, recently.*

n-usquam, adv. [n-e,

"not"; usquam, "anywhere"] **1.** *Not anywhere, nowhere, in no place.*—**2.** *In nothing, in no degree, in no respect.*

nūtrī-x, cis, f. [nūtrī-o, "to nourish"] ("She that nourishes"; hence) *A nurse.*

O, interj. *O! oh!*—at v. 19 there is an aposiopesis after O!

ŏb, prep. gov. acc. ("Towards, at"; hence) To indicate object or cause: *On account of, for* [akin to Gr. ἐπ-ί; Sans. *ap-i*].

ob-jĭcĭo, jēci, jectum, jĭcĕre, 3. v. a. [for ob-jăcĭo; fr. ŏb, "before"; jăcĭo, "to cast"] ("To cast before"; hence) With Dat. [§ 106, *a*]: *To present to.*—Pass.: **ob-jĭcĭor**, jectus sum, jĭci.

oblīquo-o, āvi, ātum, āre, 1. v. a. [oblīqu-us, "oblique"] ("To make *obliquus*"; hence) *To turn obliquely or sideways; to slant.*

ob-līqu-us, a, um, adj. [ŏb, "without force"; līqu-is, "oblique"] *Oblique, in a slanting direction.*

oblītus, a, um, P. perf. of obliviscor.

ob-lī-vīscor, tus sum, vīsci, 3. v. dep. ("To be melted" away from the mind; hence) With Gen. [§ 133, *a*]: *To forget* [prob. ŏb, without force; root LI or LIV, akin to Sans. root LI, "to melt"].

ob-nītor, nisus or nixus sum, nīti, 3.v. dep [ŏb, "against or upon"; nītor, "to lean"] **1.** *To lean, bear, or rest against or upon.*—**2.** With accessory notion of force or exertion: *To bear, push, struggle, or strive against;*—at v. 21 strengthened by contra.

obnixus, a, um, P. perf. of obnitor.

H

obrŭe, sing. pres. imperat. of obrŭo.

ob-rŭo, rŭi, rŭtum, rŭĕre, 3. v. a. [ŏb, "without force"; rŭo, "to throw down with violence"] ("To throw down with violence"; hence) *To overthrow, overwhelm.*

ob-scŭ-rus, ra, rum, adj. ("Covered over"; hence, "dark, dim"; hence) *Not known, unknown, obscure* [ŏb, "over"; scu, akin to Sans. root sku, "to cover"].

ob-stŭpesco, stŭpŭi, no sup., stŭpescĕre, 3. v. n. [ŏb, "without force"; stŭpesco, "to be amazed"] *To be amazed or astonished;*—at v. 90 with Abl. [§ 111].

obstŭpŭi, perf. ind. of obstŭpesco.

ob-torquĕo, torsi, tortum, torquĕre, 2. v. a. [ŏb, "without force"; torquĕo, "to twist"] *To twist.*—Pass.: **ob-torquĕor,** tortus sum, torquĕri.

obtortus, a, um, P. perf. pass. of obtorquĕo.

oc-cŭbo, no perf. nor sup., cŭbāre, 1. v. n. [for ob-cŭbo; fr. ŏb, "without force"; cŭbo, "to lie down"] ("To lie down" in a place; hence) *To rest,* or *repose,* in the grave.

oc-curro, curri (rarely cŭcurri), cursum, currĕre, 3. v. n. [for ob-curro; fr. ŏb, "up !or towards"; curro, "to run"] **1.** Of persons: *To run up, r un to meet* one.—**2.** Of land as Subject: *To fall in one's way.*

ŏc-ĭor, ĭus, comp. adj. *Swifter, quicker* [Gr. ὠκ-ύς].

ŏcĭus, comp. adv. [adverbial neut. of ŏcĭor, "quicker"] ("More quickly"; hence) *As a modified superlative: Very quickly* or *speedily; in much haste.*

ŏc-ŭlus, ŭli, m. ("The seeing thing"; hence) *An eye* [akin to Gr. ὄκ-ος, Sans. *aksh-a,* prob. fr. a lost verb AKSH (= IKSH), "to see"].

ŏd-Ĭum, ĭi, n. [ŏd-i, "to hate"] *Hatred, hate, ill-will.*

ŏlĕum, i, n. *Olive-oil, oil* [Gr. ἔλαιον].

ŏlim, adv. [for ollim; fr. olle, old form of ille, "that"] Of time: ("At that time"; hence) **1.** Of time past: *Formerly, once, in time past.*—**2.** Of indefinite time: *At times, sometimes, from time to time.*

ŏlīva, æ, f.: **1.** *An olive-tree.*—**2.** *An olive-branch.*—**3.** *An olive-wreath* [Gr. ἐλαία].

olle, old form of ille.

olli, old form of illi: **a.** Dat. sing., v. 10.—**b.** Masc. nom. plur., v. 197.

Olympus, i, m. *Olympus;* a lofty mountain on the borders of Macedonia and Thessaly, the fabled abode of the celestial deities [Gr. Ὀ-λυ(μ)π-ος, "the abrupt *or* steep" mountain; akin to Sans. root LUP, "to break"].

ō-men, mĭnis, n. [for or-men; fr. ŏr-o, "to speak"] ("The thing spoken"; hence) *A prognostic* or *omen* of any kind.

omn-ĭ-pŏtens, pŏtentis, adj. [omn-ĭs, "all"; (i) connecting vowel; pŏtens, "powerful"] *All-powerful, omnipotent.*

omnis, e,, adj.: **1.** *All, every.* —As Subst.: **omnĭa,** um, n. plur. *All things.*—**2.** *The whole; the whole of* that denoted by the subst. to which it is in attribution;—at v. 616 supply illis with omnĭbus.

ŏnĕr-o, āvi, ātum, āre, 1. v. a. [ŏnus, ŏnĕr-is, "a load *or* burden"] ("To load, lade, *or* burden"; hence) *To load or cover* with anything :—onerant aras, *they load the altars,* i. e with gifts or offerings, v. 101.

VOCABULARY. 99

ŏnĕr-ōsus, ōsa, ōsum, adj. [ŏnus, ŏnĕr-is, "a burden"] ("Full of *onus*"; hence) *Burdensome, heavy.*

ŏpĭbus, abl. plur. of ops; v. 41.

op-pōno, pŏsŭi, pŏsĭtum, pōnĕre, 3. v. a. [for ob-pōno; fr. ŏb, "against"; pōno, "to put"] ("To put, or place, against"; hence) **1.** *To station over against* or *opposite.*—**2.** With personal pron. in reflexive force and Dat. of person: *To put,* or *place, one's self,* etc., *in the way of* a person; v. 335.

oppŏsŭi, perf. ind. of oppōno.

op-pugno, pugnāvi, pugnātum, pugnāre. 1. v. a. [for ob-pugno; fr. ŏb, "against"; pugno, "to fight"] ("To fight against"; hence) *To besiege, lay siege to,* a city.

op-s, is (Nom. Sing. does not occur; Dat. is found perhaps only once), f. [prob. for ap-s; fr. root AP, whence ăpiscor, "to obtain"] ("The thing obtained"; hence) Mostly plur.: *Means,* or *resources,* of any kind; *wealth, riches,* etc.

optātus, a, um, P. perf. pass. of opto.

optĭmus, a, um, sup. adj. see bŏnus.

op-to, tāvi, tātum, tāre, 1. v. a.: **1.** *To wish for, desire,* something.—**2.** With Inf.: *To wish* or *desire to do, etc.*—**3.** *To choose, select.*—Pass.: **op-tor,** tātus sum, tāri [akin to Sans. root AP, in force of "to desire"].

ŏpus, ĕris, n.: **1.** *Work, labour,* etc.—**2.** *A work,* as the result of work [akin to Sans. *apas*].

1. **ōra,** plur. of ōs, ōris.
2. **ōra,** æ, f.: **1.** *The coast, sea-coast.*—**2.** *A region, country, clime.*

orbis, is, m.: **1.** *A circle, ring, orbit.*—**2.** In time: *A revolution.*—**3.** *The world the universe.*

ord-o, ĭnis, m. [ord-ĭor, "to weave"] ("A weaving"; hence) **1.** *Arrangement, order.*—**2. a.** *Order, succession, turn,* etc.—**b.** Adverbial Abl.: **ordĭne,** *In due order, regularly, properly.*—**3.** *A row* of benches or seats in a vessel; vv. 120, 271.

ŏrĭens, ntis, P. pres. of ŏrĭor.—As Subst. m. *The rising sun.*

ŏr-ĭor, tus sum, ĭri, 3. and 4. v. dep. *To rise* [root OR, akin to Gr. ὄρνυμαι].

ōr-o, āvi, ātum, āre, 1. v. a. [ōs, ōr-is, "the mouth"] ("To use the mouth"; hence, "to speak"; hence) **1.** *To beg,* or *pray, for* something; v. 617.—**2.** Used parenthetically: **ōro,** *I beg, pray, beseech, entreat;* v. 796.

1. **ōs,** ōris, n. ("That which eats"; hence) **1.** *The mouth.*—**2.** *The face, countenance;* -at v. 369 plur. for sing. [akin to Sans. root AÇ, "to eat"].

2. **os,** ossis, n. *A bone* [akin to Sans. *asthi;* Gr. ὀστέον].

os-tendo, tendi, tensum, tendĕre, 3. v. a. [for obs-tendo; fr. obs (= ŏb), "before *or* over against"; tendo, "to stretch out"] ("To stretch out, *or* spread, before" one; hence) *To expose to view; to show, exhibit, display.*

ostentans, ntis, P. pres. of ostento.

osten-to, tāvi, tātum, tāre, 1. v. a. intens. [for ostend-to; fr. ostend-o, "to show"] *To show, present to view, exhibit, display.*

ost-ĭum, ĭi, n. *The mouth* of anything; *an entrance* [akin to Sans. *osth-a,* "a lip"].

H 2

ostrum, i, n. ("The blood of the sea-snail"; hence) *Purple* [Gr. ὄστρεον].

ŏvans, ntis: **1.** P. pres. of ŏvo.—**2.** Pa.: *Exulting, rejoicing.*

ŏv-o, āvi, ātum, āre, 1. v. n. *To exult, rejoice* [prob. akin to Gr. εὔ-οι; Lat. ev-œ; and so "to shout out" *eva*].

păc-iscor, tus sum, isci, 3. v. dep. ("To bind"; hence, in moral sense, "to covenant, bargain"; hence) *To barter, hazard, stake* [akin to Sans. root PAÇ, "to bind"].

Pălæmon, ŏnis, m. *Palæmon*; see Ino [Gr. Παλαίμων].

pălans, ntis, P. pres. of pălor.

Pălĭnūrus, i, m. *Palinurus*; the pilot of Æneas. He fell into the sea and was drowned off the coast of Lucania, and gave the name to a promontory near the scene of his disaster— now prob. Punta della Spartimento [Παλίνουρος, "Fair wind astern"].

Pallăs, ădis, f. *Pallas*; the Greek name of the Roman Minerva [Gr. Παλλάς, "Brandisher or Maiden"].

palma, æ, f.: **1. a.** *The palm* of the hand.—**b.** *The hand.* —**2.** ("A palm-tree, palm"; hence) **a.** *A palm-branch.*—**b.** As a badge, or token, of victory: *The palm, prize.*—**c.** *Victory* [Gr. παλάμη].

palm-ŭla, ŭlæ, f., dim. in form only [palm-a, "the palm" of the hand; hence, from its flat shape, "the blade of an oar"] *A blade of an oar, an oar-blade.*

păl-or, ātus sum, āri, 1. v. dep. ("To wander"; hence) *To be dispersed or scattered about; to straggle.*

Pandărus, i, m. *Pandarus,* son of Lycāon; a Lycian, celebrated for his skill in archery, at the time of the Trojan war [Gr. Πάνδαρος].

Pănŏpēa, æ, f. *Panopēa,* a lengthened form of *Panopē*; a sea-nymph [Gr. Πανόπη, "All-seeing One"].

Pănŏpes, is, m. *Panopes*; a companion of Acestes [Gr. Πανόπης, "All-seeing One"].

pār, păris, adj. *Equal.*

părātus, a, um: **1.** P. perf. pass. of păro—**2.** Pa.: *Prepared, ready.*

Par-ca, cæ, f.: **1.** Sing.: *One of the (three) goddesses of fate.* —**2.** Plur.: *The Fates*: their Latin names were No a, Decuma, Morta; their Greek names Clotho, Lachĕsis, Atrŏpos [prob. root PAR, "to bring or put," whence, păr-o, "to prepare," and so, "She who brings, or assigns," one's lot;—cf. Gr. Μοῖρ-α, "The Allotter or Apportioner," fr. μείρ-ομαι, in force of "to allot," etc.].

păr-ens, ntis, comm. gen. [either for pări-ens, fr. pări-o, "to bring forth," etc.; or fr. obsol. păr-o = păr-io] **1.** *A parent.*—**2.** *A father*—each time in this book of Anchises, the father of Æneas.—**3.** Plur.: **a.** *Parents.*—**b.** *Ancestors, progenitors.*

păr-ĕo, ŭi, ĭtum, ēre, 2. v. n. ("To come forth"; hence, "to appear" at a person's command; hence) *With Dat.* [§ 106, (4)]: *To obey.*

păr-ĭ-es, ĕtis (Abl. plur. as quadrisyll., v. 589), m. ("The thing going around"; hence) *A wall* [Sans. par-i, "around"; I, root of ĕo, "to go"].

părĭo, pĕpĕri, partum, părĕre, 3. v. a. ("To bring forth"; hence) *To obtain, procure, ac-*

quire.—Pass.: **părĭor,** partus sum, pări [prob. akin to Gr. φέρ-ω, Lat. fĕr-o].

Păris, ĭdis, m. *Paris;* a son of Hecuba, who carried off Helen, the wife of Menelāus, king of Sparta, and thus caused the Trojan war [Gr. Πάρις].

păr-ĭter, adv. [par, "equal"] **1.** *Equally.*—**2.** *At the same time, together.*

păr-o, āvi, ātum, āre, 1. v. a.: **1.** *To make,* or *get, ready;* to *prepare.*—**2.** Pass. in reflexive force: *To prepare one's self, make one's self ready.*—Pass.: **păr-or,** ātus sum, āri [prob. akin to Gr. φέρ-ω; Latin fĕr-o].

pars, tis, f. ("That which is cut"; hence) **1.** *A part, piece, portion,* etc.—Adverbial Abl.: **parte,** *In part, partly.*—**2.** Of persons: *A part, some* out of many;—at v. 558 pars, as a noun of multitude, is the Subject of the plur. verb fĕrunt [Notes to Syntax, p. 133, *E*, 3]; cf. also, v. 661;—at v. 108 pars forms the Subject of părăti (erant), while, as men are spoken of, parati is in masc. gen. [see Notes to Syntax, as above] [prob. akin to φάρ-ω, "to cut"].

part-ĭo, ivi *or* ii, itum, ire, 4. v. a. [pars, part-is, "a part"] ("To part"; hence) *To divide, decide out,* etc.—Pass.: **part-ĭor,** itus sum, iri.

partītus, a, um, P. perf. pass. of partio.

partus, a, um, P. perf. pass. of părio.

parvus, a, um, adj.: **1.** In size *or* degree: *Little, small.*—**2.** In age: *Little, youthful, young.*

pas-sim, adv. [for pad-sim; fr. pando, "to spread out," through root PAD] ("By a spreading out"; hence) *On*

all sides, on every side, in all directions.

passus, a, um, P. perf. of pătĭor.

pătens, ntis: **1.** P. pres. of pătĕo.—**2.** Pa.: *Open;* i. e. at v. 552, *cleared.*

păt-ĕo, ŭi, no sup., ēre, 2. v. n. *To stand, lie,* or *be open* [akin to Gr. πετ-άννυμι, "to stretch out, extend"].

pă-ter, tris, m. ("A protector"; also, "a nourisher") **1.** *A father,* as one who protects, etc.—**2.** As a title of respect: *Father;*—at v. 14 addressed to Neptune;—at v. 241 to Portūnus;—at vv. 521, 533 to Acestes;—at v. 690 to Jŭpĭter;—at v. 130, *etc.,* used of Æneas;—at vv. 358, 867 used alone of Æneas, and at v. 424 in conjunction with satus Anchīsā;—at v. 603 = Anchīses;—at v. 341, in plur., of the Trojan elders.—**3.** *A senator* [akin to Gr. πα-τήρ; Sans. pi-tṛi, fr. root PĀ, "to protect, to nourish"].

păt-ĕra, ĕræ, f. [păt-ĕo, "to lie open"; hence, "to spread out, extend"] ("The thing spreading out *or* extending"; hence) *A broad flat dish,* especially used in making offerings: *a bowl* for libations.

păter-nus, na, num, adj. [păter, păt(ĕ)r-is, "a father"] *Of,* or *belonging to, a father; a father's;*—at v. 81 = of Anchīses.

pătĭens, ntis: **1.** P. pres. of pătĭor.—**2.** Pa.: In disposition, *etc.:* **a.** *Patient.*—**b.** In adverbial force: *Patiently.*

pătĭor, passus sum, păti, 3. v. dep.: **1.** *To suffer, bear, endure, undergo.*—**2.** *To permit, allow, suffer* [akin to Gr. πάσχω; and Sans. root BADH, *or* VADH, "to strike"].

patria, æ; see patrius.

1. **patr-ĭus,** ĭa, ĭum, adj.

[păter, patr-is] *Of*, or *belonging to, a father; a father's; paternal.* — As Subst.: **patrĭ-a**, æ, f. *Fatherland, native country.*
2. **patrĭ-us**, a, um, adj. [patri-a, " fatherland "] *Of, or belonging to, one's fatherland or native country.*
Patron, ŏnis, m. *Patron;* an Arcadian, one of the competitors in the foot-race at the funeral games of Anchises [Gr. Πάτρων].
paul-isper, adv. [paul-us, " little "] *For a little while.*
păv-ĭdus, ida, idum. adj. [păv-ĕo, " to fear "] *Terrified, alarmed, timid.*
păv-or, ōris, m. [id.] *Fear, terror, dread.*
pax, pācis, f. [for pac-s; fr. root PAC or PAG, whence păciscor, " to bind, to covenant"; pango, " to fasten "] (" The binding, or fastening, thing "; hence) *Peace.*
pectus, ŏris, n.: **1.** *The breast.*—**2.** *Heart, mind, feelings;*—at v. 816 plur. for sing.— **3.** *Soul, disposition,* etc.
pĕc-us, ŭdis, f. (" The thing fastened up "; hence, Sing.: " a single head of cattle ") Plur.: *Cattle* in general: — nigræ pecudes, *black cattle,* were offered to the deities of the lower world, v. 736. Under the term pĕcūdes are included, at v. 243, Æn. vi., jŭvenci, " steers."— N.B. When this word is applied to " sheep," it is used in an especial force [akin to Sans. paç-u, fr. root PAÇ, " to bind "].
pĕdum, gen. plur. of pes; v. 430.
pĕlăgus, i, n. *The sea,* esp. *the open sea* [Gr. πέλαγος].
Pēlīdes, æ, m. *The son of Peleus,* i. e. Achilles [Gr. Πηλείδης].
pell-is, is, f. *A skin* or *hide* [akin to Gr. πέλλ-α, ' hide '].

pello, pĕpŭli, pulsum, pe ĕre, 3. v. a. (" To cause to go hence) **1.** *To drive out* or *awa* —**2.** Of fear as Object: *To d miss, cast off.*—Pass.: **pello** pulsus sum, pelli [akin to San root PAL, " to go "].
Pĕn-ātes, ătium, m. plu [pĕn-us, " provisions, stores' (" Those pertaining to *penus* hence) *The Penates* or *guard deities,* whether of a househol or of a state as a collection households;—at v. 63 Penat patrii = the Penates of Troy.
pendens, ntis, P. pres. pendĕo.
pendĕo, pĕpendi, no su pendēre, 2. v. n.: **1.** *To ha hang down, be suspended.*—**2.** things not in use: *To ha be hung up.*—**3.** *To be suspend horizontally; to hover, flutt* etc.—**4.** Of a charioteer: *hang,* or *bend, over his horses.*
pĕnĕtrālĭa, ium; s pĕnĕtrālis.
pĕnĕtrā-lis, le, a [pĕnĕtr(a)-o, " to penetrate (" Penetrating, piercing hence) *Inner, interior, intern* — As Subst.: **pĕnĕtrālī** ium, n. plur. (" The interior, inner chambers " of a buildin hence) *A sanctuary, a chapel* at v. 744 of Vesta.
pen-na, næ, f. [for pet-n see pĕt-o] (" The flying thing hence) *A wing.*
pĕpendi, perf. ind. pendĕo.
pĕr, prep. gov. acc.: *Through, across.*—**2.** *By mec of, through.*—**3.** *Through, in midst of, amidst.*—**4.** *All ov all along* or *about.*—**5.** In tim *During, in the course of, in;* v. 6 —N.B. At v. 663 per is plac after its case.

pĕr-ăgo, ēgi, actum, ăgĕre, 3. v. a. [pĕr, "through"; ăgo, "to put in motion"] ("To put in motion through"; hence, in reflexive force, "to pass through"; hence) *To go through with, complete, finish,* etc. :—dōna pĕrăgĕre, *to finish (distributing) the gifts,* v. 362.

per-cello, culi, culsum, cellĕre, 3. v. a. [pĕr, in "augmentative" force; cello, "to impel"] ("To impel greatly"; hence) *To strike.*

perculi, perf. ind. of percello.

pĕrēgi, perf. ind. of pĕrăgo.

pĕremptus, a, um, P. perf. pass. of pĕrimo.

pĕr-erro, errāvi, errātum, errāre, 1. v. a. [pĕr, "through"; erro, "to wander"] **1.** *To wander through* or *all over.—* **2.** With reference to the sight: *To glance over, survey.*

perfectus, a, um, P. perf. pass. of perficio.

per-fĕro, tŭli, lātum, ferre, v. a. irreg. [pĕr; fĕro, "to bear"] **1.** [pĕr, "throughout"] ("To bear throughout"; hence) *To continue to bear.—* **2.** [pĕr, "without force"] **a.** *To bear, carry, convey.—* **b.** *To bring,* or *convey, word* or *tidings; to announce,* etc.;—at v. 605 folld. by Objective clause.— **c.** *To bear, endure, submit to, undergo, be subject to.*

per-fĭcĭo, fēci, fectum, ficĕre, 3. v. a. [for per-făcio; fr. pĕr, "thoroughly"; făcio, "to make"] ("To make thoroughly"; hence) With Abl. of material: *To make, form,* or *manufacture of.*—Pass.: **perficior,** fectus sum, fici.

per-fundo, fūdi, fūsum, fundĕre, 3. v. a. [pĕr, "thoroughly"; fundo, in force of "to wet or bathe"] **1.** *To wet,* or *bathe, thoroughly; to wash,* etc.— **2.** Pass. in reflexive force: *To sprinkle one's self,* etc. — **3.** Of garments: *To steep, dye.*—Pass.: **per-fundor,** fūsus sum, fundi.

perfūsus, a, um, P. perf. pass. of perfundo.

(Pergāma, ōrum, n. plur.: **1.** *Pergama,* the citadel of Troy.— **2.** *Troy.* — Hence) **Pergămĕus,** ĕa, ĕum, adj. *Trojan.*

Pergămĕus, a, um, adj.; see Pergāma.

pĕri-cŭlum, cli, n. [obsol. pĕri-or, "to try, make trial of"] ("That which serves for trying"; hence, "a trial, attempt"; hence) *Risk, hazard, danger, peril.*

pĕr-ĭmo, ēmi, emptum, ĭmĕre, 3. v. a. [for pĕr-ĕmo; fr. pĕr, "thoroughly"; ĕmo, "to take"] ("To take or take away thoroughly"; hence) *To destroy.*—Pass.: **pĕr-ĭmor,** emptus sum, ĭmi.

perjūr-us, a, um, adj. [perjūr-o, "to swear falsely"] *Swearing falsely; perjured.*

permissus, a, um, P. perf. pass. of permitto.

per-mitto, misi, missum, mittĕre, 3. v. a. [pĕr, "through"; mitto, "to allow to go"] ("To allow to go through"; hence) *To grant, permit, allow, authorize,* etc. — Pass.: **per-mittor,** missus sum, mitti.

per-mulcĕo, mulsi, mulsum and mulctum, mulcēre, 2. v. a. [pĕr, "all over"; mulcĕo, "to stroke"] ("To stroke all over"; hence) *To soothe, appease,* etc.

permulsi, perf. ind. of permulcĕo.

per-solvo, solvi, sŏlūtum, solvĕre, 3. v. a. [pĕr, "completely"; solvo, "to pay"]

("To pay completely"; hence, in figurative force) *To give, render,* etc.

per-sto, stĭti, stătum, stāre, 1. v. n. [pĕr, "continually"; sto, "to stand"] ("To stand continually"; hence) Mentally: *To stand fast, firm,* or *fixed.*

per-tædet, tæsum est, tædēre, 2. v. a. impers. [pĕr, in "augmentative" force; tædet, "it disgusts *or* wearies"] With Acc. of person and Gen. of thing" [§ 134]: *It thoroughly disgusts* or *wearies* one, *etc., of* something;—the Subject of pertæsum est (v. 714) is contained in itself, viz. tædium [§ 157].

pertæsum est; see pertædet.

per-tento, tentāvi, tentātum, tentāre, 1. v. a. [pĕr, "thoroughly"; tento, "to handle"] ("To handle thoroughly"; hence) *To seize upon, take possession of, pervade, affect,* etc.

pes, pĕd-is, m. ("The going thing"; hence) **1.** *A foot.*—**2.** Of an eagle: *A claw, talon.*—**3.** In vessels: *A sheet,* i. e. a rope attached to a sail for the purpose of setting it to the wind: —pĕdem făcĕre, *to veer out a sheet, to haul to the wind* [akin to Gr. πούς, ποδ-ός; and to Sans. *pad,* fr. root PAD, "to go"].

pes-tis, tis, f. [prob. for perd-tis; fr. perd-o, "to destroy"] ("The destroying thing"; hence) **1.** *Destruction, ruin.*—**2.** Of a destructive thing or person: *Pest, bane.*

pĕte, pres. imperat. of pĕto.

pĕtens, ntis, P. pres. of pĕto.

pĕtīvi, perf. ind. of pĕto.

pĕt-o, ivi *or* ĭi, itum, ĕre, 3. v. a.: **1.** ("To fly towards"; hence) **a.** *To seek; to proceed to*

or *towards; to direct one's course towards.*—**b.** *To seek, search for.* —**c.** *To seek, demand, ask for.*— **2.** ("To fall, or throw one's self, upon"; hence, "to attack"; hence) *To aim at* [akin to Sans. root PAT, whence Gr. πέτ-ομαι, "to fly"; and πετ, a root of πίπτω, "to fall"].

Phăëthŏn, ontis, m. *Phaëthon;* another name for the *Sun;* v. 105; where no reference is made to Phaëthon, the son of Apollo, who obtained from his father permission to drive the Sun's chariot for one day, and being unable to manage the horses, set a part of the world on fire [Gr. Φαέθων, "Shining One"].

phălĕræ, ārum, f. plur. *Trappings* for the forehead and breast of horses, *etc.* [Gr. φάλαρα].

phăretra, æ, f. *A quiver* [φαρέτρα, "a quiver," as being "that which carries" arrows].

Phēgeus (dissyll.), ĕi and ĕŏs, m. *Phegeus;* a Trojan, one of the servants of Cloanthus [Gr. Φηγεύς, "He of the oak; Oak-man"].

Phŏlŏē, ēs, f. *Pholoë;* the name of a female slave; v. 284 [Gr Φολόη].

Phorbas, ntis, m. *Phorbas;* a Trojan sailor, whose form was assumed by Somnus, when that god endeavoured to induce Palinūrus to quit his post and sleep; see Pălīnūrus [Gr. Φόρβας, "He who feeds"].

Phorcus, i, m. *Phorcus* (also called Phorcys); a son of Neptune, changed after death into a sea-god:—Phorci chŏrus, v. 240, and Phorci exercitus, v. 824, have the same meaning, viz. the sea-deities in attendance on Phorcus [Gr. Φόρκος and Φόρκυς].

VOCABULARY, 105

Phrӯges, um, m. plur. *The Phrygians;* the inhabitants of Phrygia in Asia Minor, in whose country Troy was situate [Gr. Φρύγες].

pictus, a, um, P. perf. pass. of pingo.

pĭ-ĕtas, ātis, f. [pi-us, (towards the gods) "pious"; (towards parents, *etc.*) "affectionate"] ("The quality of the *pius*"; hence) **1.** *Piety.*—**2.** *Filial affection,* etc.—**3.** *Justice;* v. 638.

(pĭgĕo, ŭi, no sup., ēre, 2. v. a. *To feel annoyance at, to repent of;* as verb personal very rare) As v. impers. in 3rd pers. sing.: **pĭget,** pĭgŭit *or* pĭgĭtum est, *etc.:* With Acc. of person, and Gen. of thing: *It repents,* etc., *one of;*—at v. 678 with Gen. of thing alone; supply *ĕas* as Acc. of person.

pig-nus, nŏris, n. [prob. for pag-nus; fr. pango, "to bind *or* fasten," through root PAG] ("The binding, *or* fastening, thing"; hence, "a pledge, security"; hence) Mentally or morally: *A pledge, token, assurance, proof.*

pĭ(n)go, pinxi, pictum, pingĕre, 3. v. a. ("To represent pictorially; to paint; to embroider"; hence) *To paint, stain, colour,* etc.—Pass.: **pĭ(n)g-or,** pictus sum, pingi [akin to Sans. root PIKJ, "to dye *or* colour"].

pīnus, ūs, f.: **1.** *A fir-tree, pine-tree; a fir, pine.*—**2.** *A ship,* as built of pine [akin to Gr. πίτυς].

pĭ-us, a, um, adj. ("Purified"; hence) **1.** With regard to religion: *Devout, pious.*—As Subst.: **pĭi,** ōrum, m. plur. *The devout, the pious,* etc ; v. 734.—**2.** With regard to parents, relatives, *etc.*· *Affectionate, tender, kind* [akin to Sans. root PŪ, "to purify"].

plăcĭd-ē, adv. [plăcĭd-us, "gentle"] ("After the manner of the *placidus*"; hence) *Gently, mildly.*

plăc-ĭdus, ĭda, ĭdum, adj. [plăc-ĕo, "to please"] ("Pleasing"; hence) *Gentle, calm, mild, peaceful, placid.*

plaudens, ntis, P. pres. of plaudo.

plaudo, plausi, plausum, plaudĕre, 3. v. n. *To clap, beat, strike,* etc.

plau-sus, sūs, m. [for plaud-sus; fr. plaud-o, "to clap"; hence, "to applaud"] **1.** *Of the noise made by the wings of a dove: A clapping sound, a clapping.*—**2.** *Applause.*

plē-nus, na, num, adj. [ple-o, "to fill"] **1.** *Filled, full.* —**2.** With Abl. (§ 118, *b*): *Filled with, full of.*

plĭcans, ntis, P. pres. of plico.

plĭc-o, avi (and ŭi), atum and ĭtum, āre, 1. v. a. *Of a snake: To fold, coil* [akin to Gr. πλέκ-ω].

plumbum, i, n. *Lead* [akin to Gr. μόλυβδος].

plūra; see plus.

plū-rĭmus, rĭma, rĭmum, sup. adj. [PLE, root of plĕ-o, "to fill"; (i) connecting vowel; rĭmus, superl. suffix: = ple-i-sĭmus; changed as follows: plei-sĭmus, pli-sĭmus, ploi-sĭmus, ploi-rŭmus, plŭ-rĭmus] ("Most, or very, full"; hence) **1.** Sing.: *Very much.*—**2.** Plur.: *Very many, most numerous.*

plūs, plūris (Plur. **plūres,** plūra), comp. adj. [contr. and changed fr. ple-or; PLE, root of plĕ-o, "to fill"; comparative suffix "or"] ("Fuller"; hence) **1.** *More.*—**2.** Neut. acc. plur.

VOCABULARY.

in adverbial force: **plūra,**
More, longer; v. 381.
pō-cūlum, cūli, n. ("That
which serves for drinking");
hence) *A cup, goblet* [akin to
Gr. πώ·ω (= πίνω), Sans. root
pā, "to drink"].
poen-a, æ, f. ("The purifying thing"; hence, "satisfaction" for an offence; hence)
Punishment [Gr. ποιν-ή; akin to
Sans. root pū, "to purify"].
Pōlītes, æ (Voc. Pōlĭtĕ,
v. 564), m. *Polites;* a son of
Priam, king of Troy [Gr. Πολίτης, "Citizen"].
polluo, ūi, ūtum, ŭĕre,
3. v. a. ("To defile"; hence)
To violate, dishonour.—Pass.:
polluor, ūtus sum, ūi.
pollūtus, a, um, P. perf.
pass. of pollŭo.
pŏlus, i, m. ("The end of
an axis, a pole"; hence, "the
North Pole"; hence) *The heaven*
or *heavens* [Gr. πόλος].
pomp-a, æ, f. *A solemn,* or
*public, procession at games,
festivals, etc.* [Gr. πομπ-ή].
pōnam, fut. ind. of *pōno;*
v. 66.
pond-us, ĕris, n. [for pendus; fr. pend-o, "to weigh"]
("A weighing thing"; hence)
1. *A weight.*—**2.** *Weight, heaviness.*
pōne, pres. imperat. of
pōno.
pōno, pŏsŭi, pŏsĭtum, pōnĕre, 3. v. a.: **1.** *To put, place,
set.*—**2.** *To erect, build, found.*—
3. *To lay down, recline.*—**4.** Of
games, a contest, *etc.: To institute, arrange, establish.*—**5.** Of
prizes: *To lay down, propose,*
etc.—**6.** *To lay aside, lay down.*
pontus, i, m. *The sea* [πόντος].
pōpŭl-ĕus, ĕa, ĕum, adj.
[pōpŭl-us, "a poplar"] *Of,* or
belonging to, a poplar; poplar-.

pŏ-pŭl-us, i, m. ("Tl
many"; hence) *The peop*
[prob. for pol-pol-us, fr. πολ-ύ
"much"; plur., "many"].
porrĭcĭam, fut. ind.
porricio.
porrĭcĭo, porrĕci, porre
tum, porricĕre, 3. v. a. [o
religious t. t. for prōjĭcĭo]
cast, or *lay,* as an offering befo
some deity;—sometimes foll
by in c. Acc.
porro, adv. ("Forwar
onward"; hence) *Further, mor
over, besides* [Gr. πόρω].
portans, ntis, P. pres.
porto.
por-tendo, tendi, tentur
tendĕre, 3. v. a. [por (= prc
"forth"; tendo, "to stretch
("To stretch forth"; henc
Religious t. t.: *To indicate, for
tell, presage, etc.*
por-to, tāvi, tātum, tā
1. v. a.: **1.** *To bear* or *carry.*
2. *To bring, convey* [prob. ak
to Gr. φέρ-ω].
Portū-nus, ni, m. [portu
uncontr. gen. portū-is, "a ha
bour"] ("One pertaining
portus") *Portunus;* a Rom
deity considered to preside ov
harbours; see Ino.
por-tus, tūs, m. *A harbor
haven, port* [prob. fr. root pr
or por, found in περ-άω,
pass through"; πόρ-ος,
way"].
posco, pŏposci, no su
poscĕre, 3. v. a.: **1.** *To a
request, demand.*—**2.** *To ask f
entreat, etc. -* **3.** Of things
Subject: *To require, dema
need.*—**4.** *To invoke;*—for for
of poscāmus, 1. pers. plur. pr
subj., see vertāmus, in verto.
pŏsĭtus, a, um, P. pe
pass. of pōno.
posse, pres. inf. of possu
possum, pŏtŭi, posse,
irreg. [for pot-sum; fr. pŏt-

"able"; sum, "to be"] **1.** *To be able.*—**2.** With Inf.: (*I*, etc.) *can,could,etc.,do,etc.,*something.
post, prep. and adv.: **1.** Prep. gov. acc.: **a.** Locally: *After, behind.* — **b.** In time: *After, since.*—**2.** Adv.: *After, afterwards.*
post-ĕrus, ĕra, ĕrum, adj. [post, "after"] *Coming after, following, next.*
pos-tis, tis, m. [pōno, "to put," through root POS] ("A putting *or* placing"; hence) **1.** *A post, door-post.*—**2.** *A door.*
post-quam, adv. [post, "after"; quam, "that"] *After that, when.*—N.B. In narrative, the adverbs postquam, ubi, simulac, and others signifying "when," "as soon as," are joined to the perf. ind., where the pluperf. would have been expected. Such perf. must be rendered as a pluperf.; v. 577; cf., also, v. 32.
pŏsŭi, perf. ind. of pōno.
præ-cep-s, cipĭt-is, adj. [for præ-capĭt-s; fr. præ, "before"; căput, căpĭt-is, "the head"] ("Having the head before"; hence) **1.** *Head-foremost, headlong.*—**2.** *In headlong haste.* —**3.** *Swift, rapid.*
præcep-tum, ti, n. [for præcap-tum; fr. præcĭpĭo, "to instruct; to order," through true root PRÆCAP (= præ; CAP, root of căpĭo)] *Instruction, injunction, order, bidding.*
præcĭp-ŭus, ŭa, ŭum, adj. [præcĭp-ĭo, "to take before"] ("That is taken before" other things; hence) *Particular, peculiar, especial.*
præ-c-o, ōnis, m. [for præ-cĭ-o; fr. præ, "before"; cĭ-o, in force of "to cry out *or* aloud"] ("One crying out, *or* aloud, before" a person, *etc.*; hence) *A crier, herald.*

præ-fĕro, tŭli, lātum, ferre, v. a. [præ, "before"; fĕro, "to bear"] ("To bear before"; hence) In figurative force: *To offer, present.* — Pass.: **præ-fĕror,** lātus sum, ferri.
præ-fīgo, fixi, fixum, fīgĕre, 3. v. a. [præ, "before"; fīgo, "to fix"] ("To fix, *or* fasten, before"; hence) With Abl.: *To tip, head, etc.,* with something. — Pass.: **præ-fīgor,** fixus sum, ĭigi.
præfixus, a, um, P. perf. pass. of præfīgo.
præiens, ĕuntis, P. pres. of præĕo;—at v. 186 the *præ* in præeunte is shortened, by poetic licence and in imitation of the Greeks, before the following *e*.
prælātus, a, um, P. perf. pass. of præfĕro.
præ-m-ĭum, ii, n. [for præ-ĕm-ĭum; from præ, "before *or* abovo"; ĕm-o, "to take"] ("A taking before *or* above" others;—"that which is taken before," *etc.*, others; hence, "profit"; hence) *A reward, prize,* etc.
præ-pe-s, tis, adj. ("Flying forwards"; hence) *Swift, quick, rapid* [for præ-pet-s; fr. præ, "forwards"; root PET, akin to Gr. πέτομαι, Sans. root PAT, "to fly"].
præ-s-ens, ntis (Abl. usually præsente of persons, præsenti of things), adj. [præ, "before"; s-um, "to be"] ("Being before" one; hence) **1.** *Present, at hand,* etc.—**2.** Of disposition or character: *Present, collected, resolute.*
præsta-ns, ntis (Abl. præstanti, v. 361), adj. [præ-st(a)-o, "to stand before"; hence, "to be superior," *etc.*] *Superior, surpassing, distinguished,* etc.

prætĕr-ĕa, adv. [for præter-eam; fr. præter, "beyond"; eam, fem. acc. sing. of is, "that"] ("Beyond that"; hence) *Besides, moreover, further.*

prætĕr-ĕo, ivi or ii, itum, ire, v. a. [præter, "past"; ĕo, "to go"] *To go past, to pass by.*

præ-vĭdĕo, vidi, visum, vidēre, 2. v. a. [præ, "beforehand"; video, "to see"] *To see beforehand, to anticipate.*

prævĭdi, perf. ind. of prævĭdĕo.

prĕcātus, a, um, P. perf. of prĕcor;—at v. 529 supply sunt with prĕcāti.

prĕces, um, plur. of prex.

prĕc-or, ātus sum, āri, 1. v. dep. *To beseech, entreat, address prayers* or *entreaties to* [akin to Sans. root PRACHH, "to ask"].

prĕmo, pressi, pressum, prĕmĕre, 3. v. a.: **1.** *To press, press against.*—**2.** *To press firmly* or *closely.*—Pass.: **prĕmor,** pressus sum, prĕmi.

pressus, a, um, P. perf. pass. of prĕmo.

prĕ-tĭum, tii, n. ("That which buys"; hence, "money"; hence) *A reward* [akin to Gr. πρί-ασθαι, "to buy"].

prex, prĕcis (obsol. in Nom. and Gen. Sing.:—mostly Plur.), f. [for prec-s; fr. prĕc-or, "to ask"] ("The asking thing"; hence) *Entreaty, prayer.*

Prĭămus, i, m. *Priam;* king of Troy, when that city was besieged and taken by the Greeks [Gr. Πρίαμος, "Chief, King"].

prīm-o, prīm-um, adv. [prim-us, "first"] *At first, in the first place, first.*

prī-mus, ma, mum, sup. adj. [for præ-mus; fr. præ, "before"; with sup. suffix mus] ("*Most before*"; hence) **1.** *First, the first* in order, *etc.*;—at v. 294 primi, plur., is predicated of the two sing. substt. Nisus and Euryălus; supply also fuĕrunt:—primus pes, *the forefoot* of a horse, v. 566.—**2.** *The first* to do something; *the first that.*—**3.** In time: *First, earliest.*—**4.** Of place, *etc.: First, foremost.*—As Subst.: **prīma,** ōrum, n. plur. ("The first, or foremost, things"; *i.e.*) *The first,* or *foremost, place* in the contest; v. 194, where it is opposed to extrēmos; cf., also, v. 338. ☞ Comp.: prior.

prin-cep-s, cĭpis, adj. [for prim-cap-s; fr. prim-us, "first"; căp-Jo, "to take"] ("Taking the first place," or "taken first"; hence) *First, foremost.*

princĭpĭo; see principium.

princĭp-ĭum, ii, n. [princeps, princip-is, "first"] ("That which pertains to the princeps"; hence) **1.** *A beginning, commencement.*—**2.** Adverbial Abl.: **princĭpĭo,** *In the beginning, in the first place, at first.*

prī-or, us, comp. adj. [for præ-or; fr. præ, "before"; with comp. suffix "or"] ("More before"; hence) *Previous, former, prior*—often to be rendered *first.* ☞ Sup.: prim-us.

pris-cus, ca, cum, adj. *Of former times, of time bygone, ancient* [obsol. pris = Gr. πρίν, "before"].

Pristis, is, f. ("A sea-monster" of any kind) *Pistris;* the name of a ship in the fleet of Æneas [Gr. πίστρις].

prō, prep. gov. abl. case: **1.** *Before, in front of.*—**2.** *For, on behalf of.*—**3.** *For, instead of, in the place of.*—**4.** *In return for, in exchange for.;* v. 230. **5.** *On account of* [akin to Sans. pra; Gr. πρό].

VOCABULARY.

prŏb-o, āvi, ātum, āre, 1. v. a. [prŏb-us, "good"] *To esteem,* or *regard, as good; to approve of.*

prō-cēdo, cessi, cessum, cēdĕre, 3. v. n. [prŏ, "forwards"; cēdo, "to go or come"] ("To go, *or* come, forwards"; hence) Of anger as Subject: *To advance, proceed.*

prōcell-a, æ, f. [prōcell-o, "to drive, *or* dash, forwards"] ("The thing driving, *or* dashing, forwards"; hence) *A violent wind; a storm, tempest, hurricane.*

prō-clāmo, clāmāvi, clāmātum, clāmāre, 1. v. n. [prŏ, "aloud"; clāmo, "to call out"] *To call out aloud, to vociferate, cry out.*

prŏcul, adv. [PROCUL, a root of prōcello, "to drive forwards"] ("Driven forwards"; hence) Of place: *At a distance, far off.*

prō-cumbo, cŭbŭi, cŭbĭtum, cumbĕre, 3. v. n. [prŏ, "forwards"; obsol. cumbo, "to lie down"] ("To lie down forwards"; hence) **1.** Of rowers: *To lean forwards,* or *bend,* to their oars.—**2.** *To fall forwards, sink down.*

prŏcurrens, ntis, P. pres. of prŏcurro.

prō-curro, cŭcurri and curri, cursum, currĕre, 3. v. n. [prŏ, "forwards"; curro, "to run"] ("To run forwards"; hence) Of rocks: *To run,* or *jut, out into the sea; to project.*

prŏcurv-us, a, um, adj. [prŏcurv-o, "to bend, *or* curve, forwards"] *Bending,* or *curving, forwards; winding.*

prō-dĭg-ĭum, ĭi, n. [for prō-dĭc-ĭum; fr. prŏ, "beforehand," root DIC, "to show"; see dico] ("A showing beforehand"; hence) *A prophetic sign, a prodigy.*

proelĭum, ĭi, n. *A battle, engagement.*

prō-fund-us, a, um, adj. [prŏ, "forwards"; fund-us, "the bottom"] ("Having the bottom forwards"; *i. e.* at some distance off; hence) *Deep, profound.*

prōgĕn-ĭes, ĭĕi, f. [prōgigno, "to beget *or* bring forth," through root PROGEN] ("A begetting *or* bringing forth"; hence) *Offspring.*

prō-hĭbĕo, hĭbŭi, hĭbĭtum, hĭbēre, 2. v. a. [for prŏ-hăbĕo; fr. prŏ, "before"; hăbĕo, "to hold"] ("To hold before one *or* in front"; hence) **1.** *To ward,* or *keep, off.—***2.** With Inf.: *To prevent,* or *hinder, from doing, etc.*

prōjĕci, perf. ind. of prōjĭcio.

prō-jĭcĭo, jēci, jectum, jĭcĕre, 3. v. a. [for prō-jăcĭo; fr. prŏ, "forwards"; jăcĭo, "to cast"] **1.** *To cast,* or *throw, forwards.*—**2.** *To cast,* or *throw, head-foremost* or *headlong.*

prōmis-sum, si, n. [for promitt-sum; fr. prōmitt-o, "to promise"] *A promise.*

prōmissu-s, a, um, P. perf. pass. of prōmitto.—As Subst.: **prōmissa,** ōrum, n. plur. *The things promised, the promised gifts* or *rewards.*

prō-mitto, misi, missum, mittĕre, 3. v. a. [prŏ, "forth"; mitto, "to send"] ("To send forth"; hence) *To promise.*— Pass.: **drō-mittor,** missus sum, mitti.

prō-m-o, psi, ptum, ĕre, 3. v. a. [contr. fr. prō-ĕm-o; fr. prŏ, "forth"; ĕm-o, "to take"] ("To take forth"; hence) Of strength, efforts, *etc.*: *To put forth, exert, etc.*

prōnus, a, um, adj.: **1.** *Inclined downwards, bending forwards, head-foremost.*—**2.** ("Inclined, or disposed, to" something or some person; hence) *Favourable;* — prona maria, "favourable seas," *i. e.* which oppose no obstacle to the vessel's course, v. 212 [Gr. πρηνής].

prŏpinqu-o, āvi, ātum, āre, 1. v. n. [prŏpinqu-us, "near"] With Dat. [§ 106. (1)]: *To draw near to, to approach.*

prŏp-ior, ius, comp. adj. [obsol. prŏp-is, "near"] *Nearer, closer,* etc. — As Subst. : **prŏpiŏra,** um, n. plur. *The nearer places;* i. e. at v. 168 the place, *or* side, nearest to the rock. ☞ Sup.: proxĭmus (for prop-simus).

prō-pōno, pŏsŭi, pŏsĭtum, pōnĕre, 3. v. a. [prō, "forth"; pōno, "to put"] *To put, place,* or *set forth* or *out; to show, exhibit, display.*

prŏprĭus, a, um, adj. *One's own property, one's own.*

prōra, æ, f. *The prow,* or *head,* of a vessel [Gr. πρῷρα].

prō-rĭpĭo, rĭpŭi, reptum, rĭpĕre, 3. v. a. [for prō-răpĭo; fr. prō, "forwards"; răpĭo, "to snatch"] ("To snatch, *or* hurry, forwards"; hence) With ellipse of personal pron.: ("To hurry one's self forwards"; *i. e.*) *To rush,* or *hurry, onwards;* v. 741.

prō-sĕquor, sĕquūtus sum, sĕqui, 3. v. dep. [prō, "onwards"; sĕquor, "to follow after"] *To follow onwards after, attend upon, accompany,* etc.

prō-sĭlĭo, sĭlŭi (less frequently silivi and silii), prps. no sup., sīlīre, 4. v. n. [for prō-sălĭo; fr. prō, "forth"; sălĭo, "to leap"] *To leap forth, spring forwards.*

prōsĭlŭi, perf. ind. of prōsilio.

prō-sum, fŭi, desse, v. n. [prō, "for"; sum, "to be"] ("To be for *or* on behalf of"; hence) *To be of benefit; to profit, avail.*

prōtendens, ntis, P. pres. of prōtendo.

prō-tendo, tendi, tensum and tentum, tendĕre, 3. v. a. [prō, "forth"; tendo, "to stretch"] *To stretch forth* or *out; to extend.*

prō-tĭnus, adv. [for prōtēnus; fr. prō, "before"; tēnus, "up to *or* as far as"] ("Up to, *or* as far as, that which is before"; hence) Of time: *Forthwith, immediately.*

proxĭmus, a, um, sup. adj. [for prop-simus; fr. obsol. prŏp-is, "near"] *Nearest, next,* whether in place or time;—at v. 320 folld. by Dat. (huic) [§ 106, (1)]; and also by Abl. of space or distance (intervallo).

prūna, æ, f. *A live,* or *burning, coal.*

pū-bes, bis, f. [prob. akin to pū-er] ("That which is nourished"; hence, "that which is grown up"; hence) *Youth* in a collective force; *young persons.*

Publĭus, ĭi, m. *Publius;* a Roman name.

pŭdĕo, ŭi (impers. ĭtum est), ēre, 2. v. n.: **1.** Personal: *To shame, feel shame.*—**2.** Impers.: *It shames, causes shame;*—at v. 196 pudeat has for its Subject the clause (nos) rediisse extrēmos [§ 157] [akin to Sans. root pūy, "to stink"].

pŭd-or, ōris, m. [pŭd-ĕo, "to feel ashamed"] ("A feeling ashamed"; hence) *A sense,* or *feeling, of shame; shame.*

pū-er, ĕri, m. ("The nourished one"; hence) **1.** *A boy, lad;*—at v. 252 puer regius = Ganymede, son of Laomĕdon

VOCABULARY.

king of Troy, who was carried off by Jupiter's eagle from Mount Ida to heaven, and there made Jupiter's *cup-bearer.*—**2.** *A grown-up youth, a young man* [prob. akin to Sans. root PUSH, "to nourish," and to πόϊρ, the Spartan form of *παῖς*].

pŭĕr-īlis, īle, adj. [pŭer, pŭĕr-i, "a boy"] *Of,* or *belonging to, a boy* or *boys; boyish, youthful;* — puerile agmen, *a troop of boys.*

pug-na, næ, f. [root PUG, whence pung-o, "to puncture or stab"] ("The stabbing thing"; hence) *A fight* hand to hand; *a battle, contest,* etc.

pul-cher, chra, chrum, adj. [for pol-cher; fr. pŏl-ĭo, "to polish"] ("Polished"; hence) **1.** *Beautiful, fair, lovely.*—**2.** Morally: *Excellent,* etc. ☞ (Comp.: pulchr-ĭor); Sup.: pulch(e)r-rĭmus.

pulcherrĭmus, a, um; see pulcher.

pulsans, ntis, P. pres. of pulso;—at v. 138 haurit pulsans = haurit et pulsat.

pulsātus, a, um, P. perf. pass. of pulso.

pul-so, sāvi, sātum, sāre, 1. v. a. intens. [pello, "to beat," through root PUL] **1.** *To beat, strike.*—**2.** Of sound: *To strike against* something *to strike.*—**3.** *To disturb, agitate, disquiet.*—Pass.: **pul-sor,**sātus sum, sāri.

pulsus, a, um, P. perf. pass. of pello.

pūmex, ĭcis, m. ("A pumice-stone"; hence) *A porous rock, soft stone.*

pūn-ĭcĕus, ĭcĕa, ĭcĕum, adj. [for pœn-ĭcĕus; fr. Pœn-i, "the Pœni *or* Carthaginians"] ("Carthaginian"; hence) *Purple-coloured, purple,* Tyre, the mother-city of Carthage, being famed for its purple dye.

puppis, is (Acc. and Abl. Sing. mostly puppim and puppi), f.: **1.** *The stern* or *poop* of a ship.—**2.** *A ship, vessel.*

purpūra, æ, f. ("The purple-fish"; hence) *Purple* [Gr. πορφύρα].

purpŭr-ĕus, ĕa, ĕum, adj. [purpŭr-a, "purple"] ("Pertaining to purple"; hence) *Purple-coloured, purple,* including very different shades of colour ; *red, ruddy,* etc.

pŭtans, P. pres. of pŭto.

pŭt-o, āvi, ātum, āre, 1. v. a. [pŭt-us, "clean, clear"] ("To make clean *or* clear"; hence, "to clear up, *or* settle," accounts; hence, "to reckon"; hence) *To deem, hold, think, imagine, suppose;*—at v. 96 pŭtet is the Subj. in indirect interrogation after ne [§ 140]; it is, also, there followed by an Objective clause.

Pyrgo, ūs, f. *Pyrgo;* the nurse of Priam's children [Gr. Πύργω].

quā, adv. [adverbial abl. fem. of qui, "who, which"] Of place: *Where.*

quærīte, plur. pres. imperat. of quæro.

quæro, quæsīvi, quæsītum, quærĕre, 3. v. a.: **1.** *To seek, search for* or *after.*—**2.** *To ask about, seek to learn, inquire.*—Pass.: **quæror,** quæsītus sum, quæri.

quā-lis, le, adj.: **1.** Interrogative: *Of what sort* or *kind.*—**2.** Relative: *Of such a sort,* or *kind, as; such as.* – **3.** *Just as, like as;* v. 213 [akin to Sans. *ka-s,* "who?"].

quam, adv. [adverbial acc. fem. of quis, "what"] **1.** *In what manner, how, as.*—**2.** After comparative words: *Than.*

quam-quam, conj. [quam,

"as," repeated] ("As as"; hence) *Though, although.*

quam-vis, adv. and conj. [quum, "as"; vis, 2. pers. sing. pres. ind. of vŏlo, "to will or wish"] **1.** Adv.: *As you will or wish, as you like.*—**2.** Conj. [§ 152, I, 5]: *However, though, although.*

quas-so, sāvi, sātum, sāre, 1. v. a. inteus. [for quat-so; fr. quăt-io, "to shake"] *To shake violently or repeatedly.*

quătĭo, no perf., quassum, quătĕre, 3. v. a.: **1.** *To shake.*—**2.** *To plague, vex, harass.*

quătŭor, num. adj. indecl. *Four* [akin to τέσσαρ-ες, τέτταρ-ες; also to Sans. *chatur* (for *chut-var*)].

quĕ, enclitic conj. *And;—que...que, both...and;—*the que at end of v. 422 is elided before the vowel with which the following line begins [akin to Gr. τέ, "and"].

queis = quĭbus; v. 511.

quemque, masc. acc. sing. of quisque; v. 561.

ques-tus, tūs, m. [quĕror, "to complain," through root QUES] ("A complaining"; hence) *A complaint.*

qui, quæ, quod, pron.: **1.** Relative: *Who, which, what, that.*—The Relative sometimes attracts the subst. out of the demonstrative clause into its own; see vv. 28, 30; ulla... quam quæ tellus, for ulla tellus... quam quæ (= ea quæ).—**b.** At the beginning of a clause instead of a conj. and demonstr. pron.: *And this,* etc.—**c.** With ellipse of demonstrative pron.: *He,* or *she, who; that which;*—at v. 713, qui = eos, qui; and quos = eos, quos.—**d.** *According to, by virtue of, such:*—quæ cuique est copia, *according to the ability* (or *means*) *each possesses,*

v. 100.—**2.** Interrogative *What.*

qui-a, conj. [adverbial o' acc. plur. of qui] [§ 152, II, (1)] **1.** *Because.*—**2.** With suffi nam (also as two words, qui nam): *For what cause, why wherefore.*

quiănam; see quia, no. 2

quicquid; see quisquis.

qui-cumque, quæ-cum que, quod-cumque, pron. rel [qui; suffix cumque] *Whoever whatever; whosoever, whatsoever*

1. **quid**; see 1. and 2. quis.

2. **quid**, adv. [adverbia nent. of 1. quis, "who o what"] *For what purpose,* etc. *wherefore, why.*

quidem, adv. *Indeed, truly*

qui-es, ētis, f. ("A lyin; down"; hence) *Rest, repose sleep* [akin to Sans. root ÇI, "t lie down"].

quie-sco, ēvi, ētum, escēre 3. v. n. [for quiēt-sco; fr. quies quiēt-is, "rest"] ("To be in state of *quies*"; hence) **1.** *T rest, keep quiet.*—**2.** *To ceas desist.*

quiĕt-us, a, um, adj. [quie sco, "to be quiet," through roo QUIET] *Quiet, calm, tranquil.*

qui-n, conj. [for qui-ne; fr qui, abl. of relative pron, qu "who, which"; ne = non] ("B which not") **1.** With Subj. *That not, but that, without, from* —**2.** In interrogations or ex hortations: *Why not, wherefor not.*

qui-ni, næ, na, num. distrib adj. [for quinqu-ni; fr. quinqu-e "five"] **1.** *Five each* or *apiece.*—**2.** *Five.*

quique = qui, que; v. 67.

1. **quis**, quæ, quid (Gen cujus; Dat. cui), pron. inter rog.: **1.** *What, what sort of, person or thing.*—**2.** *Who, what* —As Subst. n.: **quid,** *Wha*

VOCABULARY. 113

thing, what [Gr. τις, "who? what?"].
2. quis, no fem., quid, pron. indef.: **1.** *Any one, anybody; anything.*—**2. quid**, as Acc. of Respect: *In any respect or degree, at all;* v. 688 [Gr. τις, "any"].

quis-quam, quæ-quam, quic-quam *or* quid-quam, pron. indef. [quis, "any one"; suffix quam] *Any, any whatever.*—As Subst. m.: *Any one, anybody.*

quis-que, quæ-que, quod-que, pron. indef. [quis, "any"; suffix que] *Each, every, any.*—As Subst. m.: *Each one, each.*

quis-quis, no fem., quod-quod, *or* quid-quid, *or* quic-quid, pron. indef. [quis reduplicated] *Whatever, whatsoever,* person *or* thing.—As Subst.: **a.** Masc.: *Whoever, whosoever.*—**b.** Neut.: *Whatever, whatsoever.*

quō, adv. [for quom, old form of quem, masc. acc. sing. of qui, "who, which"] *To which place or spot, whither.*

quŏd, conj. [adverbial acc. neut. sing. of qui] **1.** *In that, because, inasmuch as.*—**2.** *That.*

quō mŏdŏ (v. 599), the abl. cases of qui and modus respectively. The final syllable of the adv. quōmŏdŏ is always short, and hence it cannot there be that word, used in tmesis.

quon-dam, adv. [for quom-dam; fr. quom, old form of quem, masc. acc. sing. of qui; suffix dam] **1.** *At one time, once on a time, formerly.*—**2.** *At some time, sometimes, at any time.*

quŏn-ĭam, conj. [for quom-jam; fr. quom = quum, "since"; jam, "now"] *Since now, since then, since, because.*

quŏque, conj. *Also, too:*—

placed after the word to be emphasized.

quŏt-annis, adv. [quŏt, in force of "all, every, each "; annis, abl. plur. of annus, "a year"] ("In all years, in every year"; hence) *Yearly, annually, in every or each year.*

quō-usque, adv. [for quom-usque; fr. quom, old form of quem, masc. acc. sing. of qui, "what?"; usque, "until"] Of time: *Until what time, till when, how long?*

quum (old form **quom**), relative adv. and causal conj. [for quom = quem, fr. qui, "who"] **1.** Relative Adv.: ("To the time which"; hence) *When.*—**2.** Causal Conj.: ("To the end that *or* which"; hence) *Seeing that, since, as, inasmuch as.*

răb-ĭes, ĭem, ĭe (other cases do not occur), f. [răb-o, "to rave"] ("A raving"; hence) *Rage, fury.*

răd-ĭus, ĭi, m. ("A staff *or* rod"; hence) *A ray or beam* [prob. akin to rād-ix].

răd-ix, īcis, f. ("The increasing, *or* growing, thing"; hence) *A root* of a tree, *etc.* [prob. akin to Sans. root VRIDH, "to increase"].

rādo, rāsi, rāsum, rādĕre, 3. v. a. ("To scrape *or* scratch"; hence) **1.** *To touch in passing, brush along, graze.*—**2.** *To sweep along* in flight through the air.

rā-mus, mi, m. *A bough, branch* [prob. for rad-mus; fr. same root as rād-ix; see rādix].

răp-ĭdus, ĭda, ĭdum, adj. [răp-ĭo, in force of "to hurry onwards"] *Hurrying onwards; swift, rapid.*

răp-ĭo, ŭi, tum, ĕre, 3. v. a.: **1.** *To snatch.*—**2.** *To hurry, or snatch, away.*—**3.** *To carry off forcibly.*—Pass.: **răp-ĭor**, tus

I

sum, i [akin to Gr. ἁρπ-άζω, "to snatch," etc.].
raptus, a, um, P. perf. pass. of răpĭo.
răpŭi, perf. ind. of răpĭo.
rătis, is, f. ("A float, raft"; hence) *A bark, vessel, ship* [prob. akin to rēmus].
rau-cus, ca, cum, adj. Of things: *Hoarse, hollow-sounding,* etc. [prob. akin to Sans. root ᴙᴜ, "to utter a (particular) sound"].
rĕ-cēdo, cessi, cessum, cēdĕre, 3. v. n. [rĕ, "away"; cēdo, "to go"] ("To go away, depart"; hence) *To vanish, disappear, pass away.*
rĕceptus, a, um, P. perf. pass. of rĕcĭpĭo.
rĕcessi, perf. ind. of rĕcēdo.
rĕ-cĭpĭo, cēpi, ceptum, cĭpĕre, 3. v. a. [for rĕ-căpĭo; fr. rĕ, "again"; căpĭo, "to take"] *To take* or *get again; to receive back.* — Pass.: **rĕ-cĭdĭor,** ceptus sum, cĭpi.
rĕ-condo, condĭdi, condĭtum, condĕre, 3. v. a. [rĕ, "without force"; condo, "to hide"] ("To hide, conceal"; hence) *To render of no account, to cause to be forgotten.*
rec-tor, tōris, m. [for regtor; fr. rĕg-o, "to rule"] ("He who rules"; hence) Of a ship: *A steersman, helmsman, pilot.*
rĕcur-sus, sūs, m. [for rĕcurr-sus; fr. rĕcurr-o, "to run back"] ("A running back"; hence) Of troops: *A retreat.*
rĕ-cūs-o, āvi, ātum, āre, 1. v. a. [for rĕ-caus-ŏ; fr. rĕ, "against"; caus-a, "a cause"] ("To assign a cause against"; hence) *To decline, refuse, shrink from.*
reddĭdi, perf. ind. of reddo.

reddĭtus, a, um, P. perf. pass. of reddo.
red-do, dĭdi, dĭtum, dĕre, 3. v. a. [red (= rĕ, with d for de demonstrative), "back"; do, "to give"] **1.** *To give back, return, restore.*—**2.** Pass. in reflexive force: ("To give one's self back"; *i. e.*) *To return, come back.*—**3.** *To render, yield, give,* —**4.** With second Acc.: *To render,* or *make,* an object that which is denoted by the second Acc.—Pass.: **red-dor,** dĭtus sum, di.
rĕd-ĕo, ĭvi *or* ĭi, ĭtum, īre, v. n. [red, see reddo; ĕo, "to go"] *To go* or *come back; to return.*
rĕdĭisse, perf. inf. of rĕdĕo.
rĕ-dūco, duxi, ductum, dūcĕre, 3. v. a. [rĕ, "back"; dūco, "to lead"] **1.** Of persons: *To lead,* or *bring, back.*—**2.** Of things: *To draw back.*—Pass.: **rĕ-dūcor,** ductus sum, dūci.
rĕductus, a, um, P. perf. pass. of rĕdūco.
rĕdux, rĕdūcis, adj. [for rĕduc-s; fr. rĕdūc-o, "to lead back"] ("Led back"; hence) *Returning, returned, come back;* —at v. 40 supply eos with rĕdūces.
rĕfĕrens, ntis, P. pres. of rĕfĕro.
rĕ-fĕro, (ret-)tŭli, lātum, ferre, v. a. irreg. [rĕ, "back"; fĕro, "to bring"] **1.** *To bring,* or *carry, back.*—**2.** *To give back, return.*—**3.** *To repeat, renew, restore.*
rĕ-fīgo, fixi, fixum, fīgĕre, 3. v. a. [rĕ, denoting "reversal" = "un-,"; fīgo, "to fix"] *To unfix, unfasten, take down, remove.*—Pass.: **rĕ-fīgor,** fixus sum, fīgi.
rĕfixus, a, um, P. perf. pass. of rĕfigo.

VOCABULARY. 115

rēg-ĭus, ia, ium, adj. [rex, rĕg-is, "a king"] **1.** Of, or belonging to, a king; royal.—**2.** Of royal birth or descent.

reg-num, ni, n. [rĕg-o, "to rule"] ("That which rules"; hence, "rule, authority, power"; hence) **1.** A territory, country, etc., as that over which one has power.—**2.** A kingdom.

rĕgo, rexi, rectum, rĕgĕre, 3. v. a. : **1.** To govern, rule.—**2.** Of a ship as Object : To direct, steer, etc. [akin to Sans. root RĀJ, "to govern"].

rējĕci, perf. ind. of rējĭcĭo.

rējectans, ntis, P. pres. of rējecto.

rējec-to, tāvi, tātum, tāre, 1. v. a. intens. [for rējac-to; fr. rējĭcĭo, "to throw back," through root RĔJAC (i.e. rĕ; JAC, root of jăc-ĭo] To keep throwing back or up.

rē-jĭcĭo, jĕci, jectum, jĭcĕre, 3. v. a. [for rĕ-jăcĭo; fr. rĕ, "back"; jăcĭo, "to cast"] To cast, throw, or fling back.

rĕlictus, a, um, P. perf. pass. of rĕlinquo.

rē-linquo, liqui, lictum, linquĕre, 3. v. a. [rĕ, "without force"; linquo, "to leave"] **1.** To leave or quit.—**2.** To leave behind, leave.—**3.** To give up, resign, leave.—**4.** To forsake, abandon. — Pass. : **rĕlinquor,** lictus sum. linqui.

rĕlīqui, perf. ind. of rĕlinquo.

rĕlīqu-ĭae (quadrisyll.), iārum, f. plur. [poetical form of rĕlīqu-ĭae; fr. rĕlinquo, "to leave behind," through root RĔLIQU (i.e. rĕ; LIQU, root of linquo)] ("The things left behind"; hence) The relics, remains, remnant, remainder of anything, etc.

rē-mētĭor, mensus sum, mētīri, 4. v. dep. [rĕ, "back or again"; mētĭor, "to measure"] ("To measure back or again"; hence) To trace back.

rēmex, ĭgis, m. [= rēmeg-s; for rēmig-s; fr. rēmĭg-o, "to row"] ("A rower"; hence) Sing. in collective force : Rowers.

rēmĭg-ĭum, ĭi, n. [rēmĭg-o, "to row"] A rowing.

rĕmissus, a, um, P. perf. pass. of rĕmitto.

rē-mitto, misi, missum, mittĕre, 3. v. a. [rĕ, "back"; mitto] **1.** [mitto, "to allow to go"] **a.** To allow to go back.— **b.** To give up, surrender, forego. — **2.** [mitto, "to send"] To send back.

rē-nāns, ntis, m. ... [prob. for re-nans; akin to ... rowing thing"; fr. ... row," through root ...]

reor, ratus sum, ... [found, 3. v. dep. ("To reckon"; hence) To suppose, imagine;—at v. 34 foll. by Objective clause.

rēpent-ē, adv. [rĕpens, repente, "sudden"] Suddenly, on a sudden.

rē-pĕrĭo, pĕri, pertum, pĕrīre, 4. v. a. [for rĕ-părĭo pēr- ... "again"; pārĭo, "to produce"] ("To produce again"; hence) **1.** To find or meet with.—**2.** To find out, discover.

rē-plĕo, plēvi, plētum, plēre, 2. v. a. [rĕ, "without ... "; plĕo, "to fill"] To fill up.—Pass. : **re-plĕor,** plētus sum, plēri.

replētus, a, um, P. perf. pass. of replĕo.

rē-pōno, pŏsŭi, pŏsĭtum, pōnĕre, 3. v. a. [rĕ; pōno, "to put or place"] **1.** [rĕ, "again"] ("To put, or place, again"; hence) To replace, restore, renew.—**2.** [rĕ, "aside or away"] To

I 2

VOCABULARY.

rĕ-quĭes, quĭētis and quĭēi, f. [rĕ, "without force"; quies, "rest"] *Rest, repose, respite,* etc.

rēs, rĕi, f. ("That which is spoken of"; hence) **1.** *A material thing, an object,* etc.—**2.** *A thing, matter, event, affair, circumstance.*—**3.** *Property, possessions* [akin to Gr. ῥέ-ω, "to say or speak"].

rĕsēdi, perf. ind. of rĕ-sīdo.

rĕ-servo, servāvi, servātum, servāre, 1. v. a. [rĕ, "back"; servo, "to keep"] *To keep back, reserve.*

rĕ-sīdo, sēdi, no sup., sīdĕre, 3. v. n. [rĕ, "without force"; sido, "to seat one's self"] **1.** *To seat one's self, sit down, take one's seat.*—**2.** *To settle, fix one's,* etc., *abode.*

rĕ-sŏno, sŏnāvi, no sup., sŏnāre, 1. v. n. [rĕ, "back again"; sono, "to sound"] ("To sound back again"; hence) *To resound, re-echo.*

rēspĭcĭens, ntis, P. pres. of rēspĭcĭo.

rĕ-spĭcĭo, spexi, spectum, spĭcĕre, 3. v. n. [for rĕ-spĕcĭo; fr. rĕ, "back"; spĕcĭo, "to look at"] **1.** *To look back at or upon.*—**2.** *To see behind one, at one's back or in one's rear;*—at v. 666 folld. by Objective clause.

respon-sum, si, n. [for raspond-sum; fr. respond-ĕo, "to answer"] ("An answer, reply"; hence) Of a priest, soothsayer, *etc.: An oracular response, oracle,* etc.

rĕstinctus, a, um, P. perf. pass. of rĕstinguo;—at v. 698 supply est wifa restinctus.

rĕ-stinguo, stinxi, stinctum, stinguĕre, 3. v. a. [rĕ, "without force"; stinguo, "to extinguish"] *To extinguish, put out, quench.*—Pass.: r stinguor, stinctus sui stingui.

rĕsul-to, tāvi, tātum, tār 1. v. n. [for rĕsal-to; fr. rĕsīl (*i. e.* rĕsălio), "to leap back, through root RESAL (= re; sa root of sălĭo)] ("To leap, spring, back"; hence) *To r verberate, re-echo, resoun t.*

rĕ-tĕgo, texi, tectum, tĕg ĕre, 3. v. a. [rĕ, denoting "r versal"; tĕgo, "to cover" ("To uncover"; hence) *To di close, make visible, show, reveal.*

rĕten-to, tāvi, tātum, tār 1. v. a. intens. [rĕtĭnĕo (*i.* rĕtĕnĕo), "to hold back, through root RETEN (= re; TE root of tĕnĕo)] *To hold,* or *keep back;*—at v. 278 supply ĕu (= serpentem) after rĕtentat.

rĕtexĕrim, perf. subj. rĕtĕgo.

rĕ-tĭnĕo, tĭnŭi, tentun tĭnēre, 2. v. a. [for rĕ-tĕnĕo; r rĕ, "back"; tĕnĕo, "to hold" *To hold,* or *keep, back; to detai restruin;*—at v. 669 supply ĕu as nearer Object.

re-trăho, traxi, tractun trăhĕre, 3. v. a. [rĕ, "back" trăho, "to draw"] *To draw, drag, back.*

re-tro, adv. [rĕ, "back" *Back, backwards;*—at v. 428 th e is short.

rettŭli, perf. ind. of rĕfĕr

rĕ-us, i, m. [rēs, rĕ-i, force of "a law-suit, an actio at law"] ("One pertaining t res"; hence, "one under a obligation to do or pay some thing"; hence, in figurativ force) With Gen.: *One answei able,* or *responsible, for some* thing; *a debtor with respect* something:—voti reus, (a debt with respect to, *i. e.*) bound by m vow, v. 237.

VOCABULARY. 117

rĕ-vello, velli, vulsum, vellĕre, 3. v. a. [rĕ, "away"; vello, "to pluck"] *To pluck away; to tear off or away.* — Pass.: **rĕ-vellor,** vulsus sum, velli.

rĕ-vertor, versus sum, verti, 3. v. dep. n. [rĕ, "back"; 'vertor (pass. of verto, in reflexive force), "to turn one's self," etc.] *To turn one's self, etc., back; to return, go back again.*

rĕvŏcātus, a, um, P. perf. pass. of rĕvŏco.

rĕ-vŏco, vŏcāvi, vŏcātum, vŏcāre, 1. v. a.: **1.** [rĕ, "back"; vŏco, "to call"] *To call back, recall;*—at v. 476 in figurative force.—**2.** [rĕ, "again"; vŏco, "to call out"] *To call out again or repeatedly, to keep calling out;* —at v. 167 followed by clause (quò ... Menœte) as Object.— Pass.: **rĕ-vŏcor,** ātus sum, āri.

rĕvŏlūtus, a, um, P. perf. pass. of rĕvolvo.

rĕ-volvo, volvi, vŏlūtum, volvĕre, 3. v. a. [rĕ, "back"; volvo, "to roll"] ("To roll back"; hence) Pass. in reflexive force: *To roll one's self back;* i. e. *to roll, fall,* or *sink backwards.*—Pass.: **rĕ-volvor,** vŏlūtus sum, volvi.

rĕvŏmens, ntis, P. pres. of rĕvŏmo.

rĕ-vŏmo, vŏmŭi, no sup., vŏmĕre, 3. v. a. [rĕ, "again"; vŏmo, "to vomit up"] *To vomit, or throw up, again.*

rĕvulsus, a, um, P. perf. pass. of rĕvello.

rex, rēgis, m. [for reg-s; fr. rĕg-o, "to rule"] ("He who rules"; hence) *A king:*—rex Olympi, *the king of Olympus,* i. e. Jupiter. v. 533.

Rhœtē-ĭus, ĭa, ĭum, adj. [Rhœtē-um, 'Rhœtēum," a

town and promontory of the Troad country. The town is now supposed to be represented by "Paleo Castro," and the promontory is called "Intepeh"] *Of, or belonging to, Rhœteum; Rhœtean.*

rīdĕo, rīsi, rīsum, rīdēre, 2. v. n. and a.: **1.** Neut.: *To laugh.*—**2.** Act.: *To laugh at* [prob. akin to Bœotian κρίδδω = γελάω].

rig-ĕo, ŭi, no sup., ēre, 2. v. n. *To be stiff* [akin to Gr. ῥῖγ-έω].

rīsi, perf. ind. of rīdĕo.

rīte, adv. [adverbial abl. of obsol. ritis = ritus, "a rite"; hence, "a custom," *etc.*] ("According to custom *or* usage," *etc.*; hence) *Duly, rightly, aright.*

rī-vus, vi, m. ("That which flows"; hence) ("A stream" of water, "a brook"; hence) Of perspiration: *A stream* [akin to Gr. ῥέ-ω; Sans. root sru, "to flow"].

rō-bur, bŏris, n. ("The strong thing"; hence, "an oak-tree, oak"; hence, as made of oak) *The beams,* or *timbers,* of a ship.

Rōma, æ, f. *Rome; a city of central Italy, on the banks of the Tiber, the capital of the Roman Empire.*—Hence, **Rōm-ānus,** āna, ānum, adj. *Of, or belonging to, Rome; Roman* [usually considered akin to ῥώμη, "strength"; but perhaps connected with ῥέ-ω, "to flow"; ῥεῦ-μα, "a stream *or* river"; akin to Sans. root sru, "to flow"; and so, "The stream- or river-city"].

Rōmānus, a, um; see Rōma.

rōs, rōris, m. ("Dew"; hence) *Moisture* of any kind falling in drops [prob. akin to

Gr. δρόσ-ος, and έρσ-η; also to Sans. ras-a, "water, juice"; fr. root VRISH, "to rain, to moisten"].

ros-trum, tri, n. [for rod-trum; fr. rōd-o, "to gnaw"] "The accomplisher of gnawing"; hence, "a bill *or* beak" of animals; hence) Of a ship: *The beak,* or *projecting prow.*

rōta, æ, f. *A wheel* [akin to Sans. *rutha,* "a car or chariot"].

rūdens, ntis, m.: **1.** *A rope, line, cord.*—**2.** Plur.: *The cordage,* or *rigging,* of a vessel.

rumpo, rūpi, ruptum, rumpĕre, 3. v. a. *To break, burst* [root RUP, akin to Sans. root LUP, "to break"].

rŭ-o, i, tum, ĕre, 3. v. n. ("To fall with violence, fall down"; hence) *To rush.*

rūp-es, is, f. [ru(m)p-o, "to break," through root RUP] ("The broken, *or* rent, thing"; hence) *A steep rock; a rock* in general.

rūpi, perf. ind. of rumpo.

rursus, adv. [contr. fr. rĕversus, "turned back"] ("Back, backwards"; hence) *Back again; again, anew, afresh.*

săc-er, ra, rum, adj. *Sacred, consecrated, holy.*—As Subst.: **sacr-um,** i, n.: **a.** *A sacred,* or *holy, thing.*—**b.** *A sacred rite,* etc. [root SAC, akin to Gr. ἅγ-ιος, "holy"; Sans. root YAJ, "to worship" (the deities)].

săcer-dō-s, dōtis, comm. gen. [for săcer-da-(t)s; fr. sacer, sac(e)r-i; DA, root of do, "to give"] ("One given, *or* giving himself, *etc.,* to sacred things"; hence) **1.** *A priest.*—**2.** *A priestess.*

sa-cro, āvi, ātum, āre, 1. v. a. [săcer, sacr-i, "sacred"] ("To make sacred"; hence) *To consecrate, dedicate,* etc.

sacrum, i; see săcer.

saep-e, adv. [obsol. saep-is, "frequent"] *Frequently, often, oftentimes.*

saev-ĭo, ĭi, ītum, īre, 4. v. n. [saev-us, "fierce"] ("To be fierce"; hence) **1.** *To rage, be furious.*—**2.** Of the barking of dogs: *To be furious, to rise furiously.*

saevus, a, um: **1.** *Fierce, raging, furious.*—**2.** Of things: *Cruel, fell, terrible.*

Sagăris, is, m. *The Sagaris,* called also *the Sangarius* (now the *Sacaria* or *Ayala*); a river flowing through Phrygia and Bithynia, and falling into the Pontus Euxinus (the Euxine or Black Sea) [Σάγαρις (supposed to be of Persian origin), "Bill-hook"].

săgitta, æ, f. *An arrow, shaft.*

săl, sălis, m. (rarely n.) ("Salt"; hence) *The salt water, the sea, the briny ocean* [akin to Gr. ἅλς, ἁλ-ος, and Sans. *sar-as*].

Sălĭus, ĭi, m. *Salius;* an Acarnanian, who contended in the foot-race at the funeral games of Anchises [Σάλιος].

sal-sus, sa, sum, adj. [sal, "salt"] *Salt, briny.*

sălū-s, tis, f. [for salv-ts; fr. salv-ĕo, "to be well *or* in good health"] ("The being well *or* in good health"; hence, "health"; hence) *Safety.*

salvē, salvēte; see salvĕo.

salv-ĕo, no perf. nor sup., ēre, 2. v. n. [salv-us, "well, sound" in health] **1.** *To be well,* or *sound* in health.—**2.** As a mode of salutation: Imperat. pres.: **salvē, salvēte,** *Hail (thou* or *you,* according to number of verb).

sanc-tus, ta, tum, adj

VOCABULARY. 119

[sanc-io, "to render, *or* make, sacred"; hence) *Sacred, venerable.*

sanguis, guinis, m.: **1.** *Blood:*—sanguine sacro, v. 77; Abl. of quality [§ 125, a];—at vv. 77 and 736 of the blood of sacrificial victims.—**2.** *Race, stock, family* [akin to Sans. *asan* or *asanj*].

săt-ĭs, adv.: **1.** *Sufficiently, enough.*—**2.** Used as indecl. adj.: *Sufficient, enough;* v. 786 [root SAT, whence săt-ĭo, "to satisfy"; akin to ἀδ-έω, "to be sated"].

Sāturn-ĭus, ĭa, ĭum, adj. [Sāturn-us, "Saturn"; an ancient king of Latium, who was deified, and early regarded as identical with the Greek god Κρόνος] *Of,* or *belonging to, Saturn; Saturnian;*—at v. 606 applied to Juno as the daughter of Saturn.

sătŭr-o, ăvi, ătum, āre, 1. v. a. [sătur, "full of food, sated"] ("To make *satur*"; hence) *To satisfy, appease, assuage;*—at v. 606 in Pass folld. by Acc. of "Respect" [§ 100].—Pass.: **sătŭr-or,** ātus sum, āri.

sătus, a, um, P. perf. pass. of sĕro.

saxum, i, n.: **1.** *A large rough stone; a fragment of rock.*—**2.** *A rock.*

scĕlus, ĕris, n. *A wicked deed; wickedness, guilt.*

scĭo, scīvi and scĭi, scītum, scīre, 4. v. a. *To know.*

scīrem, imperf. subj. of scio.

scŏpŭlus, i, m. *A projecting point of rock; a rock, cliff, crag* [Gr. σκόπελος, "a look-out place"].

Scylla, æ, f. *Scylla;* the name of one of the ships in the fleet of Æneas. It was named, probably, after Scylla, the daughter of Phorcys, transformed by Circe into a sea-monster, the upper part of whose body was that of a maiden, the lower part that of a fish, while dogs surrounded her waist. The poets seem to have considered that there were several monsters of this kind; whence at times the use of the plur. number [Σκύλλα, "The Render *or* Tearer," *i. e.* one who rends *or* tare her prey].

sē (reduplicated **sĕsē**), acc. and abl. of pron. sŭi.

sĕcĭus; see sĕcus.

sĕco, ŭi, tum, āre, 1. v. a. ("To cut"; hence) *To cut through the waters; i. e.* **a.** Of persons or ships: (a) *To sail rapidly through.*—(b) *To fly swiftly through.*—**b.** Of fishes: *To swim rapidly through.*

sēcrē-tus, a, um, adj. [sē-cerno, "to separate," through root SECRE (= sē; CRE, a root of cerno) ("Separated"; hence) *Of persons: Secret, apart, withdrawn.*

sĕcŭi, perf. ind. of sĕco.

sēcum = cum sē; see cum.

sĕc-undus, unda, undum, adj. [the sequ-undus; fr. sĕqu-or, "to follow"] ("Following"; hence) **1.** Of the wind: *Fair, favourable,* as following the course of the vessel.—**2.** *Favourable, propitious.*—**3.** *Favouring, showing or manifesting favour or good will.*—**4.** In order: *Second.*

sĕc-us, adv. [prob. for sĕqu-us; fr. sĕqu-or, "to follow"] ("Following"; hence, "less than" something before mentioned; hence) In comp. with a negative: *Not or none the less, nevertheless.* ☞ Comp.: sĕcĭus.

sĕd, conj. [same word as sed = sine, "without"] ("A-

VOCABULARY.

part from, setting aside"; hence) *But :*—sed enim, *but indeed, but in truth,* v. 395.
sĕdĕo, sĕdi, sessum, sĕdēre, 2. v. n. ("To sit"; hence) **1.** *To be encamped.*—**2.** *To be settled, fixed, determined on,* etc., in the mind [akin to Gr. ἕζομαι (= ἕδσομαι), Sans. root SAD, "to sit"].
sĕd-es, is, f. [sĕd-ĕo, "to sit"] ("That on which one sits"; hence, "a seat"; hence) **1.** *A dwelling-place, abode.*—**2.** Of a deity : *A temple,* as if a place of residence.
sĕd-ĭle, ilis, n. [id.] ("A thing pertaining to sitting"; hence) *A seat, bench,* etc.
segnis, e, adj. *Slow, tardy, sluggish.*
sēmĭ-nĕc-ĭs (Nom. not found), adj. [sĕmĭ, "half"; nex, nĕc-is, "death"] ("Having half death"; *i. e*) *Half-dead, half-killed.*
sem-per, adv. *Ever, always, at all times* [akin to Sans. *sam-a,* in force of "all"].
sĕm-us-tus, ta, tum, adj. [another form of sĕmĭ-us-tus; for sĕmĭ-ur-tus; fr. sĕm-ĭ, "half"; ūr-o, "to burn"] *Half-burned, half-burnt.*
sĕnect-a, æ, f. [sĕnect-us, "old"] *Old age.*
sĕnec-tus, tūtis, f. [for sĕnic-tus; fr. sĕnex, (old gen.) sĕnĭc-ĭs, "old"] ("The state, or condition, of the *senex*"; hence) *Old age.*
sĕnes, um, plur. of sĕnex.
sĕn-ex, is (originally ĭcis), adj. [sĕn-ĕo, "to be old"] *Old, aged, full of years.*—As Subst. m. : *An old man.* ☞ Comp. : sĕn-ior.
sē-ni, næ, na, num. distrib. adj. [for sex-ni; fr. sex, "six"] ("Six each *or* apiece"; hence) *Six.*

sĕnĭor, no neut., comp. of sĕnex ;—often to be rendered *old, aged.*—As Subst. : *An elder, an elderly person, an old man.*
sensi, perf. ind. of sentio.
sentent-ĭa, iæ, f. [for sentient-ĭa; fr. sentiens, sent-ĭent-is, "thinking"] ("A thinking *or* way of thinking"; hence) **1.** *An opinion.*—**2.** *A determination, purpose.*
sentĭo, sensi, sensum, sentīre, 4. v. a. : **1.** *To be sensible of, to perceive,* something.—**2.** With Objective clause : *To be sensible,* or *perceive, that,* etc.
sept-em, num. adj. indecl. *Seven* [akin to Gr. ἑπτ-ά; Sans. *sapt-an*].
sept-ēnus, ēna, ēnum, num. distrib. adj. [sept-em, "seven"] ("Seven each *or* apiece"; hence) *Seven.*
sept-ĭmus, ĭma, ĭmum, num. ord. adj. [id.] *Seventh.*
sĕqu-ax, ācis, adj. [sĕqu-or, "to follow"] ("Prone to follow"; hence) *Pursuing, chasing,* etc.
sĕquendi, Gerund in di fr. sĕquor.
sĕquens, ntis, P. pres. of sĕquor ;—at v. 227 supply ĕum (= Clŏanthum) with sĕquentem.
sĕqu-or, ūtus sum, i, 3. v. dep. a. and n. : **1.** *To follow,* in fullest sense of the word.—**2.** With accessory notion of hostility : *To follow after, pursue, chase.*—**3.** *To come next* or *after.*—**4.** *To go to,* or *towards,* a place [akin to Gr. ἕπ-ομαι, Sans. root SACH].
sĕquūtus, a, um, P. perf. of sĕquor ;—at v. 296 supply est with sĕquūtus.
sĕr-ēnus, a, um, adj. ("Glittering"; hence) *Fair, bright, calm, serene* [akin to Sans. root SUR, "to glitter"].

Sĕrestus, i, m. *Serestus;* a Trojan, who commanded one of the ships in the fleet of Æneas; vv. 487-9.

Sergestus, i, m. *Sergestus;* a Trojan, who commanded "The Centaur" at the funeral games held in honour of Anchises. From him, according to Virgil, the Sergian house, or family, at Rome were descended.

(1. **Sergĭus,** ĭi, m. "Sergius"; the name of a Roman house or family.—Hence) **Sergĭ-us,** a, um, adj. *Of, or belonging to, the Sergii; Sergian;* see Sergestus.

2. **Sergĭus,** a, um; see 1. Sergius.

sĕro, sēvi, sătum, sĕrĕre, 3. v. a.: **1.** Of a father: *To beget.*—**2.** P. perf. pass. with Abl. of Origin [§ 123]: ("Begotten by"; hence) *Sprung from:* — sătus Anchisā = Æneas, vv. 244, 424. — Pass. **sĕror,** sătus sum, sĕri [akin to Sans. root SU, "to beget"].

serpens, ntis, P. pres. of serpo.—As Subst. m. or f. ("A creeping thing"; *i. e.*) *A snake, serpent.*

serp-o, si, tum, ĕre, 3. v. n. *To creep, crawl* [Gr. ἕρπω].

sērus, a, um, adj.: **1.** *Late.* —**2.** *Too late.*

serva, æ, f. ("She who is dragged away *or* taken captive"; hence) *A female slave* [Gr. ἐρύ-ω].

servātus, a, um. P. perf. pass. of servo;—at v. 699 supply sunt with servātæ.

serv-o, āvi, ātum, āre, 1. v. a. ("To drag away" from an enemy, *etc.*; hence) **1.** *To save, preserve, protect, keep unharmed.*—**2.** *To give heed to, observe,* etc.—**3.** *To dwell in, inhabit,* etc.—Pass.: **serv-or,** ātus sum, āri [Gr. ἐρύ-ω].

sēse; see sē.
seu; see sive.
sī, conj.: **1.** *If.*—**2.** *Nearly in the force of* ut *or* quum: *When* [Gr. εἰ].

sĭbĭ, dat. sing. of pers. pron. sŭi;—at v. 61 the final i is short.

sĭbĭl-us, a, um, adj. [sibilo, "to hiss"] *Hissing;*—only found in form sibila.

Sĭ-bȳl-la, læ. f. ("A female soothsayer *or* prophetess"; esp.) *The Cumæan Sibyl* (the prophetess of Apollo at Cumæ on the coast of Campania in Italy) who was to accompany Æneas in his descent to the lower world; v. 735. This descent is described by Virgil in Æneid, Bk. 6 [Σίβυλλα, Doric form Σίβολλα = either Θε-βούλ-η (θε-ός, "a god"; βούλ-η, "counsel"), "a god's counsel"; or Δι-βούλ-η (Δι-ός, Gen. of Ζεύς, "Jove"; βούλ-η, "counsel"), "Jove's counsel"].

sĭ-c, adv. [for si-ce; akin to pronominal root HI found in hic, is, *etc.*; with suffix ce] **1.** *In this way, in such a way, so, thus.*—**2.** *In the foregoing way, thus.*—**3.** *In the following way, as follows.*

(**Sĭcāni,** ōrum, m. plur. "The Sicani"; a very ancient people of Italy on the Tiber, a portion of whom migrated to Sicily.—Hence) **Sĭcān-us,** a, um, adj. ("Of, *or* belonging to, the Sicani; Sicanian"; hence) *Sicilian.*—As Subst.: **Sĭcāni,** ōrum, m. plur. *The people of Sicily, the Sicilians.*

sicc-us, a, um, adj. *Dry* [akin to Sans. root CUSH, "to become dry"].

sī-cŭbĭ, adv. [sĭ, "if"; cŭbi (=ŭbi), "where"] *If anywhere, wheresoever.*

Sĭcŭl-us, a, um, adj.

[**Sĭcŭl-i**, "the Siculi, *or* Sicilians"] ("Of, *or* belonging to, the Siculi"; hence) *Sicilian*, *Sicilian*.

Sĭdōn-ĭus, ĭa, ĭum, adj. [Sidon, Sĭdōn-ĭs, "Sidon" (now "Said *or* Saida"), the most celebrated city of Phœnicia on the borders of the Holy Land, and the mother-city of Tyre] *Of, or belonging to, Sidon; Sidonian*.

sĭd-us, ĕris. n. ("Shape, form"; hence) **1.** *A star.*—**2.** Sts. in plur.: *The stars for the heavens, the sky;* v. 256 [Gr. εἶδ-ος].

sign-o, āvi, ātum, āre, 1. v. a. [sign-um, "a mark"] ("To set a mark upon"; hence) **1.** *To mark.*—**2.** *To mark out, note, observe*, etc.

signum, i, n.: **1.** *A mark, token, or sign.*—**2.** *A signal.*—**3.** *A figure* in relief on silver plate, etc.

sĭl-ĕo, ŭi, no sup., ēre, 2. v. n. Of things: *To be still or noiseless.*

silv-a, æ, f. *A wood* [Gr. ὕλF-η].

sĭm-ĭlis, īle, adj. With Dat. or Gen. [§ 106, (1); Notes to Syntax, p. 136, *E*]: *Like, similar to* [akin to Gr. ὅμ-οιος; and Sans. *sam-a*, in force of "like"].

Sĭmŏīs, entis (Acc. Sĭmŏenta, vv. 261, 634, 803), m. *The Simois* (now *Mendes*); a small river of Troas in Asia Minor, falling into the Scamander [Gr. Σιμόεις].

sĭm-ul, adv. *At the same time, together* [akin to Gr. ὅμ-οιος; Sans. *sam-a*].

sĭmŭlā-crum, cri, n. [sĭmŭl(a)-o, "to make like"] ("That which is made like" any object; hence, "a likeness, *image*"; hence) *A shadow, semblance, appearance:*—pugnæ simulācra, *semblances of a battle,* i. e. *sham-battles,* v. 585; so, belli simulacra, v. 674.

1. **sĭne**, pres. imperat. of sino; vv. 163, 717.

2. **sĭne**, prep. gov. abl. [akin to sē, "apart"] **1.** *Without.*—**2.** In poetry often used in combination with a noun in the place of an adj. containing the reverse of the meaning to such noun:—sine honore, *dishonoured,* v. 272.

sĭnes, 2. pers. sing. fut. ind. of sino.

sĭnister, tra, trum, adj. *Left,* i. e. *on the left hand or side.* —As Subst.: **sĭnistra**, æ, f. *The left hand* or *side*.

sĭnistra, æ; see sinister.

sĭno, sĭvi, sĭtum, sĭnĕre, 3. v. a. *To permit, allow, suffer;* —at vv. 163, 717 follld. by simple Subj., ut being understood [§ 154].

sĭnus, ūs, m. ("A bent surface, a curve," *etc.;* hence) **1.** *A bay, harbour, gulf.*—**2.** *The belly* or *bend of a sail.*

sī-quis, no fem., quid, indef. pron. subst. [si, "if"; quis, "any one," *etc.*] *If any one* or *anybody; if anything.*

Sīrēnes, um, f. plur. *The Sirens;* birds with the faces of maidens, having their habitation on the S. coast of Italy. By the peculiar sweetness of their voices they enticed on shore those who were sailing by, and then killed them:— Sirēnum scopŭli, *the rocks of the Sirens,* the name of three rocky islets off the S.W. coast of Campania, between Surrentum and Capreæ, v. 864.

sī-ve (contr. **seu**), conj. [si, "if"; ve, "or"] *Or if.*

1. **sŏc-ĭus**, ĭi (Gen. Plur. sŏcĭûm for socĭōrum, v. 174), m.

VOCABULARY.

A friend, companion, comrade [akin to Sans *sakh-i*].
2. sŏcĭ-us, a, um, adj. [1. sŏcĭ-us, "a friend"] *Of, or belonging to, a friend or friends.*
sōl, sōlis, m. *The sun* [akin to Gr. ἥλιος; Sans. *svar*].
sōlā-tĭum, ĭi, n. [sōl(a)- or, "to console"] *Consolation, comfort, solace;*—at v. 367 in plur.
sōlātus, a, um, P. perf. of sōlor.
sŏl-ĕo, ĭtus sum, ēre, 2. v. n. semi-dep. *To be wont or accustomed.*
sŏlĭtus, a, um, P. perf. of sŏlĕo;—at v. 370 supply est with sŏlĭtus.
soll-enn-is, e, adj. [for soll-ann-is; fr. soll-us (= totus), "whole, complete"; ann-us, "a year"] ("That takes place when the year is complete"; hence) *Of religious rites, etc.:* **1.** *Yearly, annual.*—**2.** *Stated, appointed, customary.*—**3.** *Religious, festive, solemn.*—As Subst.: **sollenne,** is, n. *A religious or solemn rite; a festival, solemnity, solemn games.*
sōlor, ātus sum, āri, 1. v. dep. *To comfort, solace, console.*
sŏl-um, i, n. [prob. fr. root sol = sed in sĕd-ĕo, "to sit"] ("That on which a thing is seated, placed," etc.; hence) "*the lowest part or bottom" of a thing;* hence) **1.** *The ground, soil.*—**2.** *The water beneath a vessel,* as that which supports it *or* on which it rests; v. 199.
sōlus, a, um (Gen. sōlīus; Dat. sōli), adj.: **1.** *Alone.*—**2.** *The only one who or that.*
solvĕre, 3. pers. plur. perf. ind. of solvo.
so-lvo, lvi, lūtum, lvĕre, 3. v. a. [for sĕ-lŭo; fr. sē, "a-part"; lŭo, "to loosen"] ("To loosen apart"; hence) **1.** *To unloose, untie, unbind.*—**2.** Nautical t. t.: solvĕre fūnem, *(To loose the cable;* i. e.) *To weigh anchor, set sail, put to sea.*—**3.** *To part, separate.*—**4.** Of the effects of sleep, *etc.; To relax, render powerless.*—**5.** Of fear as Object: *To banish, cast off, dismiss,* etc.
somn-ĭum, ĭi, n. [somn-us, "sleep"] ("That which pertains to sleep"; hence) *A dream.*
som-nus, ni, m.: **1.** *Sleep.* —**2.** Personified: *Somnus,* the god of sleep; v. 838 [akin to Gr. ὕπ-νος; Sans. *svap-na,* fr. root svap, "to sleep"].
sŏnans, ntis, P. pres. of sŏno.
sŏn-ĭtus, ĭtūs, m. [sŏn-o, "to sound"] **1.** *A sound.*—**2.** *A noise, crash, din.*
sŏn-o, ŭi, ĭtum, āre, 1. v. n. *To sound, resound* [akin to Sans. root svan, "to sound"].
sŏn-us, i, m. [sŏn-o, "to sound"] ("That which sounds"; hence) *Of the voice: Sound, tone.*
sōp-ĭo, ivi *or* ĭi, ītum, īre, 4. v. a. ("To lull to sleep"; hence) Of things: *To lay to rest, settle, quiet:*—sōpīti ignes, *the fires that had been laid to rest,* i. e. *that had sunk low.*—Pass.:
sōp-ĭor, ītus sum, īri [akin to Sans. root svap, "to sleep"].
sōpītus, a, um, P. perf. pass. of sōpĭo.
sōpōrātus, a, um, P. perf. pass. of sōpōro.
sōpōr-o, āvi, ātum, āre, 1. v. a. [sōpor, sōpōr-is, "sleep"] ("To endue with *sopor*"; hence) *To render, or make, soporific.*—Pass.: **sōpōr-or,** ātus sum, āri.
sors, tis, f.: **1.** *A lot by*

which a thing is determined.—
2. *Lot,* i. e. *fate, destiny, fortune,* etc.

sort-ior, ītus sum, īri, 4. v. dep. [sors, sort-is, "a lot"] *To allot, assign by lot.*

spar-go, si, sum, gĕre, 3. v. a.: **1.** *To strew, scatter.* —**2.** *To bestrew* with something. —**3.** *To spread abroad, spread,* etc.—Pass.: **spar-gor,** sus sum, gi [σπαρ, root of Gr. σπείρω, "to sow"; hence, "to scatter or strew like seed"].

sparsus, a, um, P. perf. pass. of spargo.

spătĭum, ĭi, n.: **1.** *Space, distance, interval;*—at v. 325 plur. for sing.—**2.** *A racecourse* [Gr. στάδιον, Æolic form of στάδιον].

spec-to, tāvi, tātum, tāre, 1. v. a. intens. [spĕc-ĭo, "to look at"] *To look at much* or *earnestly; to keep looking at; to gaze at;*—at v. 655 spectāre is the Historic Inf. [§ 140, 2].

spĕcŭlātus, a, um, P. perf. of spĕcŭlor.

spĕcŭl-or, ātus sum, āri, 1. v. dep. [spĕcŭl-a, "a lookout place"] ("To employ a *specula* for" any purpose; hence) *To spy out, descry, catch a sight of.*

spēlunca, æ, f. *A cave, cavern* [Gr. σπήλυγξ].

spērem, pres. subj. of spēro.

spēr-o, āvi, ātum, āre, 1. v. a.: With Inf.: *To hope,* or *expect, to do,* etc. [akin to Sans. root SPṚIH, "to desire, long for"].

spē-s, ĕi (Gen. Dat. and Abl. Plur. only in post-classical writers), f. [for spĕr-s; fr. spĕr-o; as seen by *spĕr-es,* an old Acc. Plur. in one of the earliest Roman writers] *Hope, expectation.*

spĭcŭ-lum, li, n. dim. [for spĭcŏ-lum; fr. spicum (= spīca), uncontr. gen. spicŏ-i, "a point"] ("A small point"; hence, "the point of a missile or weapon"; hence) *A dart, javelin.*

Spīo, ūs, f. *Spio;* a seanymph, one of Neptune's attendants [Gr. Σπειώ, "She of the cavern or grotto; Cavernnymph, Grotto-nymph"].

spīr-ĭtus, ĭtūs, m. [spīr-o, "to breathe"] ("A breathing"; hence) *Spirit, energy,* etc.; *a majestic,* or *dignified, bearing.*

spīro, āvi, ātum, āre, 1. v. n. *To breathe, blow.*

spissus, a, um, adj. *Thick, dense.*

spŏlĭātus, a, um, P. perf. pass. of spŏlĭo.

spŏlĭ-o, āvi, ātum, āre, 1. v. a. [spŏlĭ-um, "that which is stripped off"] ("To strip, or deprive, of covering"; hence) **1.** *To spoil, strip, rifle.*—**2.** With Abl. [§ 119, *b*]: *To deprive,* or *bereave, of; to despoil* or *strip of.*—Pass.: **spŏlĭ-or,** ātus sum, āri.

spŏlĭ-um, ĭi, n. ("That which is stripped off"; hence) **1.** *Arms, armour,* etc., stripped off a fallen foe.—**2.** *Spoil, booty, plunder* [Gr. σκύλ-λω, "to strip, flay"].

spond-ĕo, spŏpondi, sponsum, spondēre, 2. v. a. (Law and Mercantile t. t., in bargains, etc.: "To covenant, to pledge one's self"; hence) Without Object: *To promise solemnly, to make a solemn promise;* v. 18.

spūmans, ntis, P. pres. of spūmo.

spūm-o, āvi, ātum, āre, 1. v. n. [spūm-a, "foam"] *To foam.*

squā-ma, mæ, f.: *Of a*

snake, *etc.*: **1.** *A scale.*—**2.** Sing. in collective force: *Scales.*
standi, Gerund in di fr. sto.
stans, ntis, P. pres. of sto.
stă-tĭo, tĭōnis, f. [st(a)-o, "to stand"] ("A standing"; hence) *A station, post, spot,* etc.
stel-la, læ, f. [for ster-la; fr. ster-no, "to strew"] ("The strewer" of light; hence) *A star.*
ster-no, strā-vi, strā-tum, ster-nĕre, 3. v. a. ("To spread or stretch out"; hence) **1.** *To spread a thing out flat; to smoothe, level.*—**2.** *To throw down* or *on the ground; to prostrate, fell to the ground.*—Pass.: **ster-nor,** strātus sum, sterni [root STAR, by transposition STRA; akin to Sans. root STRI; Gr. στορ-έννυμι].
stĕti, perf. ind. of sto.
stirps, is, f. (rarely m.) ("The lower part of the trunk" of a tree, *etc.*, including the roots; hence) *A stem, stock, race, lineage;*—at v. 711 Acestes is said to be divinæ stirpis (Gen. of quality [§ 128]), as being the son of the river-god Crimisus.
sto, stĕti, stătum, stăre, 1. v. n. *To stand* [akin to Gr. στά-ω, ἵ-στη-μι; Sans. root STHĀ].
strāvi, perf. ind. of ster-no.
strīdens, ntis, P. pres. of strido.
strīd-o, i, no sup., ĕre, 3. v. n.; and **strīd-ĕo,** i, no sup., ĕre, 2. v. n. (both forms equally in use) ("To make a harsh sound"; hence) Of an arrow: *To whizz* [akin to Gr. τρίζω (= τρίδ-σω)].
stringo, strinxi, strictum, stringĕre, 3. v. a. ("To draw tight"; hence) *To touch lightly*

or *slightly; to graze* [akin to Gr. στράγγω].
structus, a, um, P. perf. pass. of strŭo.
strŭ-o, xi, ctum, ĕre, 3. v. a.: **1.** *To heap,* or *pile, up.*—**2.** *To build, erect, construct.*—Pass.: **strŭ-or,** ctus sum, i [akin to Gr. στορ-έννυμι, Sans. root STRI; see sterno].
stŭd-ĭum, ĭi, n. [stŭd-ĕo, "to be eager"] **1.** *Eagerness, eager desire.*—**2.** *Zeal* for a person; *goodwill, favour,* etc.;—at v. 148 plur. for sing.
stŭpĕ-făcĭo, fēci, factum, făcĕre, 3. v. n. [stŭpĕ-o, "to be astonished"; făcĭo, "to make"] ("To make to be astonished"; hence) *To astound, amaze, astonish.*—Pass.: **stŭpĕ-fīo,** factus sum, fĭĕri.
stŭpĕfactus, a, um, P. perf. pass. of stŭpĕfăcĭo.
stŭp-ĕo, ŭi, no sup., ĕre, 2. v. n. *To be struck aghast; to be amazed* or *astounded* [akin either to Gr. τύπ-τω, "to beat"; Sans. root TUP, "to hurt";—or to Sans. root STUMBH, "to stupefy"].
stuppa, æ, f. *Tow* [Gr. στύππη].
Stygius, a, um, adj. [Styx, Stȳg-is, "The Styx," a river of the lower world] *Of,* or *belonging to, the Styx; Stygian;* v. 855.
sŭb, prep. gov. abl. and acc.: **1.** With Abl.: **a.** *Under, beneath.*—**b.** *Beneath, at;* v. 785.—**c.** *Near, close to;* v. 323.—**2.** With Acc.: **a.** *Under, beneath.*—**b.** *Towards, about;* v. 327.—**c.** *Immediately upon* or *after:*—sub hæc, *immediately upon*—i. e. *in reply to—these things,* v. 394 [akin to Gr. ὑπ-ό; Sans. *up-a*].
sŭbēgi, perf. ind. of sŭbĭgo.
sŭb-ĕo, ivi or ĭi, ĭtum, ire, v. a. and n. [sŭb; ĕo, "to go"] **1.** Act.: **a.** [sŭb, "under"]

(a) *To go,* or *come, under* or *beneath.*—(b) *To enter* a place.—
b. [sŭb, "towards"] *To go towards, to approach.*—**2.** Neut. :
a. [sŭb, "towards"] *To go towards, approach.*—**b.** [sŭb, "under"] *To go under, to enter.*—**c.** [sŭb, "close after"] *To come close after,* or *next ; to follow after.*

sŭb-ĭgo, ēgi, actum, ĭgĕre, 3. v. a. [for sŭb-ăgo; fr. sŭb, "from beneath"; ăgo, "to put in motion"] ("To put in motion from beneath "; hence, "to impel, push on," a vessel, *etc.*; hence) *To compel, force.*

sŭbĭi, perf. ind. of sŭbĕo.

sŭbĭt-o, adv. [sŭbĭt-us, "sudden"] *Suddenly, on a sudden.*

sŭbĭ-tus, ta, tum, adj. [sŭb-ĕo, "to approach stealthily," through root sŭbi (= sŭb; i, root of ĕo, "to go")] ("That approaches, *or* has approached, stealthily"; hence) **1.** *Sudden, unexpected.* — **2.** In adverbial force : *Suddenly, unexpectedly.*

sub-jĭcĭo, jēci, jectum, jĭcĕre, 3. v. a. [for sub-jăcĭo; fr. sŭb, "under"; jăcĭo, "to throw"] With Dat. [§ 106, *a*]: *To throw,* or *cast, under* or *beneath ; to place beneath.*

sublātus, a, um, P. perf. pass. of tollo.

sublīmis, e, adj. *On high, aloft.*

sub-mergo, mersi, mersum, mergĕre, 3. v. a. [sŭb, "beneath"; mergo, "to plunge"] *To plunge,* or *dip, beneath* or *under* something ; *to overwhelm, submerge.*—Pass. : **submergor,** mersus sum, mergi.

submersus, a, um, P. perf. pass. of submergo.

sub-necto, no perf., nexum, nectĕre, 3. v. a. [sŭb, "beneath "; necto, "to bind or tie"]
To bind, tie, or *fasten beneath* or *below.*

subsēdi, perf. ind. of subsīdo.

sub-sīdo, sēdi, sessum, sīdĕre, 3. v. n. [sŭb, "without force"; sīdo, "to sit down"] ("To sit down"; hence) **1.** Of things as Subject : *To sink down; to remain behind.*—**2.** Of the waters, *etc.,* as Subject : *To settle down, become calm, subside.*

sub-trăho, traxi, tractum, trăhĕre, 3. v. a. [sŭb, "from beneath"; trăho, "to draw"] *To draw,* or *draw away, from beneath; to withdraw, etc.*—Pass.: **sub-trăhor,** tractus sum, trăhi.

sŭb-urgĕo, no perf. nor sup., urgēre, 2. v. a. [sŭb, "close to"; urgĕo, "to urge"] *To urge,* or *drive, close to.*

subvectus, a, um, P. perf. pass. of subvĕho.

sub-vĕho, vexi, vectum, vĕhĕre, 3. v. a. [sŭb, "from below"; vĕho, "to carry"] ("To carry from below"; hence) *To carry,* or *bear, aloft.*—Pass. : **sub-vĕhor,** vectus sum, vĕhi.

suc-cēdo, cessi, cessum, cēdĕre, 3. v. n. [for sub-cēdo; fr. sŭb, "towards *or* up to"; cēdo, "to go"] With Dat. [§ 106, *a*]: *To go towards* or *up to ; to approach, draw near to.*

successi, perf. ind. of succēdo.

succes-sus, sūs, m. [for succĕd-sus ; fr. succēd-o, "to succeed"] *A succeeding, success.*

(**sūdes**), is (Nom. Sing. does not occur), f. *A stake,* etc.

sūd-or, ōris, m. [sūd-o, "to sweat"] *Sweat, perspiration.*

sŭes, acc. plur. of sus ; v. 97.

sŭē-sco (in poets dissyll.), vi, tum, scĕre, 3. v. a. [sŭē-o,

VOCABULARY. 127

"to be accustomed"] *To ac-custom, habituate.*

suētus (in poets dissyll.), a, um, P. perf. pass. of suesco: *Accustomed, habituated, wont.*

suf-ficio, fēci, fectum, ficĕre, 3. v. n. [for sub-făcio; fr. sŭb, "under"; făcio, "to make"] ("To make, *or* cause, to be under"; hence, "to furnish, afford, supply"; hence, in neut. force, "to be supplied"; hence) *To suffice, be sufficient.*

1. sŭi, sĭbi, se, pron. pers. sing. and plur. *Of*, etc., *himself, herself, itself, themselves.*

2. sŭi, ōrum; see sŭus.

sulc-o, āvi, ātum, āre, 1. v. a. [sulc-us, "a furrow"] *To furrow, plough*, i. e. of a ship, *to pass through, sail over.*

sulcus, i, m. *A furrow*;—at v. 142 applied to *the track* of vessels through the water [Gr. ὁλκός].

sum, fŭi, esse, v. n.: **1.** *To be.*—**2.** With Dat. [§ 107, c]: *To be to* one; *i. e.* with the Lat. Dat. used in Eng. as Subject, *to have* [in pres. tenses akin to ἐσ-μί = εἰ-μί, and to Sans. root AS, "to exist, to be"; in Perf. tenses akin to φύ-ω, φύ-μι, and Sans. root BHÛ, "to be"].

sūme, pres. imperat. of sūmo.

summum, i; **summus**, a, um; see sŭpĕrus.

sū-mo, mpsi, mptum, mĕre, 3. v. a. [contr. fr. sŭb-ĕmo; fr. sŭb, "up"; ĕmo, "to take"] *To take up, take*;—at v. 533 supply ĕā (= mūnĕra) after sūme.

sŭper, adv. and prep.: **1.** Adv.: **a.** *Above.*—**b.** *Besides, moreover.*—**2.** Prep. gov. Acc. *Above, over* [al-in to Gr. ὑπέρ].

sŭpĕrandus, a, um, Gerundive of sŭpĕro.

sŭpĕrans, ntis, P. pres. of sŭpĕro:—superans animis, *sur-passing in a haughty spirit*, i. e. *highly elated*, v. 473.

sŭper-bus, ba, bum, adj. [sŭper, "above"] ("That is above others; hence) **1.** *Proud, haughty, elated.*—**2.** *Distinguished, illustrious*, etc.

sŭpĕresse, pres. inf. of sŭpersum.

sŭpĕri, ōrum; see sŭpĕrus.

sŭpĕr-o, āvi, ātum, āre, 1. v. n. and a. [sŭper, "over"] **1.** Neut.: ("To go over, surmount"; hence) **a.** *To have the upper hand; to be, or prove, superior.*—**b.** *To abound, or surpass, in something.*—**c.** *To remain, or be left*, out of a certain number.—**d.** *To survive.*—**2.** Act.: **a.** *To go past, or beyond; to pass by.*—**b.** *To overcome, conquer*—iterum superare priorem, to acquire the first place, i. e. to obtain the first place by conquering.—**c.** *To get the better of, surpass, subdue.*

sŭper-sum, fŭi, esse, v. n. [sŭper, "over and above"; sum, "to be"] ("To be over and above"; hence) *To remain, to be left as a remainder.*

sŭpĕr-us, a, um, adj. [sŭper, "above"] **1.** Pos.: *That is above, or on high.*—As Subst.: **sŭpĕri**, ōrum, m. plur. *The gods above, the celestial deities.*—**2.** Sup.: **a. suprēmus**, a, um; ("Highest"; hence) In time or succession: *Latest, last, final.*—**b. summus**, a, um: (a) Locally: (α) *Highest, loftiest.*—As Subst.: **summum**, i, n. *The highest place or part*; v. 180.—(β) *The top, or highest part, of that to which it is in attribution.*—(b) In degree: *Highest, greatest, utmost.*

supplex, lcis, adj. *Suppliant.*—As Subst. comm. gen. *A suppliant.*

sŭpra, prep. gov. acc.

[contr. fr. sŭpĕrā, adverbial abl. of sŭpĕrus, "that is above"] *Above, over.*

sŭprēmus, a, um; see sŭpĕrus.

surgens, ntis, P. pres. of surgo.

sur-go, rexi, rectum, gĕre, 3. v. n. [contr. fr. sur-rĕgo, for sub-rĕgo; fr. sŭb, "upwards, up"; rĕgo, "to lead straight or direct"] ("To lead straight, or direct, upwards or up"; hence, in reflexive force) *To rise, arise.*

sūs, sŭis, comm. gen. *A hog; a sow;*—Plur.: *Swine* [Gr. ὗς, "a hog"].

sus-cĭto, cĭtāvi, cĭtātum, cĭtāre, 1. v. a. [for subs-cĭto; fr. subs (= sŭb), "from beneath"; cĭto, "to move violently"] ("To move violently from beneath"; hence, "to lift up"; hence) **1.** *To stir or rouse up; to arouse.*—**2.** Of fire as Object: *To stir up, rekindle.*

sus-pendo, pendi, pensum, pendĕre, 3. v. a. [for subs-pendo; fr. subs (= sŭb), "beneath"; pendo, "to hang"] ("To hang" a thing "beneath" something else; hence) *To hang up, to suspend.*—Pass.: **suspendor,** pensus sum, pendi.

suspensus, a, um: **1.** P. perf. pass. of suspendo.—**2.** Pa.: ("Suspended"; hence) Of the mind: *Wavering, doubtful, hesitating, in suspense, anxious.*

sustŭli, perf. ind. of tollo.

sŭ-us, a, um, possess. pron. [sŭ-i, "of himself," etc.] ("Belonging to *sui*"; hence) **1.** *Of, or belonging to, himself (herself, etc.); his,* etc., *own.*—As Subst.: **sŭi,** ōrum, m. plur. *Their friends or countrymen;* v. 577.—**2.** *Favourable, friendly, propitious,* as if inclined or devoted *to one;* v. 832.

Syrtĭs, is, f. *Syrtis;* the name of two sand-banks in the sea on the N. coast of Africa; viz. Syrtis Major (now "Sidra"), and Syrtis Minor (now "Cabes");—at v. 51 the plur. number includes both of them [Σύρτις].

tædet, tædŭit *or* tæsum est, tædēre, 2. v. a. impers. *It wearies* or *offends one,* etc.;—at v. 617 with clause pelăgi perferre labōrem as Subject [§ 157].

tænĭa, æ, f. *A band, fillet* [Gr. ταινία].

tænĭs, for tænĭis, abl. plur. of tænia.

tălentum, i, n. ("A thing weighed") *A talent;* a sum of money: **a.** In silver = about £243 15s. sterling.—**b.** In gold, the amount would depend upon the value that gold bore with respect to silver. Under the republic the common rate of gold to silver was as 10 to 1; but in the time of Julius Cæsar as 7½ to 1 [Gr. τάλαντον].

tā-lis, le, adj. *Of such a kind, such.*—As Subst.: **tālĭa,** ium, n. plur.: **a.** *Such things.*—**b.** *Such words,* etc. [prob. akin to demonstr. pron. root το, "this," and Gr. article τό].

tam, adv. [prob. akin to tālis, "such"; see tālis] *So.*

tămen, adv. [prob. a lengthened form of tam] ("In so far"; with adversative qualification) *For all that, notwithstanding, yet, nevertheless, still, however.*

tan-dem, adv. [for tamdem; fr. tam, "so"; demonstr. suffix dem] ("Just so far"; hence) *At length, at last.*

tantāne = tanta, neut. acc. plur. of tantus, with ne enclitic; see 2. ne.

tantum, adv. [adverbial

VOCABULARY.

neut. of tantus, "so much"] **1.** *So much.*—**2.** *Only, merely, alone.*

tant-us, a, um, adj.: **1. a.** *So much.*—**b.** *Of such a quantity, so small,* etc.—**2.** *So great,* whether in size or number [akin to Sans. *távant*, "so much"].

tardans, ntis, P. pres. of tardo.

tardātus, a, um, P. perf. pass. of tardo.

tard-o, āvi, ātum, āre, 1. v. a. [tard-us, "slow"] ("To make *tardus*"; hence) **1.** *To hinder, delay, retard.*—**2.** Of old age as Subject: *To render one slow* or *infirm.*—Pass.: **tardor**, ātus sum, āri.

tar-dus, da, dum, adj. [prob. for trah-dus; fr. trăh-o, "to draw"] ("Drawing one's self along"; hence) *Slow, tardy.*

Tartăra, ōrum; see Tartărus.

Tartărus, i, m. (Plur. **Tartăra**, ōrum, n.) *Tartarus* or *Tartara; the lower world* [Gr. Τάρταρος, Τάρταρα].

taur-us, i, m. *A bull* [Gr. ταῦρ-ος; akin to Sans. *sthūr-in*, "a beast of burden"; compare Anglo-Sax. "steor"; English, "steer"].

te, acc. and abl. sing. of tu.

tec-tum, ti, n. [for teg-tum; fr. těg-o, "to cover"] ("The covering thing"; hence) **1.** *The roof* of a building.—**2.** *A building* as covered by a roof.—**3.** *A house, dwelling, abode.*

tecum = te cum; see cum.

Tĕgĕ-æus, æa, æum, adj. [Těgě-a, "Tegea" (now "Paleo-Episcŏpi")]; a town of Arcadia, the central state of ancient S. Greece] *Of,* or *belonging to, Tegea; Tegeæan.*

tellūs, ūris, f.: **1.** *The earth.*—**2.** *Earth, ground,* etc.—**3.** *A land, country;* v. 30.

tēlum, i, n. *A weapon* whether for hurling or for close combat;—at v. 438 těla = crestūs; —at vv. 501, 514 = săgittas;— at v. 520 tělum = săgittam [usually referred to Gr. τῆλε, "far off"; but rather for tendlum, fr. tend-o, in force of "to launch *or* hurl" a weapon; and so, "the thing launched or hurled"].

tempes-tas, tātis, f. [for temper-tas; fr. tempus, old gen. tempěr-is, as proved by existing adverbial abl. tempěr-i] ("The state, *or* condition, of *tempus*"; hence) Of weather; in a bad sense: **1.** *Storm, tempest.*—**2.** Plur.: Personified as deities: *The Storms* or *Tempests;* v. 772.

tem-plum, pli, n. ("A piece cut off"; hence, "an open space" marked by an augur for taking auspices; hence) *A temple,* as dedicated to some deity [akin to Gr. τέμ-νω, "to cut"].

tempŏra, um; see tempus.

tem-pus, pŏris, n. ("That which is cut off; a section, portion," etc.; hence) **1.** ("A portion of time; a time"; hence) **a.** *Time* in general.—**b.** *A proper or fitting time; an opportunity.*— **2.** Plur.: *The temples* of the head [root TEM, akin to τέμ-νω, "to cut"].

tendens, ntis, P. pres. of tendo.

ten-do, tětendi, tensum *or* tentum, tendĕre, 3. v. a. and n.: **1.** Act.: **a.** *To stretch out or forth; to extend.*—**b.** Of the eyes as Object: *To strain, direct earnestly.*—**c.** Of weapons, etc.: *To shoot, hurl, launch;*—at v. 508 tetendit is used, by the figure zeugma, with both ocŭlos and tělum; see no. b above.—**2.** Neut.: **a.** *To bend one's way, to go.*—**b.** With Inf.: *To exert one's self, to endeavour* or *attempt, to*

K

do, *etc.* [akin to Gr. root τεν, whence τείν-ω].

tĕn-ebræ, ebrārum, f. plur. *Darkness* [akin to Sans. *tam-as*, "darkness"].

tĕnebr-ōsus, ōsa, ōsum, adj. [tĕnebr-æ, "darkness"] ("Full of, or abounding in, *tenebræ*"; hence) *Dark, gloomy*.

tĕnens, ntis, P. pres. of tĕnĕo.

tĕn-ĕo, ŭi, tum, ēre, 2. v. a. [akin to ten-do] **1.** *To hold; to keep, or have, in the hand.*—**2.** *To lay hold of, hold fast.*—**3.** *To hold, or retain, what one already has.*—**4.** *To hold, or keep, to something.*—**5.** With *iter* as Object: *To hold on one's way or course.*—**6.** *To have, or hold, possession of; to occupy.*—**7.** *To reach, arrive at.*—**8.** Of a name as Object: *To hold or have.*—**9.** *To hold, or keep, back; to hinder, detain, retard*—at v. 154 without nearer Object.

ten-to, tāvi, tātum, tāre, 1. v. a. intens. [tĕn-ĕo, "to hold"] ("To hold greatly"; hence, "to handle, feel," *etc.*; hence) *To try, attempt, essay.*

tĕnŭ-is, e, adj. ("Stretched out"; hence, "thin"; hence) **1.** Of the atmosphere, *etc.*: *Light*, as opposed to "dense, heavy."—**2.** Of the wind: *Light, slight, gentle.*—**3.** Of circumstances: *Low, reduced, etc.* [akin to Sans. *tanu*, "thin"; fr. Sans. root TAN, "to stretch out, extend"; whence Gr. τεν, root of τείνω].

tĕnus, prep. (put after its case) gov. abl. *As far as, up to.*

tĕr-es, ĕtis, adj. [tĕr-o, "to rub"] ("Rubbed"; hence) *Rounded, round, smooth.*

tergum, i. n. : **1.** *The back*, whether of men or beasts;—at v. 87 in plur. for sing.—**2.** *The back or hinder part; the rear.*—**3.** *The skin, hide* of an animal.—**4.** As being made of bull's hide: *A cæstus*; v. 419.

ter-ni, næ, na, num. distrib. adj. [tres, t(e)r-ĭum, "three"] **1.** *Three each.*—**2.** *Three*; v. 560. —**3.** For triplex: *Three-fold, triple*; v. 120, where an abl. sing. *terno* is used.

terno; see terni, no. 3.

tĕro, trivi, tritum, tĕrĕre, 3. v. a. *To rub, rub against* [Gr. roots τερ, whence τε(ί)ρ-ω; and τρι, whence τρί-βω].

ter-ra, ræ, f. ("The dry thing"; hence, "the earth" as such; hence) **1.** *Land*, as opposed to water; v. 243.—**2.** *The earth, ground.*—**3.** *A land, country*;—Plur.: *The lands, countries*, i. e. *the earth*; v. 803 [prob. akin to Gr. τέρ-σομαι, "to be, or become, dry"; Sans. root TRISH (TARSH), "to thirst"].

terr-ĕo, ŭi, ĭtum, ēre, 2. v. a. *To frighten, terrify, alarm.* —Pass.: **terr-ĕor**, ĭtus sum, ēri [akin to Sans. root TRAS, "to tremble"; in causative force, "to cause to tremble"].

terr-ĭ-fĭc-us, a, um, adj. [for terr-ĭ-făc-us; fr. terr-ĕo, "to frighten"; (i) connecting vowel; făc-ĭo, "to make"] ("Making to frighten"; hence) *That causes fright, fear, or terror; terrific.*

territus, a, um, P. perf. pass. of terrĕo.

ter-tĭus, tĭa, tĭum, adj. [tres, t(e)r-ĭum, "three"] ("Pertaining to *tres*"; hence) *Third*;—at v. 314 supply victor with tertius.

testis, is, comm. gen. *A witness.*

test-or, ātus sum, āri, 1. v. dep. [test-is, "a witness"] *To call upon, or invoke, as witness; to call to witness.*

tĕtendi, perf. ind. of tendo.

Teucri, ōrum ; see Teucrus.

Teucrum, for Teucrōrum gen. plur. of Teucri ; v. 592.

Teucr-us, a, um, adj. [Teucer, Teucr-i, "Teucer"; an ancient king of Troy] ("Of, or belonging to, Teucer"; hence) *Trojan.*—As Subst. : **Teucri,** ōrum, m. plur. *The Trojans* [Gr. Τεῦκρος].

tex-o, ŭi, tum, ĕre, 3. v. a. ("To fabricate"; hence) **1.** *To construct, build,* etc.—**2.** ("To interweave"; hence) *To mix, mingle, intermingle, blend.*—Pass. : **tex-or,** tus sum, i [akin to Sans. root TAKSH, "to fabricate"].

textus, a, um, P. perf. pass. of texo.

Thalia, æ, f. *Thalia ;* a seanymph [Gr. Θάλεια, "Blooming One"].

theātrum, i, n. : **1.** *A theatre.*—**2.** *An open space* for exhibiting games [Gr. θέατρον; "that which serves for seeing, or beholding," sights].

Thētis, ĭdis *or* ĭdos, f. *Thetis ;* a sea-nymph [Gr. Θέτις].

Thrāces, um, m. plur. *The Thracians.*—Hence, **Thrācius,** ĭa, ĭum, adj. *Of, or belonging to, the Thracians; Thracian* [Gr. Θρᾷκες].

Thrācius, a, um ; see Thrāces.

Thrēicius, a, um = Thrācius [Gr. Θρηίκιος].

tĭgris, is *or* ĭdis, comm. gen. *A tiger* or *tigress* [Gr. τίγρις, fr. a Persian word signifying "an arrow"].

tĭmens, ntis, P. pres. of timĕo.

tĭm-ĕo, ŭi, no sup., ĕre, 2. v. n. and a. : **1.** Neut. : *To fear, be afraid.*—**2.** Act. : *To fear, dread, be afraid of.*

tĭm-or, ōris, m. [tim-ĕo, "to fear"] ("A fearing" hence) *Fear, terror.*

tĭtŭbātus, a, um, P. perf. pass. of tĭtŭbo.

tĭtŭbo, āvi, ātum, āre, 1. v. a. ("To make to stumble or reel"; hence) Pass. in reflexive force: ("To make one's self, etc., to stumble," etc.; hence) *To stumble, reel.*—Pass. : **tĭtŭbor,** ātus sum, āri.

tŏlĕrā-bĭlis, bĭle, adj. [tŏlĕr(a)-o, "to bear *or* endure"] *That may, or can, be borne* or *endured; tolerable :*— non tŏlĕrābĭle, *unendurable, intolerable;* see non, no. 2.

tollo, sustŭli, sublātum, tollĕre, 3. v. a. : **1.** *To lift up, raise, uplift, elevate.*—**2.** With Personal pron. in reflexive force : *To lift one's self up; to rise, rise up.*—**3.** *To take,* or *curry, away.*—Pass. : **tollor,** sublātus sum, tolli [root TOL, akin to Sans. root TUL, "to lift"; Gr. τλάω, "to bear"].

tŏnans, ntis, P. pres. of tŏno.

tondĕo, tŏtondi, tonsum, tondēre, 2. v. a. : **1.** Of the hair : *To clip, cut short,* etc.—**2.** Of trees : *To lop, cut, prune, trim,* etc.

tŏn-ĭtrus, ĭtrūs. m. [tŏno, "to thunder"] ("That which effects the thundering"; hence) *Thunder.*

tŏn-o, ŭi, ĭtum, āre, 1. v. n. *To thunder* [akin to Sans. root STAN, "to thunder"].

tonsus, a, um, P. perf. pass. of tondĕo.

torqu-ĕo, torsi, tortum, torquēre, 2. v. a. : **1.** *To turn, turn about* or *round; to twist.* —**2.** Of weapons: *To hurl, fling with force,* etc. [akin to Gr. τρέπ-ω, "to turn"].

torrĕo, torrŭi, tostum, torrēre, 2. v. a. ("To dry *or* burn" hence) Of food: *To roast, dress* [akin to Sans. root TRISH, "to thirst"; Gr. τέρσ-ομαι, "to become dry"].

torsi, perf. ind. of torqueo.

tor-tus, tūs, m. [for torqutus (trisyll.); fr. torqu-ĕo, "to twist"] *A twisting.*

tŏr-us, i, m. ("The thing filled" out; hence) *A couch* [akin to Sans. root TUL, "to fill"; Gr. τύλ-η, "a cushion, bolster," etc.].

tŏt, num. adj. indecl. *So many.*

tŏt-ĭdem, num. adj. indecl. [tot, "so many"] *Just so many* or *as many.*

tŏt-ies, adv. [id.] *So many times, so often.*

tō-tus, ta, tum (Gen. tōtīus; Dat. tōti), adj. ("Increased"; hence) *The whole* or *entire; the whole of* [akin to Sans. root TU, in meaning of "to increase"].

trăde, pres. imperat. of trādo.

trā-do, dĭdi, dĭtum, děre, 3. v. a. [tra (= trans), "across"; do, "to give"] ("To give across"; hence) With Dat. [§ 106, (3)]: *To give,* or *hand over, to; to commit, confide,* or *entrust, to.*

trăhens, ntis, P. pres. of trăho.

trăho, traxi, tractum, trăhěre, 3. v. a.: **1.** *To draw, drag, drug along,* etc.—**2.** In figurative force: *To draw, drag;*—at v. 709 without nearer Object.

trājectus, a, um, P. perf. pass. of trājĭcĭo.

trā-jĭcĭo, jēci, jectum, jĭcěre, 3. v. a. [for trā-jăcĭo; fr. tra (= trans), "across or over"; jăcĭo, "to cast"] ("To cast across or over"; hence) *To pass,* or *tie,* something *around* an *object.*—Pass.: **trā-jĭcĭor,** *jectus sum, jĭci.*

trăme-s, trămĭtis, m. [for trame-t-s; fr. trămĕ-o, "to go across"] ("That which goes across"; hence, "a crossway, cross-path"; hence) **1.** *A way, path, road.*—**2.** *A course, flight,* etc.

tranquillum, i; see tranquillus.

tranquillus, a, um, adj. *Calm, quiet, tranquil.*—As Subst.: **tranquillum,** i, n. *Calm weather, a calm.*

tran-scrībo, scripsi, scriptum, scrībĕre, 3. v. a. [trans, "across or over"; scribo, "to write"] ("To write across or over" from one book to another; "to transfer" in writing; hence) *To transfer, remove, to another place.*

trans-curro, curri and cŭcurri, cursum, currĕre, 3. v. n. [trans, "across"; curro, "to run"] *To run across.*

trans-ĕo, ivi or ĭi, ĭtum, ire, v. a. and n. irreg. [trans; ĕo, "to go"] **1.** [trans, "across"] **a.** Act.: *To go across* or *over* a thing; *to cross,* or *pass, over.*—**b.** Neut.: (a) *To go,* or *cross, over* to the enemy for the purpose of spying.—(b) Of time: *To pass by, elapse.*—**2.** [trans, "beyond"] Act.: *To go beyond, pass by;*—at v. 326 supply ĕum after transĕat.

transii, perf. ind. of transĕo.

trans-trum, tri, n. [trans, "across"] ("That which crosses over"; hence) *A cross-bench* in a vessel.

transversa; see transversus.

transver-sus, sa, sum, adj. [for transvert-sus; fr. transvert-o, "to turn across"] ("Turned across"; hence) **1.** *Transverse, cross-, oblique.*—**2.** Neut. acc. plur. in adverbial

force: **transversa,** *Crosswise, transversely, obliquely, sideways.*
traxĕrim, perf. subj. of trăho.
traxse, for **traxisse,** perf. inf. of trăho; v. 786.
trĕmens, P. pres. of trĕmo.
trĕm-isco, no perf. nor sup., iscĕre, 3. v. n. [trĕm-o, "to tremble"] *To tremble, to quake.*
trĕ-mo, mŭi, no sup., mĕre, 3. v. n. *To tremble, quake, quiver,* etc. [akin to Gr. τρέ-ω].
tres, tria (Gen. trium), num. adj. *Three.*—As Subst. m. *Three persons, three* [Gr. τρεῖς, τρία].
trī-dens, dentis, adj. [tres, tri-um, "three"; dens, "a tooth"; hence, "a prong"] *Having three teeth* or *tines; three-pronged.*
trī-līx, līcis, adj. [for trī-lic-s; fr. tres, tri-um, "three"; līc-ĭum, "a thread" of anything woven] *Having,* or *with, three threads; triply-woven.*
Trī-n-ăcr-ĭa, iæ, f. *Trinacria,* a name given to *Sicily,* from its three promontories, *viz.* Pachȳnus, Pelorus, and Lilybæum.—Hence, **Trīnăcrĭ-us,** a, um, adj. *Of,* or *belonging to, Trinacria* or *Sicily; Trinacrian, Sicilian* [Τρινακρία; fr. τρεῖς, τρί-a, "three"; (ν) epenthetic; ἄκρ-α, "a point"; hence, "a headland *or* promontory"; and so, "the land, *or* island, of the three promontories"].
Trīnăcrĭus, a, um; see Trĭnăcrĭa.
trī-plex, plĭcis, adj. [for trī-plic-s; fr. tres, tri-um, "three"; plĭc-o, "to fold"] *Three-fold, triple.*
trĭpŏdes, um, plur. of trĭpus.
trĭpus, ŏdis, m. *A three-footed seat,* a *tripod* [Gr. τρίπους].
tris-tis, te, adj. *Sad, sorrowful, mournful,* etc. [prob. akin to Sans. root TRAS, "to tremble"; and so, literally, "trembling"].
Trīton, ōnis *or* ōnŏs, m.: **1. a.** *Triton;* a sea-god, who, at the bidding of Neptune, blew through a shell to rouse or calm the waters.—**b.** Plur.: *Tritons;* i. e. sea-gods in general; v. 824.—**2.** *Triton;* a river and lake in Africa, near the lesser Syrtis, where according to some mythological accounts Pallas (or Minerva) was born.—Hence, **Trīton-ĭus,** ĭa, ĭum, adj. *Of,* or *belonging to, Triton; Tritonian.*
Trītōnĭus, a, um; see Triton, no. 2.
Trŏădes, um, **Trŏes,** um, **Trŏĭus,** a, um, **Trŏja,** æ, **Trŏjānus,** a, um, **Trŏjānus,** i; see Trŏs.
Trŏ-s, is, m. [Trŏ-s, "of, or belonging to, Tros," a king of Phrygia, from whom Troy took its name] ("One belonging to *Tros*"; hence) *A Trojan, a man of Troy.*—Plur.: **Trŏ-es,** um, *The Trojans.*—Hence, **Trŏ-ja** (= Trŏ-ĭa), jæ, f.: **a.** ("The city of Tros") *Troy;*—the taking of Troy by the Greeks is said to have occurred B. C. 1184.—**b.** *Troja,* or *the game of Troy;* a Roman game performed on horseback and representing a fight; at v. 602 the origin of it is ascribed to Æneas.—Hence, **a. Trŏj-ānus,** āna, ānum, adj. *Of,* or *belonging to, Troy; Trojan.*—As Subst.: **Trŏjānus,** i, m. *A Trojan.*—Plur.: **Trŏjāni,** ōrum, *The Trojans.*—**b. Trŏ-ĭus,** ĭa, ĭum, adj. = Trŏjānus.—**c. Trŏ-as,** ădis, f. *A Trojan woman.*—Plur.: **Trŏ-ădes,** ădum, *The Trojan women* [Gr. Τρώς].
tū, tŭi (plur. **vos,** vestrum), pers. pron. *Thou, you;*—at v. 420 emphatic [τύ, Doric form of σύ].

tŭba, æ, f. *A* (straight) *trumpet.*

tŭens, ntis, P. pres. of tŭĕor.

tŭ-ĕor, ĭtus sum, ĕri, 2. v. dep. *To look upon, behold, see.*

tŭli, perf. ind. of fĕro.

tŭlissem, pluperf. subj. of fĕro.

tum, adv. *Then* [prob. akin to tălis; see tălis].

tŭm-ĭdus, ĭda, ĭdum, adj. [tŭm-ĕo, "to swell"] *Swelling, swollen.*

tŭm-ŭlus, ŭli, m. [id.] ("The thing swelling up"; hence) **1.** *A rising ground.*—**2.** *A sepulchral mound, a tomb.*

tun-c, adv. [contr. and altered fr. tum-ce; *i. e.* tum, "then"; demonstrative suffix ce] *At that time, then.*

tu(n)do, tŭtŭdi, tunsum and tūsum, tundĕre, 3. v. a. *To strike, beat, smite.*—Pass.: **tun(d)or,** tunsus and tūsus sum, tundi [akin to Sans. root TUD, "to strike"].

turba, æ, f.: **1.** *Turmoil, disturbance, uproar,* etc.—**2.** *A crowd, multitude, throng* [Gr. τύρβη].

turbātus, a, um, P. perf. pass. of turbo.

turb-ĭdus, ĭda, ĭdum. adj. [turb-o, "to disturb"] ("Disturbed"; hence) *Wild, stormy, boisterous.*

turb-o, āvi, ātum, āre, 1. v. a. [turb-a, "a disturbance"] ("To make a *turba* with regard to"; hence) *To disturb, agitate, throw into disorder* or *confusion.*—Pass.: **turb-or,** ātus sum, āri.

turma, æ, f. *A troop,* or *squadron, of horse.*

turpis, e, adj. *Filthy, foul, nasty.*

tŭtā-men, mĭnis, n. [tūt-(a)-or, "to protect"] ("That which protects"; hence) *A protection, defence, means of protection,* etc.

tūt-or, ātus sum, āri, 1. v. dep. [tūt-us, "safe"] ("To make *tutus*"; hence) *To protect, defend, support; to take the part of* a person.

tū-tus, ta, tum, adj. [tŭ-ĕor, "to protect"] ("Protected"; hence) *Safe, in safety.*

tŭ-us, a, um, pron. poss. [tŭ, "thou"] *Thy, thine; your.*

Tўbris, ĭdis (Acc. Tybrim, vv. 83, 797), m. *The Tybris* or *Tiber* (now *Tevere*); the river on which Rome was built.

ūber, ĕris, n. *A mother's breast* [akin to Gr. οὖθαρ; Sans. *údhar*; cf. Eng. "udder"].

ŭbi, adv. [akin to qu-i, "who, which"] **1.** Of time: *When;*—for force of ubi with perf. ind. in narrative see post-quam.—**2.** Of place: *Where.*

ū-dus, da, dum, adj. [for uv-dus; fr. obsol. ŭv-ĕo, "to be damp"] *Damp, moist, wet.*

ul-lus, la, lum (Gen. ullīus; Dat. ulli), adj. [for un-lus; fr. ūn-us, "one"] *Any.*

ultĭmus, a, um, sup. adj.: **1.** *Furthest; most distant* or *remote.*—**2.** *The furthest,* or *most distant, part of* that denoted by the subst. to which it is in attribution;—at v. 317 supply spatia with ultima.—**3.** *Last.*

ultr-o, adv. [obsol. ulter, ultr-i, "beyond"] ("Beyond, on the further side"; hence) **1.** *Besides, moreover, too.*—**2.** *Of,* or *by, one's self,* etc.; *i.e.* without any external impulse, etc.; v. 446.

umbra, æ, f.: **1.** *Shade, shadow.*—**2.** *The shade, spirit,* or *Manes,* of a departed person;—at v. 81 in plur. of the shade of Anchises.

ūn-ā, adv. [adverbial abl.

VOCABULARY. 135

of ûn-us, "one"] *In company, at the same time, together.*
unc-us, a, um, adj. [unc-us, "a hook"] ("Having an *uncus*"; hence) Of an eagle's talons: *Curved, bent inwards.*
und-a, æ, f. ("That which wets") **1.** *Water.*—**2.** *The water of the sea.*—**3.** *A wave* [akin to Sans. root UND, "to wet or moisten"].
undans, ntis, P. pres. of undo.
u-nde, adv. [for cu-nde (= qu-nde); fr. qu-i, "who, which"] **1.** Of place: *Whence.* —**2.** Of persons: *From whom, whence.*
und-i-que, adv. [und-e; (i) connecting vowel; que, indefinite suffix] ("Whencesoever"; hence) *From all parts or every quarter; on all sides, on every side.*
und-o, ävi, ätum, äre, 1. v. n. [und-a, "a wave"] ("To rise in waves; to surge, swell"; hence) Of reins: *To wave, undulate, hang loosely,* etc.:—undantia lora, *reins hanging loosely, flowing reins.*
unguis, is, m. ("A nail" of persons) Of animals: *A talon, claw* [akin to Gr. ὄνυξ; Sans. *nakha*].
un-quam, adv. [un-us, "one"] *At any (one) time; ever.*
ün-us, a, um (Gen. ünīus; Dat. üni), adj.: **1.** *One.*—As Subst. m. *One man, one:*—ad unum, *to a man,* v. 687.—**2.** *Alone, only.*—**3.** *Most of all, above all, especially.*
urb-s, is, f. [prob. urb-o, "to mark out with a plough"] ("That which is marked out with a plough"; hence) **1.** *A city, walled town.*—**2.** *A city for the people of a city.*
urgeo, ursi, no sup., urgēre, 2. v. a. ("To press, urge,

etc.; hence) *To press hard, beset closely;*—at v. 442 without nearer Object.
üro, ussi, ustum, ürēre, 3. v. a. *To burn, burn up, destroy or consume by fire* [akin to Sans. root USH, "to burn"].
urs-a, æ, f. *A she-bear; a bear* [like urs-us, "a bear," akin to Sans. *riksh-a*; Gr. ἄρκτος, ἀρκ-ος].
u-s-que, adv. [akin to qui; with (s) epenthetic; que, indefinite suffix] Of time: *As far, or as long, as; until;* see quousque.
ūsus, a, um, P. perf. of ütor.
ūt, adv. and conj.: **1.** Adv.: **a.** *As.*—**b.** *When.*—**2.** Conj.: *That, in order that.*
üter-que, utrā-que, utrumque (Gen. utrius-que; Dat. utrique), pron. adj. [ūter, "one or the other"; que, suffix] *One and the other; both, each.*
ūtor, ūsus sum, ūti, 3. v. dep. With Abl. [§ 119, (a)]: *To use, make use of, employ.*
utrăque, neut. acc. plur. of üterque; v. 855.
utrŏque, adv. [adverbial neut. abl. sing. of üterque, "both"] *On both sides, to each side.*

văc-ŭus, ŭa, ŭum, adj. [văc-o, "to be empty"] ("Empty"; hence) Locally: *Open, free, unobstructed,* etc.
vāde, pres. imperat. of vādo.
vā-do, no perf. (in classical Latin) nor sup., dĕre, 3. v. n. *To go, to come* [akin to Gr. βαίνω (dissyll.), "to go"].
vădum, i, n. [vād-o, "to go"] ("That through which one can go"; hence) **1.** *A shallow, shoal.*—**2.** *A body of water, the sea,* etc.

văg-or, ātus sum, āri, 1. v. dep. [văg-us, "wandering"] *To wander, rove, roam at large, etc.*

văle, pres. imperat. of văleo.

vălens, ntis, P. pres. of văleo.

văl-ĕo, ŭi, ĭtum, ēre, 2. v. n.: **1.** *To be strong* or *powerful.*—**2.** With Inf.: *To have strength* or *power to do, etc.; to be able to do, etc.*—**3. a.** *To be well* or *in good health.*—**b.** In leave-taking: **văle,** (*Be in good health;* i. e.) *Farewell, adieu* [prob. akin to Sans. *bal-a,* "strength"].

văl-ĭdus, ĭda, ĭdum, adj. [văl-ĕo, "to be strong"] *Strong, powerful, mighty.*

vallis, is, f. *A valley.*

văp-or, ōris, m.: **1.** *Steam, exhalation, vapour.*—**2.** *Cause for effect: Fire* [akin to Gr. καπ-νός, "smoke"].

văr-ĭus, ĭa, ĭum, adj. ("Party-coloured, spotted"; hence) *Various, different, manifold* [akin to Gr. βαλ-ιός].

vastus, a, um, adj. *Vast, huge, immense.*

vā-tes, tis, comm. gen. ("A speaker"; hence) **1.** *A soothsayer, prophet,* etc.; v. 524. —**2.** *A prophetess,* etc.; v. 636 [prob. akin to FA, root of (for), fā-ri, "to speak"; and to φα, whence φά-σκω, φη-μί, "to say"].

vĕ, enclitic conj. *Or* [akin to Sans. *vâ,* a particle denoting "option"].

vĕho, vexi, vectum, vĕhĕre, 3. v. a. *To carry, convey.*—Pass.: **vĕhor,** vectus sum, vĕhi [akin to Sans. root VAH, "to carry"].

vĕl, conj. [akin to vol-o, vel-le, "to wish"] ("Wish *or* choose"; hence) *Or if you will, or.*

vēlātus, a, um, P. perf. pass. of velo.

vĕlim, pres. subj. of 2. volo.

vēl-o, āvi, ātum, āre, 1. v. a. [věl-um, "a covering"] ("To furnish a *velum* to"; hence) *To cover, wrap, envelope, etc.*—Pass.: **vēl-or,** ātus sum, āri.

vēlox, ōcis, adj. *Swift, fleet, rapid, quick.*

vē-lum, li, n. [for vehlum; fr. věh-o, "to carry"] ("The carrying thing"; hence) *A sail:*—vēla dăre tūta, (*to give safe sails* to the wind; *i. e.*) *to sail in safety,* v. 796.

vĕl-ut, adv. [věl, "even"; ut, "as"] *Even as, like as, just as.*

vĕn-ĕror, ĕrātus sum, āri, 1. v. dep. *To worship, reverence with religious awe, revere, adore* [akin to Sans. root VAN, "to worship"].

vēni, perf. ind. of věnĭo.

vĕnĭens, ntis, P. pres. of věnĭo.

vĕnĭo, vēni, ventum, věnīre, 4. v. n. *To come.*

vent-us, i, m. ("The blowing thing"; hence) *Wind* [akin to Sans. root vâ, "to blow," through part. pres. *vânt,* "blowing"; cf. Sans. *vât-a,* "wind," as "the blowing thing"].

Vĕn-us, ĕris, f. ("Loved One") *Venus;* the goddess of beauty and love, and the mother of Æneas [akin to Sans. root VAN, "to love"].

verber, ĕris (Nom., Dat., and Acc. Sing. do not occur), n. [prob. for fer-ber; fr. fĕr-ĭo, "to beat"] ("That which brings about the beating"; hence) "a lash, whip, scourge"; hence) *A stripe, blow, etc.*

verbĕr-o, āvi, ātum, āre, 1. v. a. [verber, "a lash"] *To lash, beat, strike.*—Pass.: **verbĕr-or,** ātus sum, āri.

verbum, i, n. *A word.*

vĕr-o, adv. [vĕr-us, "true"] **1.** *Truly, in truth, indeed.*—**2.** *But indeed, but however, but.*

ver-ro, ri, sum, rĕre, 3. v. a. ("To sweep"; hence) *To sweep, or skim, along* or *over the waters*, etc.

versans, ntis, P. pres. of verso.

ver-so, sāvi, sātum, sāre, 1. v. a. intens. [for vert-so; fr. vert-o, "to turn"] **1.** *To turn over much* or *frequently; to keep turning over.*—**2.** *To turn with force or violence; to knock over or about.*—**3.** Mentally: *To ponder, meditate.*

1. versus, a, um, P. perf. pass. of verto.

2. ver-sus, sūs, m. [for vert-sus; fr. vert-o, "to turn"] ("A turning"; hence) *A row, line*, etc.

vert-ex, ĭcis, m. [vert-o, "to turn"] ("The turning thing"; hence, "the crown, or top," of the head; hence) **1.** *The highest point, peak, top or summit* of anything;—at vv. 35 and 759 of the summit of a mountain. — **2.** Phrase: *A vertice, (From the top;* i. e.) *From above, down from above.*

vert-o, verti, versum, vertĕre, 3. v. a.: **1.** *To turn:*—vert āmus, *let us turn*, v. 23. The first pers. plur. pres. subj. is sometimes used (as here) to express a wish, or exhortation, in which the speaker includes both himself and those whom he addresses. This is called Subjunctivus Adhortativus.—**2.** Pass. in reflexive force: *To turn one's self*, or *itself; to turn.*—**3.** Of the sea as Object: *To turn up* with oars, etc. — **4.** *To overturn, overthrow, destroy.*—Pass.: **vert-or**, versus sum, verti.

vĕru, ūs, n. *A spit* for roasting.

vĕr-us, a, ͏͏͏͏, adj. *True.*—As Subst.: **vēra**, ōrum, n. plur. *True things.*

vesper, ĕris and ĕri, m. ("The evening"; hence) *The West* [Gr. ϝέσπερ-ος].

Ves-ta, tæ, f. *Vesta;* one of the principal Roman deities, in whose temple were said to be preserved the Penates and the sacred fire which Æneas had brought from Troy. No statue was erected in it, but the sacred fire was kept burning, night and day, on the altar. The goddess, herself, was regarded as pure and chaste, and her priestesses (the Vestal virgins, originally four, afterwards six, in number, taken from the noblest families of Rome) were bound by a vow of chastity. If any one of them violated this vow, she was to be buried alive in the Campus Sceleratus, and her paramour scourged to death in the Forum [akin to Sans. root vas, "to dwell"; hence, "The Dweller" in households, as their presiding deity].

ves-ter, tra, trum, pron. poss. [for vos-ter; fr. vos, plur. of tu, "you"] *Your.*

vestīg-ĭum, ĭi, n. [vestĭg-o, "to track"] ("A tracking; that which is tracked"; hence) **1.** *A foot-print, foot-track.*—**2.** *A foot-step, a step.*—**3. a.** *The sole* of the foot.—**b.** Of a horse: *The hoof.*

ves-tis, tis, f. *A garment; clothing, dress* [akin to Gr. ϝέσ-θής, "a garment"; Sans. root vas, "to wear" as clothes; "to put on"].

vĕt-us, ĕris, adj. ("That has existed for years"; hence) **1.** *Old, aged.*—**2.** *Ancient* [prob. ak'n to ϝέτ-ος, "a year"].

vĭ-a, æ, f. ("The thing that carries or conveys"; hence) **1.**

VOCABULARY.

A way, road.—**2.** *A way or course.*—**3.** *A way, journey, voyage* [prob. akin to Sans. *vaha*, "a road," fr. root VAH, "to carry"].

vĭā-tor, tōris, m. [vĭ(a)-o, "to travel"] *A traveller.*

vīc-īnus, īna, īnum, adj. [vīc-us, "a street, village," etc.] ("Of, or belonging to, a *vicus*"; hence) With Dat. [§ 106, (1)]: *Near to, near.*

vīcis-sim, adv. [vīcis, "change"] ("By a change"; hence) *On the other hand, in turn.*

vīc-tor, tōris, m. [vinco, "to conquer," through root VIC] *Conqueror, vanquisher, victor.*—As Adj.: *Conquering, victorious.*

victus, a, um, P. perf. pass. of vinco;—at v. 156 supply ĕam (= Pristin *or* navem) with victam.

vĭdĕo, vidi, visum, vidēre, 2. v. a.: **1.** *To see.*—**2.** Pass.: *To seem, appear.*—Pass.: **vĭdĕor,** visus sum, vidēri [akin to Gr. *ἰδ-εῖν*; Sans. root VID, "to perceive"; originally "to see"].

vĭdissem, pluperf. subj. of vĭdĕo.

vĭgĭlans, ntis, P. pres. of vĭgĭlo.

vĭgĭl-o, āvi, ātum, āre, 1. v. n. [vĭgĭl, "watchful"] *To be watchful* or *vigilant, to watch.*

villus, i, m. *Shaggy hair of a wild-beast or animal.*

vincĭte, plur. pres. imperat. of vinco.

vinc-lum, li (-ŭlum, ŭli), n. [vinc-ĭo, "to bind"] ("The binding thing"; hence) *A band, cord, fastening, etc.*

vinco, vici, victum, vincĕre, 3. v. a. [root VIC] *To conquer, overcome, subdue,* etc.—Pass.: **vincor,** victus sum, vinci.

vincŭlum, i; see vinclum.

vīn-um, i, n. *Wine;*—only in plur. in this book of Virgil [Gr. *Ϝοῖνος*].

vĭr, vĭri (Gen. Plur. virûm for virōrum, vv. 148, 369), m. *A man* [akin to Gr. *ἥρ-ως*; Sans. *vīr-a*, "a hero"].

vīres, ĭum, plur. of vis.

Virgĭlĭus, ĭi, m. *Virgilius* (with prænōmen *Publius* and cognōmen *Maro*) *or Virgil,* a Roman poet, was born at Andes, a small village near Mantua, in Cisalpine Gaul, on 15th October B.C. 70, and died at Brundusium (now Brindisi) on 22nd September B.C. 19.

vir-go, gĭnis, f. *A virgin.*

virgŭl-tum, ti, n. [virgŭl-a, "a little twig"] ("A thing furnished with *virgula*"; hence, "a bush, thicket," etc.; hence) Plur.: *Brushwood, faggots,* etc.; v. 661.

vĭrĭdans, ntis, P. pres. of vĭrĭdo.

vĭr-ĭdis, ĭde, adj. [vĭr-ĕo, "to be green"] **1.** *Green.*—**2.** *Fresh, blooming,* etc.

vĭrĭd-o, no perf. nor sup., āre, 1. v. n. [vĭrĭd-is, "green"] *To be green* or *verdant.*

vir-tus, tūtis, f. [vĭr, "a man"] ("The quality of the *vir*"; hence) **1.** *Valour, bravery.*—**2.** *Excellence, merit, worth.*

virûm, for virōrum, gen. plur. of vir.

vis, vis (plur. **vīres,** ĭum), f.: **1.** *Strength.*—**2.** *Force, violence.*—**3.** *Power, efficacy* [Gr. *Ϝίς*].

viscĕra, um, plur. of viscus.

viscus, ĕris (mostly plur.), n.: **1.** *The inner parts* of the body; *the entrails, bowels, viscera.*—**2.** *The flesh.*

vīsūrus, a, um, P. fut. of vĭdĕo.

1. **vī-sus,** sūs, m. [for vidsus; fr. vĭd-ĕo, "to see"] ("A

seeing"; hence, "the faculty of seeing, the sight"; hence) *A thing seen; a sight*, etc.

2. **vīsus**, a, um, P. perf. pass. of vĭdĕo;—at v. 610 folld. by Dat. [§ 107, *d*];—at v. 637 supply est with visa;—at v. 768 visa (supply est) belongs to both făcies and nōmen, but takes the gender of facies, nearest to which it is placed; both aspĕra and tolerabile are complements [§ 87, *D, a*].

vī-ta, tæ, f. [for viv-ta; fr. viv-o, "to live"] ("That which is lived"; hence) **1.** *Life.*—**2.** *A spirit*, or *shade*, in the lower world.

vī-tta, ttæ. f. [prob. fr. vīĕo, "to bind"] ("The binding thing"; hence) *A band, fillet, garland*.

vĭtŭlus, i, m. *A calf* [Gr. Ϝίταλός].

vīv-ĭdus, ĭda, ĭdum, adj. [viv-o, "to live"] ("Living"; hence) *Full of life* or *vigour; vigorous, energetic*.

vīvo, vixi, victum, vivĕre, 3. v. n. *To live*;—at v. 681 used figuratively of burning tow [akin to Sans. root जीव्, "to live"].

vix, adv. *Scarcely, hardly, with difficulty*.

vōbis, dat. and abl. plur. of tu.

vŏcans, ntis, P. pres. of vŏco.

vŏcātus, a, um, P. perf. pass. of vŏco.

vŏc-o, āvi, ātum, āre, 1. v. n. and a.: **1.** Neut.: *To call.*—**2.** Act.: **a.** *To call.*—**b.** *To call upon*, or *invoke*, a deity, etc.;—at v. 686 vŏcăre is the Historic Inf.—**c.** *To call for*, or *implore*, aid, etc.—**d.** *To call to*, or *upon*, a person for aid, etc.—**e.** *To call*, or *summon*, for any purpose.—Pass.: **vŏc-or**, ātus

sum, āri [akin to Sans. root वाच्, "to speak"].

vŏlans, ntis, P. pres. of 1. vŏlo.

vŏlens, ntis: **1.** P. pres. of 2. vŏlo.—**2.** Pa.: *Willing, ready*.

vŏl-ĭto, ĭtāvi, ĭtātum, ĭtāre, 1. v. n. freq. [vŏl-o, "to fly"] (Of birds, etc.: "To fly to and fro"; hence) Of th'ngs as Subject: *To hover, float about*, etc.

1. **vŏlo**, āvi, ātum, āre, 1. v. n.: **1.** Of birds, etc.: *To fly.*—**2.** Of persons *or* things: *To fly*, i. e. *to move rapidly* or *swiftly; to speed, hasten along*, etc.

2. **vŏlo**, vŏlŭi, velle, v. irreg.: **1.** *To be willing.*—**2.** *To wish, desire.*—**3.** Of the gods: *To will, ordain*, etc. [akin to Gr. βολ, root of βόλ-ομαι (= βο(ύ)λ-ομαι), "to wish"; and Sans. root वृ, "to choose"].

vŏl-ūcer, ūcris, ūcre, adj. [vŏl-o, "to fly"] ("Made, or formed, for flying"; hence, "winged"; hence) *Swift, rapid*.

vŏlŭi, perf. ind. of 2. vŏlo.

vŏlū-men, mĭnis, n. [for volv-men; fr. volv-o, "to roll"] ("The thing rolled"; hence) **1.** Of a snake: *A fold, coil.*—**2.** *A fold* of a cord, etc.

vŏlū-to, tāvi, tātum, tāre, 1. v. a. intens. [for volv-to; fr. volv-o, "to roll"] ("To roll about"; hence) Of the voice as Object: *To cause to roll, roll along* or *onwards*.

volvo, volvi, volūtum, volvĕre, 3. v. a.: **1.** *To roll.*—**2.** Pass. in reflexive force: ("To roll one's self," etc.; hence) *To roll along* or *onwards*.—Pass.: **volvor**, vŏlūtus sum, volvi [akin to Gr. Ϝελύ-ω, "to roll"].

vŏmens, ntis, P. pres. of vŏmo.

vŏm-o, ŭi, ĭtum, ĕre, 3. v. a.

("To vomit up *or* forth"; hence) *Of smoke as Object*: *To pour forth*, etc.
vōs, vestrum, plur. of tu.
vŏ-tum, ti, n. [for vovtum; fr. vŏv-ĕo, "to vow"] ("That which is vowed"; hence) *A vow*.
vox, vōcis, f. [for voc-s; fr. vŏc-o, "to call"] ("That which calls *or* calls out"; hence) **1.** *The voice.*—**2.** *A word, speech, cry,* etc.
Vulc-ānus, āni, m.: **1.** *Vulcan;* the ancient mythic fire-god of the Romans.—**2.** *Fire* [sometimes referred to Sans. *ulkā,* "a fire-brand, fire-ball"; sometimes to root JVAL, "to shine, to blaze"].
vuln-us, ĕris, n. *A wound* [akin to Sans. *vran-a,* "a wound"; fr. root VRAN, "to wound"].
vul-tus(old form **vol-tus**), tūs, m. [prob vŏl-o, "to wish"] ("The wishing, *or* expressing one's wish," by the looks; hence) **1.** *Expression of countenance, aspect, mien.*—**2.** *Face, countenance.*

Xanthus, i, m. *The Xanthus;* a river of Troas [Gr. Ξανθός, "Gold-coloured" stream]

Zĕphўrus, i, m.: **1.** *Zephyrus* or *the West-wind;*—at v. 33 in plur.; cf. vespĕre ab atro Consurgunt venti, vv. 19, 20.—**2.** *Wind* in general [Gr. Ζέφυρος].